Percy Hetherington Fitzgerald

Principles of Comedy and Dramatic Effect

Percy Hetherington Fitzgerald
Principles of Comedy and Dramatic Effect
ISBN/EAN: 9783744778282

Printed in Europe, USA, Canada, Australia, Japan

Cover: Foto ©Thomas Meinert / pixelio.de

More available books at **www.hansebooks.com**

PRINCIPLES

OF

COMEDY

AND

DRAMATIC EFFECT.

BY

PERCY FITZGERALD, M.A.,

AUTHOR OF 'THE LIFE OF DAVID GARRICK,' ETC., ETC.

> 'But when from Nature's pure and genuine source
> These strokes of acting flow with generous force,
> To me they seem from quickest feelings caught:
> Each start is Nature and each pause is Thought.'
> CHURCHILL. *The Rosciad.*

LONDON:
TINSLEY BROTHERS, 18, CATHERINE STREET, STRAND.
1870.
[All rights reserved.]

CONTENTS.

PART		PAGE
I.	THE DRAMATISTS	9
II.	COMEDY	58
III.	BURLESQUE	149
IV.	THE FRENCH STAGE	200
V.	ACTORS PAST AND PRESENT	245
VI.	THE ACTORS OF THE DAY	297
VII.	THE MUSIC HALL QUESTION	324
	POSTSCRIPT	349
	APPENDIX	356

PART I.

THE DRAMATISTS.

In some of the old essays of the past and present centuries, are passages which allude to the play-house—that good old-fashioned word—the actors, and general entertainment of the stage, in a manner very significant, when we come to think of the present condition of our stage. In the 'Spectator,' 'Adventurer,' and 'Connoisseur,' in the essays of Hunt, Hazlitt, and Lamb, we find a certain sense of reverence, and even awe. They seem to approach the subject as if it were some fifth estate; it appeared something akin to Parliament, or the Law: the actors were potentates. Not so many years ago Hazlitt ushered in his volume of criticisms, with a sort of apology, in which he appealed to the existing interest in the stage. 'It was always in our thoughts,' he said; 'the new play of the night before was eagerly discussed next day at the clubs, and other places of resort; it was greedily bought up and read: we followed the passing actor, if some rare chance exhibited him to us in the street, with eyes of sympathy, reverence, and admiration.' The delightful strains in which Lamb fondly recalls his old actors—as much associated with hours of unspeakable delight as any of his poets or pet books, are familiar to all. Now, there can be no question but that this peculiar tone came of nothing artificial, but followed directly from the healthy condition of the stage itself, and the object of the following inquiry is to show that such a respect and interest waits on true dramatic art only; that contempt, or at least indifference, follows false dramatic art; and that the present apparent prosperity is in reality only decay.

At the present moment there are about twenty theatres open in London. We hear of three or four being built, and of as many more being projected. Within ten years it is not unlikely that this number may be doubled. Competition seriously affects such ventures, and if it were possible to conceive such a palmy state of the drama, as that there was something substantially good and attractive played at each house simultaneously, public support sufficient to ensure overflowing audiences, 'continued and triumphant success,' 'uninterrupted run!' 'two hundredth night!' with all the variety of dramatic and mural panegyric, could hardly be reckoned on for each establishment, without interfering with the other's prosperity. The fault, wherever it rests, does not lie with those who are called patrons of the drama, always faithful, eager, generous, and overpowering in their approbation and support, when they are pleased. Though such support seems coarse, selfish; and like our ' patronage' of those who minister to other people's pleasure. The 'actors' patrons' seems to be a relic of that obsequious homage, due from those who were in the law's eye no better than ' vagabonds' and belonging to an inferior caste, and who, on country circuits, had to go round and humbly beg the countenance of the squires. This multiplication of theatres, and this never-failing or flagging popular taste, is often appealed to as proof of the flourishing state of the stage at the present moment. Actors, too, even of the common rank and file, are in demand, and managers complain of the difficulty of procuring them. Play-writers receive sums nearly as large as was paid in the days of Garrick, when even a mediocre drama that ran its nine nights was worth its three or four hundred pounds to the author.

Scenery has almost reached perfection,—at least the perfection of splendour, though not of dramatic propriety; and, what Garrick, Kean, or Kemble could not have hoped to see, the most complicated and familiar objects about us are fearlessly laid hold of by the property man, and dragged upon the stage. Thus, when we take our dramatic pleasure, we have the satisfaction of not being separated from the objects of our daily life, and within the walls of the theatre we meet again the engine and train that set us down almost at the door; the interior of hotels, counting-houses, shops, factories, the steam-boats, waterfalls, bridges, and even fire-engines. The complaint that Charles Lamb made some forty or fifty years ago may, indeed, be repeated now with infinitely more propriety. 'We have been spoiled,' he writes, ' not with sentimental comedy, but a tyrant far more pernicious to our pleasures, which has succeeded to it, the exclusive and all-devouring drama of common life . . . . . where, instead of the fictitious half-believed personages of the stage (the phantoms of old comedy), we recognize ourselves, our own brothers, aunts, kinsfolk, allies, patrons, enemies, the same as in life. . . . . We carry our fireside concerns to the theatre with us. We do not go thither, like our ancestors, to escape from the pressure of reality, so much as to confirm our experience of it. . . . . We must live our toilsome lives twice over.' This applied only to character and to action: it seemed a decay to Elia, whose agreeable ramblings on actors and plays fill only too few pages of his delightful essays; but are sufficient to set us wondering at the life, variety, and animation with which 'the stage' was then bubbling over. Yet this practical tone, this bare shifting of daily objects from the street to the stage, merely illuminating them by the glare of gas or electric light, is at the bottom of the decay of the stage in the present day. For with all these theatres built and being built, this 'three hundredth night of School,' the true fascination and attraction of the drama is becoming more and more enfeebled every day. The number of theatres is no proof of a healthy taste, as they are mere favourite subjects of speculation, like a 'favourite stock,' for the Englishman who wishes to gamble a little. A theatre brings power and a little sovereignty. But the players are constantly shifting, and in three-fourths of the houses money is slowly or swiftly lost. It is a purely mechanical arrangement, like the 'finding the money' for opening a business. A theatre is not found or built because a place must be got for good actors, but the actors are found because a theatre must be opened. Let the money be forthcoming, the rest follows, as of course. With the dramas a good name is all that is needed—one that will figure on the poster—huge black letters on a yellow ground. In the actors, name also is chiefly what is looked for; and to other advertising devices is now added, that of pasting a grotesque and buffoonery caricature of the actor in his favourite character upon every dead wall and boarding. This cannot help to refine our association of the stage. This is all no more than a purely mercantile and material view of the stage and its attractions,—a dealing with it as if it was a business which, by forcing and pushing, and outlay and management, must draw the public in crowds. With all these houses there arises competition, and the competition of trade, and therewith disastrous results. A particular writer is in favour, and his pieces are forthwith played against each other. The rivalry in scenic shows, the introduction of objects of art and nature upon the stage, is still more desperate. All is material, scenes, construction, furniture, and, above all, the play, and the acting. We go not so much to hear as to look. It is like a gigantic peep-show, and we pay the showman, and put our eyes to the glass and stare. The vulgar of all ranks, therefore, as much in the highest as in the lowest, have been always drawn in overflowing crowds to see anything that takes the shape of a splendid show. The *prestige* and popularity of such spectacles spreads with an enthusiasm, beside which the colder but more substantial approbation accorded to intellectual enjoyments seems tame. *Curiosity* to see a popular piece spreads with all the contagion of an epidemic; but its hold on the public mind is quite as temporary. Rarely, however, is such a 'run' obtained; at every fresh draught the palate requires higher and higher spicing.

But the truth is that these twenty or thirty theatres are properly not London theatres, but have country audiences as well. The universal centralization, the diffusion of theatrical news by journals and newspapers, makes every one in the country follow stage matters with as much interest as people living in London. The run of a new piece or a new show stimulates eagerness in the provinces. But this attendance brings with it a risk and drawback. This country crowd, being at a distance, and more impressionable, follows the cry of fashion; but it has no other guide, and will fall away as readily as it flocked to see. In Germany, where every little town has a good theatre and sometimes a magnificent one, there are comparatively few houses in the capitals. This seems to show that the provincial populations are content with their own local entertainments. In truth, a multitude of theatres is no criterion of prosperity; and the ever-changing proprietors, as just noticed, prove that all cannot flourish together. Rival houses in business are 'killed off' by the laws of competition; but the fascination of rule and control, like that of having a seat in the House of Commons, makes the theatre an exception.

The true cause of this multiplication of theatres is really to be found in the decay of dramatic art.

When merely talent was in demand, the fact of having money to build and open a theatre would be as nothing: money could not create the article that the public would care to see. But when it came merely to shows and dioramas and *spectacles* on the stage, where the chief labour of the evening was to feast the eye with decorations, dresses, and beautiful scenes, it was plain that any one with capital might compete with the rest. And this, as in the recent re-opening of the wine trade and banking business, every one might rush in, and try to draw custom to himself. But it may be predicted, it will be with the theatres as with these great joint stock banking houses and wine companies, depending on mere *ocular* support, as it may be called. Frail and fickle as it is, that organ will soon feel *ennui* or fatigue, and when the revival of a better taste sets in, there will be neither actors nor plays in sufficient abundance, nor of sufficient merit, to draw the public.

If we look round, too, at the comparative condition of all these theatres, we shall see that each only enjoys health at long and uncertain intervals. At two or three houses only at a time do 'successes' set in; the rest languish on, making experiments, several times renewed, until they blunder on a hit. During this struggle managers have to come and go; and a return of those who, during the last twenty or thirty years, have been, like Mr Micawber, 'the victims of pecuniary embarrassment,' would show, at least, that the degradation of the stage does not turn to profit. No less curious a return would be the names of those pieces which have restored sinking ventures, or brought most money to the treasuries; and we should find the list swelled by pieces, like 'Our American Cousin,' the screaming burlesques of 'Black-Eyed Susan' and 'Ixion,' and 'The Field of the Cloth of Gold,' the 'Peep o' Day,' 'The Colleen Bawn,' 'Arran na Pogue,' 'The Streets of London,' 'After Dark,' 'The Turn of the Tide,' and others of kindred sort. In most of these the eye settles on some mechanical prodigy which drew the whole town. A tree that bent over a precipice (bent, too, by means of a very palpable hinge); the slow rising of water in a cave, a house on fire, a tunnel and locomotive, some vulgar slang songs, a steamboat—these are the triumphs on which we plume ourselves.

Another cause of failure is the confusion in the

choice of pieces, no one house having an avowedly special character, every one scrambling for popular favour with melodrama, comedy, or farce, according to the whim of the day. Neither are there traditions, which gain a certain respect, nor do actors claim any fixity of tenure, but migrate according to humour or pay. All this produces uncertainty, and makes the success of any piece mere gambling speculation. The actors are untrained, and have no schools to train themselves in; though, by this time, burlesque has its traditions, i. e. its tunes, and breakdowns, and impertinent fashion of repeating doggrel; and it is hard to blame a manager if he prefer not to lean upon frail reeds, and concentrate all his powers upon paint, timber, and lime-light, which can be perfectly depended upon. And here nothing strikes us more, in the writers of the present time, than their extraordinary rapidity of production. This is scarcely the writer's fault, for it is a curious and unhealthy characteristic of the age, that any popularity must become extravagant popularity, and when the public fancies anything, it must surfeit itself. Formerly, too, reputations were of slow and steady growth; now celebrity comes up, mushroom-like in a night, and is, perhaps, as easily produced. Mr Byron—whose 'name' is at present 'well up'—a short time since enjoyed the satisfaction of seeing no less than five new pieces of his own writing played at different London theatres on the same nights; and yet, considering the class of play the public requires to be furnished with, this rate of production seems not too hasty; for pieces turning on the mere physical order of life, which, where they deal with character, are meant only to bring out the external peculiarities of a particular player, can be supplied with rapidity, if the writer have Mr Byron's skill, and knowledge of the stage. But to produce a drama that will endure, that will equally please when *read*, and which is founded on long study and observation of human character, and of those points of human character which, to belong to every generation, requires deep study and long preparation. All the great writers of the last century produced, and were able to produce, only very few works. Goldsmith has left us but two comedies; Sheridan, three; Hoadley, one; Macklin, two; Colman, half-a-dozen; Cumberland, three or four; Holcroft, four or five; Murphy—excluding his translations—

the same; and yet most of these were professional play-writers. Each piece was written slowly, and often under the eye of the manager, usually a writer himself; often condemned wholesale, and re-written, laid by, and re-touched and altered. All this was done in awe of a healthy and competent public opinion, which was something substantial that had 'stuff' in it, that should not be rickety under the weight of the grand talents of a fine actor that would bear seeing again and again and each time discover something that had been unobserved before.

Mr Tom Taylor, Mr Byron, Mr Halliday, Mr Boucicault, Mr Robertson, and Mr Oxenford, are the writers whose works are now most in demand. Mr Boucicault has had a long career, and is perhaps a specimen, often given, of the well-trained professional dramatist, perfectly skilled in foreign as well as home traditions, and a master of all known stage devices and effects. All through his career he has had his finger on the very pulse of the Pit, and has nicely followed every change in its beatings. His earliest pieces reflect the tone of the good old school of character, and his comedy of 'London Assurance,' with its extraordinary vivacity, its unflagging *character*, its Dazzle, and

Lady Gay Spanker, which, in the cant phrase, act themselves, will never be dropped out of the list of acting plays. Yet a single fact in connection with this play should have warned existing actors of the hopeless incapacity into which they have drifted. Not long since a performance of 'London Assurance' was given, in which was combined, for some charitable benefit, the strength and flower of every company in London. The list of names represented all the acknowledged chiefs in the respective walks. Yet the failure was disastrous—more disastrous from the very pretension. The actors seemed not at home in such old-fashioned parts: their line was the imitation of extreme eccentricities; they had lost the famous old art of getting within the mere rind of a character, possessing themselves by study of the key-note, the leading principle, which would, without effort, supply the true illustrative accompaniments of voice, gesture, and oddity.

Practising himself, and improving his cunning by skilful French adaptations of powerful pieces, made, like 'Janet's Pride,' with wonderful skill, Mr BOUCICAULT turned to domestic melodrama, and produced the charming 'Colleen Bawn,' one of the few legitimate successes of the last twenty years. There is a tone and flavour about this piece infinitely characteristic, touching, and national; and though dealing with 'low' life, and the humour of 'low' life, the feeling that remains is one of perfect refinement. Much is, of course, owing to Gerald Griffin, on whose story the play is founded; but the whole is really treated in an original manner. Here, too, is introduced, and with the most perfect legitimacy, that remarkable 'sensation scene,' as it was called, of the water-cave,—brought in without violence, following naturally in the situation *which required it*, and therefore increasing the attraction of the play. After some more attempts of this *genre*, the author changed his hand, and began producing that curious class of pieces to which 'The Streets of London,' 'Lost at Sea,' 'After Dark,' and the 'Long Strike' belong. These seem to have for model the old Porte St Martin pieces; but without the romance and passion which gave life to so many of those really admirable productions. The taste of the town now requiring great scenic *tours de force*, and the theatres competing with each other in the attraction of objects from outside, which seemed to defy reproduction on the stage, it was necessary that the writer should, like Mr Crummles' dramatist, construct his piece in the interest of 'the pump and washing-tubs,' or kindred objects. Hence the panorama of fires, underground railways, music halls, steamboat piers, dry arches, and such things. The characters are meant to be 'London characters,' or rather figures, and the plots of the kind which Miss Braddon has made so popular. Lost and found wills, forgers, scheming Jews, bigamy, suicides, crafty scheming men, who stick at nothing,—in short, *mechanical* figures and incidents are the elements. It must be conceded that the pieces are done as skilfully as possible, and are really interesting.

The plea on which the author offers dramas of this nature is, that they really are reflections of the incidents and fashion of the time, and therefore hold the mirror up to London. These Jew speculators, forgers, and particularly humorists out of the lower London ranks—play-bill sellers, &c.—are all about us; and though such elaborate tissues of ingenious crime may not be actually woven near us, the police reports show that something very like these delinquencies exist. Now this argument is so frequently urged, in many other arts, too, besides the dramatic, and on its moral side, with reference to the notorious 'Formosa,' that it becomes worth while to look into the whole a little closely.

It comes back to the distinction, to be often insisted on in these pages, between what is dramatic and what is mimetic. Acting that is not founded on character, is mere mimicry; acting that is, is the pure drama. This does not exclude story, and story of the most exciting sort; but the story should be born of the clash of character with character; not the character of the story. To set off a narrative of interest by colourless figures—and we are now speaking merely in reference to the relative *prominence*, for Mr Boucicault does give us characters, and good ones, too; figures whose function it is to be story-tellers, as it were, and help on the action—would, if unassisted, result in simple tedium. But Mr Boucicault and his audience both know that this is set off by, or leading up to, the scenic 'sensation;' and the expectancy, or actual enjoyment, supplies other interest. The result may be a single play or two of exciting interest, like 'After Dark,' but see the result in the future, which is, as it were, discounted. In a few short rounds the whole compass of these scenic prodigies is spent. With infinite labour of thought and mechanical skill something is discovered, but by-and-by all wonder and surprise is exhausted; anything astonishing is found to be like what has gone before; and the bill-forgers, bigamists, Jew bill dealers, and suicidal work-girls, left to themselves, without bridges to leap from, dry arches to sleep under, or burning houses to be saved from, tumble over like card-board soldiers. The worst of these great effects is, that here are almost always excrescences, for which either the piece has been written, or which have been imported into the piece. In any case they dwarf the play. In Mr Robertson's 'Nightingale' there is a fine effect of the great sea, with the heroine exposed in an open boat; but this exposure does not grow out of the course of the piece, or influence its future fortunes. It is the most prominent feature of the whole, and yet is no more than an interpolated portion of a diorama. Nearly all these costly and pretentious *tours de force* could be cut out: they are, as it were, lugged in, head and shoulders; and thus does true dramatic art indemnify itself. So with the comic figures, taken from the streets,

—the cads and cadgers, whose slang and readiness does such service in these dramas. Here we may compare Mr Boucicault with himself, and see what is the real principle in dealing with such characters. In the 'Colleen Bawn' we saw the Irish 'low' element of humour elaborated; but it was all in the interest of the play. It tended to bring about the action, and the result was interest, and a feeling of respect and sympathy; but with this cockney street humour, which is on the *outside*, the effect is the same as on ourselves passing by, *in* the street; just as we feel amusement mingled with contempt—a sense of distrust, and a wish to have as little contact as possible with such characters. So from our house window we might look out, and be amused at some such spectacle; but if it was repeated two or three mornings it would grow tedious, and we would ask the police to see that such performers 'moved on.' And this is the fatal Nemesis for an 'oddity' actor, or an 'oddity' part, that is, such a part as is founded on 'cant' words, and, perhaps, on 'cant' dress, and is brought in merely to exhibit the same. There is nothing of 'cant' in real human character.

While, however, play-maker, play-actor, and

play-goer admit reluctantly that there is something wrong in the British drama, they can point triumphantly to what has done the mischief—the glories of British scenery. This, at least, flourishes; and has almost reached perfection. Every Christmas sees new and yet newer triumphs, and Callcott and Grieve confound us with a fresh paradise in every new pantomime. Set scenes, perfect structures that have to be 'built,' have taken the place of the old 'flats'; side scenes have given way to regular enclosures; and drawing-rooms and boudoirs appear ready furnished with hangings, buhl, clocks, &c.; in short, as the bills are careful to inform us, 'the furniture in Act IV. by Messrs —— and ——, of Oxford Street.' This surely is a conscientious support to the piece, and the manager is thus said to spare no expense to mount his play properly. Yet the question arises whether this, considered to be the cause of the decay of the dramatic portion, is not itself a decay. A few reflections will show that the whole is based on false principles.

The confusion arises from the idea, that the closer reality is imitated, the more nearly *effect* is produced. If actual *reality*—the thing itself—can be introuced, the *acme* is reached. A landscape defies such an introduction, though partial attempts can be made at producing a street. But the simplest illustration, by which the whole principle can be tested, is that of the common Drawing-room Scene. In many of the leading plays now acting, there is some such elaborate room, richly furnished and appointed, on which great trouble and cost have been expended. As the drop scene rises, we see the French windows to the right, with cornices and rich rep curtains, Louis Quatorze chairs, a pier table and mirror, buhl cabinets, marquetry tables, chimney-piece, fender, &c.; in short, 'Messrs —— and ——, of Oxford Street,' have done their best. Yet it may be said, that the more realistic and complete the attempt, the more there is of failure; of a sense of something wanting. The completeness of these additions makes the poorness of its background felt. Thus, let any one look at the real cornices, and see how clumsily they hang on the canvas background, revealing that it is anything but a firm wall. The marquetry tables look dull and shabby and prosy; the accessories overpower the groundwork, they are discordant with the poor flat painting about them, painting of mouldings, ceiling, cornices, surbases, all produced by colour. And this leads us to the curious conditions under which things are seen upon the stage. There is no sunlight, no casting of shadows, which makes the whole richness of objects in average daily life. *There* every little depression, every 'bit of work,' has its faint shadow. On the stage the glare of gas is equable—coming from above, below, and from the side; and such shadows as there are, are the coarse shadows of limelight. Hence it is that in painting, it is necessary to paint shadows with colour; and hence the effect and appropriateness of scenery. Further, there is another condition, and a very remarkable one, often lost sight of. This drawing-room, with its appointments, is one not seen, as other drawing-rooms are, from the inside or the doorway, but is gazed at after an Asmodean fashion—its side taken out—by people who are from thirty to a couple of hundred feet away. No ordinary room is seen under such conditions. In real life, statues placed at a height or distance are made coarse and gigantic. On the stage the actors' faces have a glare thrown on them; but real distant objects cannot be so strongly illuminated. Take the marquetry table with the 'console' legs, to be seen at one of the leading theatres. It is self-evident that the work of Messrs —— and ——, of Oxford Street, was meant to be seen a couple of feet off, and not hundreds of feet away, where it looks muddy and dull.

Now let us see what should be the true principle. In this matter the scenic artist need only stick to his own original canons. He paints falsely to produce a true effect. The inexperienced goes up to a scene, and is amazed at the coarseness and roughness—the absolute no-shape and no-colour—all streak and daub. Yet the artist has in his own mind a finished picture utterly dissimilar, and sees it as a result all the time. The costumier uses not laces and delicate gold edgings, but coarse things—spangles, cotton velvets, and such matters—while Dutch metal flares more brilliantly on his soldiers' helmets than would real gold. The furniture should be under the same law; and instead of calling in Messrs —— and ——, of Oxford Street, the manager should say to his artist: 'Make me a table that will *look* like a marquetry table under the glare of gas and at a great distance.' A number of angular dashes in sienna and lake, with some judicious gilding, will give this effect. There must be a consistency in this mysterious stage world, and all must be of a piece. There is a Library Scene at a certain theatre, used always as Sir Charles Surface's room, where there are crimson curtains, and shelves upon shelves of books stretching away, which has no 'building in,' and is infinitely more like a real library than if we saw real shelves, and some hundred real books strewn about. Yet the whole—the library chairs, the shadows, the perspective of the recesses—all are on one flat surface; and the effect is rich, warm, agreeable, and theatrical—that is, touched with that sort of romantic, exaggerated air which stage scenery should have. Once lose this, and the stage begins to have an air of something infinitely low and vulgar; *e. g.* when a *real* crowd, in its everyday working clothes, is actually fetched out of the street to figure there, as now often happens. Anything more dirty or unpleasant than their coarse clothes, exposed to the fierce illumination—a condition to which they are not subject in real life—is not conceivable. Those groupings of London-life stories, with policemen, &c., break down the romantic barriers, to let us out again into the thoroughfares, and are really little better than that representation of the Coronation in the days of Garrick, when the back wall of the theatre was removed, and the audience were shown the street behind, with bonfires blazing.

Some of these triumphs of set-scenery which lately drew the whole town to look—witness a snow-view of Charing Cross—seemed after the first surprise ineffably poor and bungling. The great frames of wood and whitened canvas were but too plainly revealed: their joinings, and readiness for being wheeled away: the whole was ambitious and clever; but anything but a delusion. And thus we arrive at what seems a paradox—that the more complex and elaborate the imitation, the further off travels the sense of illusion; for this reason, that by the very laborious minuteness of reproduction, deficiencies are made more conspicuous. Thus with these drawing-room scenes: the more the refined disorder of such a room is attempted, the more we are called on to require *everything* found in such places; and no upholsterer, however eminent, *could* furnish and arrange any room, on stage or elsewhere, within the few minutes between the acts. There is always something crooked and awry; and if not, the door always betrays its lath and canvas nature—an astonishing relic of stage barbarism. Who has not noticed the fashion in which it sticks, or flaps-to lightly, as if made of pasteboard? We might suggest to the realists a device which would mend this—a real door-case, with real door, which would fit into a hole in every interior. Thus indignant maidens and virtuous sons, in their sortie, might be indulged in a real sonorous slam.

These remarks, however, scarcely apply to 'Little Emily,' which, taken by itself, apart from all æsthetic views, the fashion in which it has been played on the stage, its elaborate brilliance of scenery, makes up a most agreeable entertainment. In this piece there is an average of good acting, distributed fairly among all the characters, which is rarely found. It is on the whole a brilliant piece, and deserves the success it has. But in the reason for this success we may find a lesson. Real *characters* were given to the actors to learn; characters for whose proper representation Mr Dickens had, as it were, given the minutest instructions in the pages of his novel; and thus we are supplied with round, finished pictures, instead of the meagre, unfurnished figures which crowd ordinary plays.

It is curious what rude principles still obtain

in the treatment of scenery, notwithstanding all the perfection they have reached to. It is not uncommon, at even the great theatres, to see a castle divide in two—half going up, half downwards; and in 'Faust,' at Covent Garden, the 'cathedral' goes swinging and swaying up in the air, with a most absurd effect. The real difficulty in the intricate 'set pieces' is to bridge over the space between them and human life. No matter how minute and careful the reproduction, there are always jagged edgings and shadows, which show the profile of canvas. It must be owned that at the gay Olympic—now a miracle of brilliance and richness where it was formerly no less a miracle of darkness and dinginess—are some surprising attempts at scenic effects. There is a close—the illuminated cathedral running round—with an additional effect of moonlight falling in front. The cloister seems to be 'built up,' and as the organ begins to play, a procession of choristers is seen to pass through the cloister. But at this moment the human element dwarfs the whole, and sends it away out of the realms of delusion. Living figures in the distance look gigantic, and though seen in the distance, become a standard, by which we find the whole cathedral to be about double the height of the choristers. Then the moonlight is certainly very effective in this, as in other cases; but when the characters come to the front, they cast awkward shadows, and bring out the boards of the stage; and the blackness of these shadows is so violent as to force on us at once that it is artificial light. And this proves, what I have said before, the danger of over-elaboration of stage effect. The more realism is aimed at, the more surely will the eye discover where it falls short. So with the effects so common now of banks to rivers, placed in front of one another, in the construction of some brilliant landscape. Concealed jets of light are placed in front of each: but the foremost 'profile' bank, having no stronger lights than the footlights, which are at a distance from it, are in comparative shadow and have the look of being cut out of card. There is room, too, for improvement in the 'fly pieces' which hang overhead, and which really do not affect to be more than what they are, pieces of painted canvas. The French fashion of constructing a room closed in, and only open to the audience, is fatal to the idea of distance and space. Even in the changing of scenes there are some old-fashioned blemishes still unthought of; and night after night in the best London theatres we see the halves of a flat 'carpenter's scene' joined together swiftly, with a loud report from their contact. It is only on a large stage like Covent Garden that these attempts at construction can be carried out successfully, and some of the recent pantomimes at that house were miracles of exquisite effect. On that vast stage the absolute effects of open country and landscape, stretching far away in the distance, and the enormous length of scenes and aerial space thus gained, present the appearance of a great waste of sky and atmosphere.

But, in truth, this mimicry, once begun, is endless; it becomes gigantic and insupportable. Whole houses and streets have to be built up with infinite toil and cost; mountains have to be constructed, bridges thrown across, whose canvas flutters as the pursued girl staggers over. Yet still we are not in the least beguiled; we may venture to say that the skilfully, effectively painted flat scene is far more welcome to the eye, has more illusion, and certainly no points of weakness or make-shift, which the most careless eye can detect. In fact, we would venture to say that the true theory lies somewhere in a certain generalization, certain conventional shapes of scene and furniture, so general in style and figure as to fit all. This was the usage of the old days of Garrick and his Drury Lane. And there was a certain propriety in this course. Once we descend into archæological minuteness, the eye is disturbed, criticism is challenged, or we become pledged to a minuteness of detail which the play does not require, and which is an insufferable burden to those who get up the play.

A more intricate question as to stage effect arises, when we consider what amount of *exaggeration* an actor is allowed to indulge in, so as to produce effect on the audience. As to tragedy, and especially in certain forms of tragedy, a certain stateliness is necessary to raise the subject out of mere homeliness, and is due to the dignity of the piece. And this can be seen a good deal on the French stage, where stately and even pompous declamation seems in keeping with certain subjects, nay, seems even necessary. But in any ordinary acting there must be exaggeration to produce an effect which shall not seem exaggerated, as can be seen in the case of amateurs doing so simple a thing as walking across the stage, which itself requires acting to look like ordinary walking. The reason for this is, that players are not seen under the conditions of ordinary life. They are under a glass, as it were; placed in a conspicuous position, with strong light flaring on them, and every motion brought into prominence.

In common life we are too close, and ourselves generally too much engaged in what is going on, to take notice of these things. So with speeches and conversation. It is obvious that the mere careless tones of every remark would not do for the publicity of a great theatre, and must be overdone to attract attention and have weight. But here comes in the abuse. The true actor learns nicely the exact force and weight of such exaggeration, and so proportions it that it does no more than produce the effect of what is natural, and unexaggerated. Just as the well-known figures of boys in St Peter's, that support the holy water vase, prove to be of gigantic dimensions. The vulgar actor, on the contrary, seizes on this as an opening for making himself more conspicuous, and to this we owe the stampings and stridings and roarings which have actually become established, as a necessary part of stage effect.* Hence it is that we have this laboured enforcing of interior thoughts and emotions, by violent and obstreperous outward manifestation, as though it were possible to have an alphabet and language of thought. Hence the common actor's limited categories of various expression may be divided for him under heads—joy, rage, &c., into some one of which everything must be forced.

That view of Charles Lamb's as to the unsuitableness of Shakespeare's tragedies for the stage has always seemed to have much weight, and may be noticed here. There is so much that is impalpable—so airy and delicate; so much that is mental and philosophical, and which cannot possibly be expressed by the machinery of the stage. A great deal, as in 'Lear' and 'Hamlet,' is pure dreamy fluctuation of the mind; whose existence it is wholly a false principle to convey to a large and mixed crowd, by the agency of declamation and gesture. Such emotions are concealed from the spectator in real life, though to such a spectator

---

* A French dramatist has lately been lecturing on this very matter, but I have not been able to discover whether the lectures have been published.

they are often *betrayed*, by the play of feature or tone of voice. Thus in the late Mr Charles Kean's system of overloading Shakespeare's plays with dresses, and pageantry, and scenic effects, there was a very coarse and false mode of illustration. But the remarks of Elia are so just, and commend themselves so strongly—to say nothing of his quaint and charming language, always welcome under any pretext—that I shall have no scruple of introducing them here.

'Talking is the direct object of the imitation here. But in all the best dramas, and in Shakespeare above all, how obvious it is, that the form of *speaking*, whether it be in soliloquy or dialogue, is only a medium, and often a highly artificial one, for putting the reader or spectator into possession of that knowledge of the inner structure and workings of mind in a character, which he could otherwise never have arrived at *in that form of composition* by any gift short of intuition. We do here as we do with novels written in the epistolary form. How many improprieties, perfect solecisms in letter-writing, do we put up with in Clarissa and other books, for the sake of the delight which that form upon the whole gives us. But the practice of stage representation reduces everything to a controversy of elocution. Every character, from the boisterous blasphemings of Bajazet to the shrinking timidity of womanhood, must play the orator. The love-dialogues of Romeo and Juliet, those silver-sweet sounds of lovers' tongues by night; the more intimate and sacred sweetness of nuptial colloquy between an Othello, or a Posthumus, with their married wives, all those delicacies which are so delightful in the reading, as when we read of those youthful dalliances in Paradise—

> "As beseem'd
> Fair couple link'd in happy nuptial league,
> alone:"

by the inherent fault of stage representation, how are these things sullied and turned from their very nature by being exposed to a large assembly; when such speeches as Imogen addresses to her lord come drawling out of the mouth of a hired actress, whose courtship, though nominally addressed to the personated Posthumus, is manifestly aimed at the spectators, who are to judge of her endearments and her returns of love. But Hamlet himself—what does he suffer meanwhile by being dragged forth as the public schoolmaster, to give

The Dramatists. 43

lectures to the crowd! Why, nine parts in ten of what Hamlet does, are transactions between himself and his moral sense, they are the effusions of his solitary musings, which he retires to holes and corners and the most sequestered parts of the palace to pour forth; or rather, they are the silent meditations with which his bosom is bursting, reduced to words for the sake of the reader, who must else remain ignorant of what is passing there. These profound sorrows, these light-and-noise-abhorring ruminations, which the tongue scarce dares utter to deaf walls and chambers, how can they be represented by a gesticulating actor, who comes and mouths them out before an audience, making four hundred people his confidants at once. I say not that it is the fault of the actor so to do; he must pronounce them *ore rotundo*, he must accompany them with his eye, he must insinuate them into his auditory by some trick of eye, tone, or gesture, or he fails. *He must be thinking all the while of his appearance, because he knows that all the while the spectators are judging of it.* And this is the way to represent the shy, negligent, retiring Hamlet!'

This is all true and excellent; and though men,

who believe in the surpassing excellence of Shakespeare, and that he was made to be read, and acted, and would bear every possible test, could not bring themselves to accept Elia's view, still his remarks are valuable in this place, as illustrating a genuine principle of acting—namely, the true and natural fashion of a player revealing his private thoughts to the audience.

Passing now to the *moral* view of certain plays, which was lately under discussion, it will be seen that the exhibition of a piece like 'Formosa' cannot in any way be justified. The exhibition of the career of a lady whose profession need not be named, with the persons whom she usually influences, and the supposed life of both, was defended on the ground that the stage was to reflect the manners of the time: that people took 'dramatic' interest only in what struck a chord, by reminding them of the ordinary or average life of the day; and finally, if people countenance, and are interested in, what is disreputable, they will require to meet the same on the stage. In short, the question of dramatic morality is entirely on their own heads. The stage is merely ministerial, and the dramatists must supply what they demand at their own risk.

Now, all these positions are mistakes. In the first place, it is a principle in art that there must be *selection*, and that the whole art lies in the selection ; and it was on this point that the early Pre-Raphaelites made shipwreck. Some would produce a piece of decayed brick wall, copied with amazing exactness; or, more singular still, a patch of weeds in ditch-water, with stoats and decomposition faithfully given. So with the old Dutch painters, who copied lighted candles, and lemon peels, and crusts of bread, with the same amazing power of imitation. This might be called the holding the mirror up to nature. But the true principle lies in selecting what is *beautiful*, —finding out the common principle which underlies a number of beautiful objects of the same class, and making us familiar with it. The mere slavish copying of an inanimate object is worth nothing beyond the mere momentary admiration at the trouble and mechanical skill; there must be the hint of a sentiment, something drawn from the artist's own soul, and which he has worked in with his colours. So with dramas like 'Formosa.' Vice and its ways are as utterly coarse and uninteresting, as the Pre-Raphaelite garbage and ditch-water; and the presentment of the 'Villa at Fulham,' and what goes on there, is as morbid and undramatic as wax-work models of the human figure, and its diseases, which are exhibited under scientific pretences. Further, it may be wholly disputed whether this is holding the mirror up to the lives of the public who flock to look at its life. There is a conventional standard of human life which, by common consent, is regulated by rules of decency, and to which we appeal officially. Our laws, customs, family affairs, police, are all regulated on a *soi-disant* moral basis; and such enters into every relation. And it is impossible to deny this, or shut one's eyes to it; honesty is not only the best, but the recognized policy, and this should be reflected back from the stage. Yes, it will be said, a *soi-disant* hypocritical policy; but our heart of hearts will go with the truth of the picture; to all it will come home as a fact, true but unrecognized. No: for we need only turn to the French stage to see a more legitimate way of dealing with such subjects. To the French, whose manner of life corresponds, and to whom Mr Boucicault's arguments would apply, such a mode of 'holding up the mirror' would be eminently inartistic, at the least. Let any one turn to the 'Dame aux Camelias,' or to the 'Adrienne Le Couvreur,'—both lives of courtesans,—and it will be seen with what true dramatic art they are treated, even in reference to the character of the audience. Pictures of the vicious life are there not the end in view; such for a French audience would be mere grossness. Those plays are a hundred times more dangerous than any scene in 'Formosa.' In the French pieces the immoral element is assumed as a foundation, as in most French books and plays: after that assumption enters sentiment, tenderness, and passion; all which interpose between it and the audience. The true test would be this: exhibit 'Formosa' in diorama shape, or with dissolving views; 1. 'Interior of a courtesan's villa at Fulham;' 2. 'Arrival of lady visitors;' 3. 'Supper at the Villa;' and public indignation would soon be roused. However, the manager of this theatre, when 'Formosa' was played, took the matter out of the province of argument by a statement which amounted to this:—that virtue did not pay; that vice did; and that he was obliged to play what paid.

And his view shows what a serious responsibility rests upon the heads of our theatres, and certainly should justify the interference of the State as censor. The stage has an incredible influence, even with the most educated. We are amused at the ranting virtue of the transpontine theatres; but the shouts of approval from an unwashed audience have some significance, though their practical value is little. But a more weighty proof may be found in witnessing a play like the 'Colleen Bawn,' from which it would be hard to come away without feeling a generous sympathy with the virtues of the poor, and, through the skill of the author, a better enlightenment as to their kindness and goodness, disguised from us by a cloak of what we think vulgarity. That there should be such an officer as censor, and that he should have 'passed' such a piece as 'Formosa,' is an argument not against Mr Boucicault, but against one more of the many miserable shams which still endure.

The most popular writer of the day cannot be passed over in a review of the stage. An abundant supply of Mr ROBERTSON's pieces have been familiar to the public for many years, and the list is a tolerably long one. It included 'David Garrick,' an adaptation from the Ger-

The Dramatists.

man; 'Society,' 'Ours,' 'Caste,' of which the first differs so much from the rest in boldness and marked character, that it has the air of an adaptation; also 'Home,' from the French, 'For Love,' 'Shadow-tree Shaft,' 'Dreams,' 'The Nightingale,' and 'School.' More than half of these have been failures. Garrick, criticising some one with Boswell, said what he wanted was 'beef.' This is the want in Mr Robertson's plays. Like all men of true taste, he sees and admires the delicate touchings of the French writers, this mastery of the airy measures of speech and character; but he forgets that it is merely so much skin and colouring, under which the French have a strong skeleton. We can quite fancy a poetical man being possessed with an interesting or dramatic idea, and pleased with it. Thus, Tennyson's Lady Clara Vere de Vere and the love of a young German artist, or the notion, as in 'The Nightingale,' of an opera singer persecuted by a mysterious Eastern; the loss of her child, &c. Such topics have a picturesque air; but they are mere crude notions, the colours, the tools with which to work. Such is the mere machinery without steam. A dramatic writer of sound principles would begin at the other end. Some powerful situation, some original clashing of the passions, would seize on his mind; and, turning it all sides, he would work his way outwards, trying various persons and characters, until, perhaps, he found that an Eastern and the opera singer together would be the best persons to bring out what is desired. The same fault runs through all Mr Robertson's pieces: they are skilful sketches and groupings. But this 'Nightingale' was so utterly destitute of vitality, motion, character, and meaning, that it seemed merely a collection of profiles, painted and labelled.

Mr Tom Taylor is a writer of far greater firmness and vigour, with, besides, the nicest skill and touch. His knowledge of the stage is thorough; and though he has 'adapted' freely, he has virtually only taken the 'motif,' as though some one should say, 'Here is a good subject,' and made the rest his own. 'Still Waters run Deep,' 'The Contested Election,' 'The Overland Mail,' and 'The Unequal Match,' are all fresh, and gay, and entertaining, and will certainly keep the stage. The characters are treated legitimately, both causing the situations and being developed by them. His last production—a play in blank verse, with the scene laid in Shakesperian times—seemed the most daring of ventures, the most forlorn of hopes. But the dry bones of remote era and costume and diction were vivified by strong situation, marked character, and poetical lines; and the result is that audiences crowd to where they know they will be interested. A good and original comedy of the same writer has been drawing crowded houses at the Haymarket; and it is not often that two legitimate successes from the same hand have to be recorded for a single year.

This leads us to consider a special shape of play which often finds its way to the stage, namely, the dramatized novel. The fashion that has so often obtained, of putting a story that has acquired great popularity on the stage, throws some light on what is the true nature of the dramatic. A great master attracts a vast audience, whom he approaches through their intellect only, and the same public is seized with a desire to see and hear his characters in more material shape. The guide to the result of such experiments may be summed up thus: failure generally, but the higher and more artistic the writer, the more certain the failure. Mr Dickens's best story is now being submitted to this test; and though the performance is successful, and 'draws,' this result is owing, not to its being a presentation of Mr Dickens's story, but to some good scenery, the amusing acting of an American player, and the level merit of the actors.

This practice has become so common, that it is really assumed that every story requires only some skilful mechanical arrangement to take the shape of a drama. Yet happily the genius of a great writer is not to be thus dealt with, and his very genius is his protection. The spectators of 'Little Em'ly' must feel a curious sensation, half of pleasure, half of disappointment, and the disappointment takes the shape of some such expression as, 'Well, Peggotty could hardly have been this sort of man; Miss Trotwood scarcely this sort of person.' Nay, had Mr Dickens accurately copied these characters from living originals, and were these set before us to speak and act, even here we might find the same want of recognition. The truth is, that a writer of genius works more by association, by hints, by 'striking chords' which the reader can lay his ear to. There is a bloom, an airiness—hints—touches as delicate as the powder on a butterfly's wing, which defy dramatist's or actor's touch. This is specially the case in a novelist like Mr Dickens, where there is so much that depends on the story-teller himself, so much that is outside the characters. But this will be more evident by a comparison with other story-tellers.

Sir Walter Scott's novels were regularly dramatized when they came out, and it is quite apparent that the best of the versions—those which now keep the stage, 'Rob Roy' and 'Guy Mannering' —were accepted as perfect representatives of the original novels. They are both admirably done, and the story and character, so far as they go, happily sketched and dramatized. We accept the Dominie Sampson of the play as the Dominie of the story, the same in quality, though not in quantity; so with Dandie Dinmont; while the Bailie Nicol Jarvie and the Dougal Creature were confessed by Sir Walter himself to be perfect embodiments in the flesh of what he had written. The reason of this success is, that the novels are dramas with very bold characters; that is, natures that reveal themselves by very marked tokens of speech and action. The situations are all strong, and a little coarse, speaking in a relative sense. Alexandre Dumas is another writer who has been immensely 'dramatized'; but his 'Monte Christo,' whether in drama shape or novel shape, is precisely the same. The characters are either distinct, or mark themselves by bold actions and witty speeches: but they are all more or less conventional. Thus D'Artagnan, whom we have read of in the 'Three Musketeers,' would be acceptable to us on the stage, when played by any dashing, spirited actor, with a wig and pointed moustaches, a hat and plume, jerkin, sword, and Louis XIV. boots. We might see half-a-dozen good actors in the part, and find nothing discordant with what we had read. The character has a few bold, broad touches on the outside, and here we find them. So with Dominic Sampson. The wig and scholastic dress, the abstraction, the bookishness, the frequent 'prodigious!' can all be seen and heard upon the stage as well as in the book.

It is very different with a work of the class of 'David Copperfield.' One of the charms of Mr Dickens's humour are those sudden analogies between objects of mind and matter—strange and surprising likenesses—and which is indeed opening a new world. Another feature lies not so much in making the characters, as in 'bringing them out' by the curious comments, hints, and remarks of the novelist himself. It is as though we were witnessing all the scenes of the story, with a mysterious spirit by our side, who had privileged and Asmodean access to secret interiors of house and of mind. Thus is given for behaviour and speech and deportment, otherwise unmeaning, a secret key, which makes all intelligible. Now it is obvious that on the stage all this must be lost. Numbers who go to the Olympic see David Copperfield himself on the boards, in a strange coat and gilt buttons, follow him as he moves among the other characters, and would own that he fulfils his duty to the play respectably. He has about the same business that he has in the story—friend of Steerforth and Peggotty, unmasker of Uriah Heep, and so forth. Given that selection of episodes now being played, it might be asked, What more could be added to the part? Yet this is a superficial view. Turn to the story, and we find that his is the mind which reflects and colours the whole course of events to us. Through him, as it were, we see every character: it is his mind, his feeling, the mind of the author himself, and his own life— that fills up the whole. Through the eyes of David look forth the eyes of the writer; his quick wit, his genius, illuminates that figure, brings out the wit and humour of others, as steel does with flint, and illustrates their doings with a sort of commentary. Thus Copperfield becomes the soul of all. We turn to the stage, and all this must disappear; there remains but a figure in a long coat and gilt buttons, who walks on and walks off, and is about as purposeless as one of Madame Tussaud's images. Not but that the adapter has done his part with a surprising tact and self-abnegation: and we only use his skilful adaptation to illustrate a principle. But a most judicious and elegant expounder has laid down the true view in a lucid judgment. Charles Lamb, in a well-known essay, explains the reverence due to such great masters, and, allowing something for a fantastic exaggeration, which makes the charm of his style, he wishes that the plays of Shakespeare were never acted—'there is so much in them which comes not under the province of acting. . . . . The glory of the scenic art is to promote passion, and the more coarse and palpable the passion the more hold upon the eyes and ears of the spectator the performer has. . . . . . So to see Lear acted—to see an old

The Dramatists. 57

man tottering about the stage with a walking-stick, turned out-of-doors by his daughter on a rainy night, has nothing in it but what is painful and disgusting. This is all the feeling which the acting of Lear ever produced in me. But the Lear of Shakespeare cannot be acted. The contemptible machinery by which they mimic the storm which he goes out in, is not more inadequate to represent the horrors of the real elements than any actor can be to represent Lear. . . . . The greatness of Lear is not in corporal dimensions, but in intellectual . . . . it is his mind which is laid bare. . . . . On the stage we see nothing but corporeal infirmities and weakness, the impotence of rage : while we read we see not Lear, but we are Lear,—we are in his mind. . . . .' Every word of this applies to the works of great novelists.

We shall now pass to an examination of what appear to be the true principles of interest and entertainment in comedy,—those which should attract, and hold, an intelligent audience.

PART II.

COMEDY.

'THE stage,' magic word! and its costly and magnificent *entourage*, seems to point at some source of exquisite enjoyment, now gone from us. Granting that there are some who enjoy the play as heartily as they could desire, each must own that the elements we have been dwelling on are not the ones which minister to their relish. It, of course, cannot be denied that the play-house rings with as loud and perhaps more boisterous laughter than ever Drury Lane did in the days of Garrick; but this is no test. Laughter is common to both fools and wise men, but signifies a very different form of enjoyment in each case, and there is an admirable passage in Leigh Hunt which will more than illustrate this.

'Some of these performers think they gain no applause unless they have raised a tempest of laughter: they forget that the most exquisite humour is that which provokes the least mirth;

that wit, so superior to mere humour, disdains the acknowledgment of external laughter, and is content with that feeling of pleasure and surprise which may be called the laughter of the mind; *that a pantomime clown, in short, when he breaks his nose against a door, boasts a wilder burst of applause than genuine comedy perhaps ever obtained.'*

This brings us to the inquiry what ought to be the true source of enjoyment in stage representation, for we have now got into such confusion and indistinctness, that to go and see *something on the stage,* 'a medley of colours under a strong light, amounts to that phrase, so delightful to children, of 'going to the theatre.'

We often hear the phrase, in illustration of some good story of real life, 'Quite a drama! like what you would see on the stage.' This would seem to hint at something that is very *rare* and exceptional indeed, or something exciting and interesting. But surely, at this present moment, such an illustration has lost its force; and one would be inclined, reviewing the dull progress of a stage-story, rather to say, 'This is nearly as prosy as real life;' or 'Like what you would see in the street.'

The stage is but a poor copy of life—a selection, as it were, not so much of *material* events, as the vulgar and superficial suppose, but of mental conflicts, mental struggles, which may, indeed, give such results as powerful material events, but in themselves become the substantial support, the leading ideas, of the whole. In real life there are stories of absorbing and overwhelming interest always going on about us; but they are unmanageable, because spread over a long period—because encumbered with the 'padding' of common dead-level life. Still, making all deductions, there is something in *life*, in what is *living*, and in what genuinely attaches itself and belongs to life, that always will interest, and even absorb. Hence the public is never weary of trials. Hence a private history has always a strange charm of its own, as if a reflection of life, and which it seems to lose when it gets into print. Hence housemaids listen at the keyhole to what 'master and missis' are saying. Hence the truth of what Walpole has said so justly —if any one were to set down honestly and faithfully all that he has seen, thought, or observed, the result would be a most interesting book—'ir whatever hands,' adds the lively letter-writer. For this is the whole secret of interest—the candour, not the manner, of the revelation. Once let affectation overlay what is being told, and it becomes so much deceit. In short, a man's mind 'a kingdom is,' not merely 'to me,' but to all others; it furnishes variety inexhaustible. It is not in colours, lights, groupings, gorgeous and fantastic scenery, dresses, handsome faces and figures, dances, flowers, jewels, puns, and poor songs, that, true interest or amusement is to be sought and found. These are the mere inanimate stocks and stones of life; and in time—after the few seconds' surprise is over—produce about as much entertainment as a day's pleasuring to the British Museum does to the country bumpkin, or even to persons of far higher training and refinement.

A quarrel takes place in the street; a crowd gathers at once. We hear two people discussing something in a railway-carriage, naturally, of course, and not talking for us; it becomes more interesting than the book or newspaper we are reading. A shrewd observant member of a family travels abroad; his little adventures, trifling but told well, linger on the memory far more than the pretentious scenes of official tourists. We ourselves may have figured in some little rencontre at an inn, or coach, or boat; have come in contact with some 'characters,' as we call them; and we turn back to these with a surprising relish and longing. They are dramatic, more or less. They are bits of *life*.

Now a play exhibits in a small space what is an extract from human life. Some concessions must be made to the limitations of time, and the skill of the writer is shown in leaving out, with as little violence as may be, the dead-level monotonous bits during which nothing can be done. Hence there will always be a rather unnatural gathering together of incidents in a play, which will require from the spectator a certain allowance. This is common to all plays; but it is more *comedy* —that art now as much lost to us as is the rich red of old stained glass—with its principles of entertaining, that we have now to consider.

Human action, as just shown, is always interesting, and rivets the attention. Human character also attracts; and the two mainly constitute the interest of conventional comedy. In fact, that much-hackneyed 'holding up the mirror-to-Nature' is the true secret; but it must be to *Nature*; for a sort of holding up is always attempted, but it is to something artificial or accidental. The mirror is held up to gaudy dresses, to painted faces, to antics of all sorts, to twitches of expression, to positive 'grinning through a horse-collar;' but not to Nature. It will be said, the skilful scene-painters of our time do at least deserve this credit, that they reflect the most exquisite hills, vales, and woods, the old ruins of abbeys and castles; but this is outside the dramatic art, and belongs to the panorama. The houses on fire, coal-pits, machinery-rooms, steamers, and railway-trains, do not deserve recognition. The truth is, a really good comedy, with good judges present, would be as amusing on the old Thespian cart, without scene, curtain, or foot-lights, as it would be at Drury Lane.

For 'character' to interest, several things are necessary, all which were duly attended to in the old days of comedy. It must be genuine and spontaneous—a quality rarely found in even the attempts at character of our modern pieces, which are done with a certain heavy laboriousness, and to order, as it were, just as a workman would make a chair. But the real mistake grows out of the corruption that has spread over the modern drama, which appeals entirely to the eye and ear, instead of to the mind; for a 'character' is now entirely made up out of external accidents, strange-coloured hair, false forehead, comically-cut coats, particoloured trousers; also out of tricks of elocution, of strange sounds, and jerks of manner. These are ludicrous when seen once or twice, and such are, no doubt, grotesque enough in this way; but it should be noted why.

In real life, such oddities of manner, and even of dress, are but the grotesque effects of a cause yet more grotesque—of a mind and habit of thought of which these are but faint tokens—an expression of something within. To take an instance. One may have seen in a coffee-room the oldest frequenter—a little shrunken and shrivelled old man, with a high-collared coat of a pattern forty years old, a hat singularly tall, which, with his ancient and corresponding gloves, he puts on the rail always precisely in the same spot. This being is all rusty—soul, body, and clothes; talks in a chirping way of fifty years ago as though it were yesterday. His mind goes back, as do his clothes; so there is a perfect correspondence. From the old hat being always in the one spot, it may be augured that he will grow testy should another take it. Here then is a correspondence between the inward character and its external side. But could we fancy a rational modernized old gentleman, whose ideas were in exact accordance with the tone of the day, but who wears a dress thus eccentric, there would be an utter discordance—there would be neither interest nor 'fun'—the dress would be unmeaning. So, too, with his manner and tricks of voice and expression. These should be the result of some odd tone of mind, and reveal it; just as hesitations and stammerings show an uncertainty of mind, and twitchings and 'pluckings' at a wig; and those queer movements of figure and limbs, those strange tones of voice, which go to make up the modern notion of character, betoken corresponding oddities of thought and feeling.

Yet, giving the utmost license, how limited all this is, as a mere gamut of expression! And as we look down the line of 'funny men' now in possession of the English stage, what a little variety in their tricks, and how hard to call to mind anything more than what we have just been mentioning! As there are but eight notes in an octave, so we can sound in a very short time the dull tones of dress, caricature, 'making faces,' and voice. These are what make up character-parts—strange beings formed on no human model, wearing clothes seen in no known street, talking as no human being ever talked: and these are the creatures that figure in the pieces where anything comic is required. We think of the hundred-and-one ingenious actors at the provincial theatres, who are doing the round of Box and Cox business, Slasher and Crasher, and the rest: there is no other model but the one—the ridiculous Cockney in pink trousers, talking very fast and glibly. The cleverness of the actor made something approaching a character of Lord Dundreary; but a great deal was owing to dress and outer eccentricity. When a new figure was wanted out of the same family, the device was to change the colour of the hair, complexion, and dress—make him all white hair, white cheeks, and white dress — but character was not to be expected.

On far different principles were the old comedies written. They are amazing for their likeness to life; for their flow, and spirit, and character. The impression they leave is like that of one of Fielding's or Smollett's, or even Thackeray's, stories; their characters are round, and seem to have lived; the whole is like an incident out of real life, told by a lively and vivacious storyteller. Modern plays beside these round richly-coloured figures seem like profiles cut out of card —quite poor and flat. Indeed, the art of drawing character, save in the hands of a leader or two, seems gone, in the novels; and instead we have faint weak *labelling* of characters—for it is no more —such as we find in the common circulating-library novel—mere bits of canvas stretched upon a poor framework of lath.

The chief secret of the success of the dramatic work of the old times was, that such 'characters' were not mere isolated figures in the piece— coming on merely for their *own sake*, and the more selfish sake of the actor that played them—but were real *aids to the story*. They were not formed so as merely to arrive in their turn, grimace awhile, do their regulation bit of fun, and then withdraw, to allow the story to go on. With far more artistic views the oddities of the character were made to influence the story, consciously or unconsciously. Place an oddity in a drawing-room, where he is merely to come and go, make a few speeches, even exhibit his humour in the most effective manner, and we shall soon grow tired of him. It becomes repetition. But entangle him in some serious and complicated business, the details of which embarrass him at every turn, against which he struggles vainly—here his oddities, the attitudes of his mind in contact with circumstances, become ever changing and ever new. It is the *action*, in short, that is necessary to the character. The character should exist for the story; and, in return, the character will find itself repaid by the discovery of innumerable fresh 'points' of which it would otherwise have been deprived. But the foolish players of our time confound monopoly with effect, and think that, unless the chief attention of the audience—quite apart from the story—be concentrated on them and their antics, there is loss of interest and effect. They little think that a vast deal more could be procured for them on the old system. But this is the grand weakness and the grand temptation in all worldly things—discounting the present more showy advantages, to the sacrifice of what would be ten times as effective.

The simple answer to the question, what it is that entertains us in the drama, must, in part, be an answer to what it is that, in a lower degree, entertains us in life. The spectacle of human character, and the action which the conflict of character brings about, makes up the enjoyments of life. If we were confined to the use of our eyes only, and passed on, looking at all the beautiful shows in the world, and merely following out some formal labour, life would lose all its charm. But, the looking at the turns and freaks of character, and at the *action* of various minds, unexpected and surprising, this is what gives us a relish for society. Now, this very surprise and consequent delight cannot be ordered at pleasure; we cannot command the dramatic interest of life and character; but we can go to the theatre. There skilful students of human nature, by an instinct which is born with them, can divine these curious emotions of character and humour, and show us what we could not hope to see elsewhere, except by a rare accident. And our entertainment is in exact proportion to the power of this instinct. The whole is independent of scenery, painting, electric light, dresses, and mimicry.

Last year, at a foreign watering-place, a French comic actor came on his tour, and was announced at the little theatre of the place to give a 'Lecture on the Needle-Gun.' We have seen some comic performances of this sort in England,—some of those free and too familiar addresses, in which the player thinks only of laughter, and of saying what is 'funny' without its being appropriate. We could understand how an English lecture on the needle-gun would be written by some of the 'smart' men of the day,—full of puns, and jokes, and familiarity; but the French player, even in this light exercise, showed himself a true artist, and a more interesting and dramatic quarter of an hour could not be conceived. And it is worth while pausing a little, to see on what principles real 'fun' was to be got out of such a subject. The English actor's theory would be something of this sort— to amuse the audience by jesting, possibly by a queer tone of voice, in imitation of some popular lecturer, or of the generic type of lecturer. It would take the shape of a comic lecture, perhaps after the style of one of the late Albert Smith's addresses. In nine cases out of ten, such would be the view taken by an English actor to whom a manager might propose such a performance. He would be certain to get laughter out of it. The French artist went to work on quite a different system. He, as it were, said to himself, 'Lecturing, like every other grave thing, has its comic side.' We could conceive a grave and simple-minded college-professor enraptured at the science, and delighted with the elegant ingenuity of the Chassepot. To see a little man carried away by his enthusiasm, and handling one of those terrible weapons, is in itself a ludicrous contrast. He is humane, bookish, would faint if he heard a shot; yet he has this murderous engine in his hand, and is expatiating on it with affection, mixed with a little timidity. On this view he would start with perfect gravity and a painful *earnestness*, and from this basis the whole humour of the lecture actually did flow. The most delightful portion was this very sincerity and eagerness, which caused him, as it were, to forget the whole theory of the mechanism; and his enthusiastic flourishes about the perfection of the machinery would be abruptly checked by a hopeless confusion; a bewildered look coming on his face as he drew back a bolt, or pushed out some piece, having at last to stop,—then extricating himself by light generality; but in his face was trouble and uncertainty; and he would again gradually approach the really substantial portion of his lecture, the explanation of the mechanism, which, by the end, never was explained.

Now, the entertainment produced by this performance—and it was very great—is the pure entertainment of dramatic art. Plays, comedies, and tragedies are all no more than a development of this feeling. The source of pleasure here is the earnestness and sincerity, which in itself was the cause of the embarrassment and distress. It was, in short, character in movement, and taking a certain shape.

Of tragedy it is useless to speak, as we have no tragedy, or indeed tragedians. It is, as it were, out of fashion, and the sympathy of the age does not go with, at least, the conventional shape of tragedy. That stilted tone which attends on the best of the old tragedies seems to interpose a barrier of stout buckram between them and our hearty sympathy: and the stiff, stereotyped sufferings which heroes and heroines endure, with the established stalkings and mouthings to which the most respectable of modern players are partial, make us believe that these are people and events belonging to another dispensation altogether, and who are really outside our fashion of life. Their exaggerated and overdone woes we do not see or hear of in the daily round of human affairs. It will be otherwise when writers of imagination, with instinct for character, and with a deep knowledge of the passions, arise ; and who, studying the course, the sympathies of our everyday life, will hold up a true picture of real *tragedy*, — of the conflict of those special passions which are felt, are raging about us, and belong to our time. Then shall the true chord of sympathy be touched.

With comedy it is very different. We should not be inclined to lay much stress on that view of it, so often insisted on by so many critical writers, which looks on it as a sort of censor for the time, the *castigator morum*, which is a mere utilitarian view. But the process of 'lashing' the follies and eccentricities of the time by 'holding up the mirror' to human character, and its efforts at outward manifestation at the same time, is a precious homage to the value of the stage, as a part of public education; and with a correct public taste and really good dramatic writers, it can be the most effectual reformer and corrector of morals and vulgarities. That there is nothing Utopian or painful in this view will be seen in a moment. The whole stream of dramatic life is marked by such triumphs; and a play written by some master of satire and ridicule, and at the same time thoroughly successful, has, over and over again, routed from society some miserable folly that would otherwise have held its ground. But here again we find the difference between the genuine, and the false, dramatic art which now obtains. The latter affects, indeed, to ridicule, as it fancies; but it merely exhibits. Often we see upon the stage some foolish type of character of the time, offered in a ridiculous shape, indeed, but still overdrawn and only a caricature. The attempt on the part of writer, and of player especially, is to produce a 'funny' effect; the exceptional and odd portions are extravagantly developed. The result is sympathy with, rather than contempt for, the originals. As an instance, the well-known dramatic Lord Dundreary, who, as a character, has taken with the public more than other characters during the last twenty years,

must have been originally suggested by the type of
vapid, languid, vacuous swell, who is undoubtedly a
figure of society. That such a demeanour was and
is growing 'fashionable' there can be no doubt,
as well as that it was a bitter social malady which
needed check and cure. A student of character,
like Foote for instance, would study carefully the
evils to which such a temperament leads; its selfishness, heartlessness, and ignorance; or, taking
a lighter view, the contemptible life, the useless-
ness, blundering, and stupidity of such a nature.
His part in the story would be marked by the
exhibition of these defects: he would be attended
in his course by laughter and enjoyment, but the
laughter of contempt. Of such a treatment of a
drama it is needless to say that Mr Tom Taylor is
quite capable; but the point was to make a good
character for a particular actor. Mr Sothern, too,
could have given this legitimate view; but the
result was a wonderful *tour de force*, an extravagant
piece of farce, exceedingly amusing and grotesque,
but having no dramatic significance whatever. It
neither invites nor repels; it is detached from the
story; we go to see it and laugh.* The 'swell'

* At the same time it would be impossible not to do justice to the

reigned triumphant, and perhaps enjoyed the spectacle the most of any. He knew it could not apply to him; and the weekly 'funny' papers had many pictures on this truly comic unconsciousness. An admirable passage of Leigh Hunt here recurs :—
'The author thinks, not how he may improve his audience by painting its likeness, but how he may flatter it by making its features beautiful, or amuse it by showing how merrily he can distort them. As nobody therefore finds his likeness on the stage, nobody is improved by it; virtue is not encouraged by the representation of its *unpresuming* countenance, nor is vice alarmed at the deformity of its passion-tortured features: the scene is so far drawn forward, as it were, into the part appropriated to the audience, or in other words it is so evidently the intention of the author, and consequently of his actors, to stand before the spectator as mere candidates for applause, that the stage becomes literally abstracted from its abstraction, its professed absence from an overlooked multitude is forgotten.'

On the other hand, there is a class of this

excellence of this extraordinary performance. All through it there are real *dramatic* details; but they are isolated, and do not relate to the whole. But the intention was caricature.

'languid swell' whose languor is the result of slowness of temper, and who has good-nature at the bottom of his absurdities. Such are often judged a little unjustly; but the stage may stand their friend; and that lightly-sketched character of 'Jack Poyntz' in 'School' has, in a small way, brought home to many what good there may be below such eccentricity. Such is the exquisite art of a drama: it takes the place of acute judgment, and teaches us what outside oddities there are, and humours that have no connection with heart or character, and what outside peculiarities flow legitimately from within. These latter are what *really interest;* and the vice of our time, both in writer and actor, is in mistaking mere outside *accidents* for a legitimate signification of what is within. It would take too long to examine the other writers, but the single name of Foote will be sufficient, who, in play after play, delighted and amused, and at the same time so covered with ridicule, the vicious nabobs, macaroni parsons, demireps, and other odious types of his day, as actually to make them unfashionable, and subjects of public contempt.

That same meagreness of intellect which teaches

that the servile imitation of material objects is the highest dramatic art, has also seriously affected the *soi-disant* comedy of the day. We may be thankful for some little break in the clouds; and the extraordinary success of one play at a little theatre, which has long passed its three hundredth representation, shows that the taste for a comedy of manners is not wholly dead. In 'School' the audience who fill stalls and boxes, some of whom have been again and again to see the piece, find the faint beginnings of that pleasurable sensation, which arises from having the mirror held to their lives. Yet surely, without disparagement of the writer's cleverness, this mirror is rather of a wavy surface, and presents distorted outlines and reflections. As is well known, it is a German play adapted. German manners meet us at every turn, forced into contact with English character. Thoroughly foreign is the patriarchal character of the professor, who is at the head of the young ladies' school; so, too, is the importance attached to the examination, &c. Quite foreign, too, is the publicity, the admission of officers to an examination of young ladies, the love-making, the fetching cream, the wanderings in the woods, the moonlight scenes, the marriage, with the arrival of the lady in her bridal dress. The admirable acting makes us forget this discordance; but the whole is a sort of hybrid—a German lady with English feet. But some of the British characters are so good, and so excellently played, that we pass by the discordance; we are glad to get something that approaches to the play of character on character, and an evening at 'School' was a most agreeable and enjoyable one.

Still, using this play as an illustration, it will be said that here is presented a very fine reflection of some characters in English society, and that therefore this is good comedy. There is the good-natured soldier 'swell,' Jack Poyntz, the young lord, the old beau, the hoyden school-girl. But there is more wanted than this, as will be seen by a comparison with the other comedies. The play, as was said, is very light and sketchy; it has no story, and is really no more than a series of scenes and a number of pleasant agreeable conversations. Far more than this is required. The substance of the drama is action, and this the dialogue and characters should help forward. Every sentence should be part of the means to this end. All mere phases of character, mere smart speeches, however good in themselves, which do not belong to a situation, which in itself belongs to the plot, is surplusage, and in truth uninteresting. A great deal in 'School' is open to this objection, being put in to show the author's command of what is called 'epigrammatic dialogue.' Even if this show the *general* character of the person, it is not enough. *The situation should do that.* For how is it in real-life? There is so much of what is affectation and artificial in our social relations, so much that is indifferent in visits, talks, dinners, &c., that three-fourths of what is done and spoken has no special significance. But let a strong situation arise, something where our interest and inclinations are concerned, and then genuine character is brought out; every word has thus a purpose. So with comic peculiarity or humour—a situation is the talisman for that. But in truth 'School' in its original shape is little more than a poem or pastoral, and is merely a delicate idealization of German scholastic life. As such it went home to the hearts of those for whom it was written. So, too, in a later piece, 'The Nightingale,' there is a young ensign played by Mrs Mellon. It was clearly the intention of the author to give a picture of a boy officer, fresh from school, and always talking nonsense from sheer spirits. Such a type undoubtedly exists, but it is no character for the stage, nor character at all. Such is too trifling and too harmless to be worthy of serious satire; taken by itself, is so purposeless, and the childish speeches have so little connection with interior character, that the whole has merely the effect of careless and unmeaning rambling on the author's part. As was said before, for stage character a certain strength and meaning and consistency is necessary,—external peculiarities alone will not do. When it comes to represent folly by foolish words, which have no connection with action, interior or exterior, there is absolutely no effect produced, or rather a wrong effect. In short, mere servile copying is not sufficient, as can be shown by this illustration from novel-writing. It might be assumed that people of rank writing about high life would, without any gifts, be able to give the most satisfactory picture of its manners and customs. But how do they go about it? We find a 'state' dinner party described minutely—the ornaments, servants, courses, &c.; 'a perfect photograph,' their friends will tell them. Yet the *effect* is pure vulgarity; the writer unintentionally appears like a parvenu who has seen such an entertainment for the first time. The skilful writer, on the contrary, who has studied what may be called the art of indication, knows how to convey the effect, without at all appearing to be struck by these objects. And the skilful dramatic writer will convey the *effect* of a boy-officer's folly by some outward action operating in such a nature, or would make the spectator draw such a conclusion for himself. The opposite plan is no more than a mere labelling, 'This is a foolish fellow,' 'this is a joke,' &c.

The taste for 'sensation,' as it is called, has effected more than scenery; and the characters in a drama, to 'draw,' must be of that startling 'raree-show' description popularized by burlesque, laid in such staring gaudy colours as all who run may read. But they are indeed of a quality which would more suit those who *cannot* read. Mr Byron has been lately playing, in one of his own pieces, an eccentric character, which has in had very great success. This is 'Sir Simon Simple,' in 'Not such a Fool as he looks.' Now here we are enabled by comparison to see after what different principles the French and English go to work. The English piece might be expected to turn on apparent stupidity being a match for cleverness; and the basis of pleasure for the audience would be found in the defeat of those who would take advantage of mere physical deficiencies. And, again, there would be this further moral, the unfairness of judging character hastily, because of such outward deficiencies. This, naturally, was the view taken by the French writer, Charles de Bernard, whose outlines and principle— and only these—Mr Tom Taylor has taken for that excellent play, 'Still Waters run Deep,' substituting indifference and apparent weakness of purpose for imbecility. Mr Byron, on the contrary, worked on the surface, merely following to the established principles of the day. The first object was the reaction of a purely eccentric character, who would stand alone, and whose oddities of dress, speech, and manner might cause laughter. A great deal of effect is produced by a dull sheepish manner, an eye-glass permanently fixed in the eye, sleek yellow hair, &c. Nearly every speech he utters is written to produce a point and convey variety. He is sent to distribute tracts to workmen, and relates how he was received. 'I knocked at Crump's door. The door was opened by Crump, and out came Crump;' which produced loud laughter. He says he produced a great effect on Crump. 'No doubt he was softened by your kindness?' the giver of the tract asks. 'Well, n-no, not exactly that.' 'Well, perhaps you reasoned with him on the course he was pursuing?' 'N-no, I can't say that I did.' 'Well, what *did* you do?' '*I stood him a pot of porter and a screw.*' This produced another roar. Now, Mr Byron is undoubtedly a clever writer, and he merely writes 'this sort of thing,' following the existing fashion of his school. But a play or a character, made merely on a series of 'jokes' like this, is a play and character constructed on false dramatic principles. A French writer would have studied such a character from within, and would have seen the *situation* best calculated to bring it in strange lights and attitudes. But mere grotesque dress and grotesque speeches will never make character, or indeed interest.

The same false 'tack' in the case of both writer and actor is to be seen in another modern piece, by Mr Craven, a writer who has 'a name'—the grand point to be looked to,—in a piece called 'Philomel,' lately playing at the Globe Theatre. The scene is laid in Jersey; and the author, casting about for novelty in the conception of a comic character, naturally thought of the steam-packets between Southampton and Jersey; and the steam-packets then suggested a funny steward. What direction this fun was to take was naturally the next question; and the opposition between his apparent nautical character, and his really landsmanlike avocation, seemed to promise a legitimate dramatic opening. But the conventional treatment suggested itself at once. The comic steward must *advertise* himself in that line, and tell the audience, in so many words, that he is trying to imitate a sailor. Thus he was always ostentatiously 'hitching up' his trousers, lifting his legs in a nautical hornpipe fashion, and went off always with a declaration that 'he was a true British *Tar!*' Now, tested by real life and character, this was all false. The real steward, who was zealously ambitious to be thought a sailor, would never *assert* it, would be hurt if any one else were to do it. He would assume that the fact was self-evident; but a skilful writer would make him betray his eagerness by various signs and tokens, which the audience would see with enjoyment, but of which he himself would be assumed to be unconscious.

Mr ANDREW HALLIDAY's last piece, 'Love's Doctor,' will bear being tried by the true dramatic tests of genuine character; and the relative situations of the characters make it a bit of genuine comedy. The stages by which such a piece might have been evolved would have been something after this fashion. First, it might be supposed a sort of inspiration would be suggested, either by experience or by instinct, as to the dramatic contrast afforded by high and low life, each with their distinct sympathies, being forced violently into contact, and how unpleasantly they would lie upon each other in every way. We may suppose a little sketch of the plot had just suggested itself to the author, a 'young gentleman' falling in love with a girl of very low family, and cured by the father's welcoming and forwarding the proposal. Now, this bare outline is dramatic in itself, as it brings a sort of surprise, founded still on study of human nature; for the ordinary course would seem to be, that *opposition* would be the natural means for carrying out the father's end. The mind that would take such a course would be a superior one, from its knowing human nature better, and its proceedings would *excite our interest and respect*. Having got thus far, the true dramatist would see that there also existed a dramatic element in the contrast of two social ranks brought into such peculiarly intimate contact, and would ask himself how would he make this relation operate on his plot. By developing an honest and natural vulgarity in the lower characters, who shall have a thorough sympathy with their calling, —say a greengrocery business,—believe in it, and *respect* it. A false principle, and a common one, would be to make 'funny' parts for the players, as would be done in a farce, in which case the effect is lost. Next the dramatist would think of his individual characters; how *they* would forward, or be developed by, the story; and it was a happy instinct that suggested the tippling 'hero,' trading on his Crimean 'charge,'—a vapouring, worthless fellow, whose sham dignity seemed to bring him a little nearer at first sight to the family with whom his daughter was to be connected, but which, in reality, *sank him lower* than his own rank. Further, a real and moral dignity was given to that low family by the honest independence of the wife and daughter,—their true dignity, which made them find support for the worthless husband, and in the end sets them, in the eyes of the audience, on a level with the genteel family who rejects them. This is all *dramatic*, and it shows how a well-chosen subject in good hands will work itself out. There are minor contrasts of a humorous sort, as when Mr and Mrs Onion go on a visit to the genteel house, when, as is to be expected, the ' hero's ' dignity and bearing helps to bring out the contrast. There is only one failure in the working out, and that, it may be conceived, was due to the exigence of the acting caste. The ' young gentleman ' who was in love should have been thoroughly *genuine*, just as his cure and awakening are genuine. His character should have been that of a foolish, ardent, and unsophisticated lad. Instead, he is forced, by the eccentricity of the actor, into the London cockney of farce. This is felt to be a false and artificial idea all through, and it jars upon us. The piece is, in short, written on those principles on which it would have been written in the last century; and it is a healthy and genuine 'success.'

But in truth all the good dramatic pieces are constructed on such principles. Over a hundred years ago came out a farce which still keeps the stage, and which for humour is worth whole bales of farces of the 'Box and Cox' pattern. This is the amusing 'High Life below Stairs,' long attributed to the pen of a clergyman, but which really seems to have been the work of Garrick, who was always reluctant to have his name *affichéd* as an author. The motive of this situation is the contemptible and comic result of those in a low station aping merely the *outside* airs and manners, dress, &c., of their betters, which is the first feeling. Thus the jarring opposition between the internal 'valet' nature and the borrowed plumes in which it has decked itself, brings about what is ludicrous and dramatic, with even a moral. In the hands of great actors, who had studied human nature, with the way it would manifest itself under such conditions, it must have been a treat of the highest order. The moderns will, of course, only think of getting 'fun' out of their characters, exaggerate absurdly, and take care to show all the time that they are merely masquerading. The *sincerity* and genuine belief of 'My Lord Duke' and 'Lady Betty' that they were bearing themselves correctly, and quite on a level with the demeanour of their august masters and mistresses, would never enter their heads. But we shall come back to this piece later.

It is when we pass from some of the things now playing, to Goldsmith's 'She Stoops to Conquer,' at the St James's Theatre, that we may well despair of the English drama. Light and darkness, brilliancy and stupidity, nature and affectation, life and death, are not more opposed. But it seems a wonder how this immortal comedy 'got into this galley;' it is as strange among its fellows, as was Rip Van Winkle after his return. It is, alas! a little strange also to the audience, who, though amused, seem but half satisfied, as though this was not the sort of thing they liked. The truth is, their stomachs are so accustomed to rich loaded sauces and greasy stews, they cannot as yet relish prime well-dressed meats. Audiences have to be educated as well as actors, who are now unequal to such a task, and really find it far above their strength. Their tongues are itching for the easy and rollicking familiarities of the every-day farce, or their limbs yearning for the easy 'breakdown.' And, indeed, this play, like others of the same importance, was written for very great players, and was meant to be a stock piece at that one house. It was not intended to be carried over the kingdom and played by every journeyman corps that could get permission to do so. It belonged to the original actors. So long as they survived, and young Marlow was to be convertible with Lee Lewes, and Miss Hardcastle with Mrs Bulkeley, it made no itinerant course.

That delightful comedy, 'She Stoops to Conquer,' would indeed deserve a volume, and is the best specimen of what an English comedy should be. It illustrates excellently what has been said as to the necessity of the plot depending on the characters, rather than the characters depending on the plot, as the fashion is at present. How would our modern playwright have gone to work, should he have lighted on this good subject for a piece—that of a gentleman's house being taken for an inn, and the mistakes it might give rise to? He would have an irascible old proprietor, who would be thrown into contortions of fury by the insults he was receiving; visitors free and easy, pulling the furniture about, ransacking the wardrobes, with other farcical pranks, such as would betray that they were *not* gentlemen, or such as guests at an inn would never dream of doing. But farce would be got out of it somehow. We might almost swear that the real 'fun' of the whole would be fetched out of the servants, the part of a drawling flunkey being specially 'written up' for Mr ——, or Mr ——. The visitor's 'hown' valet, a fine London domestic, would have a great deal of 'business,' and his love-makings and freedoms with the 'landlady' would have a great share in the piece.

Very different were the principles of Goldsmith. He had this slight shred of a plot to start with; but it was conceived *at the same moment with the character of Marlow* — the delicacy and art of which conception is beyond description. It was the character of all others to bring out the farce and humour of the situation, viz. a character with its two sides—one that was forward and impudent with persons of the class he believed his hosts to belong to, but liable at any crisis, on the discovery of the mistake, to be reduced to an almost pitiable state of shyness and confusion. It is the consciousness that this change is *in petto* at any moment, that the cool town man may be hoisted in a second on this petard, that makes all so piquant for the spectator.

To make Marlow a mere exquisite would have furnished a conventional dramatic contrast: but the addition of bashfulness—and of bashfulness after this artistic view—more than doubled the dramatic force. A further strengthening was the letting his friend into the secret; so that this delightfully self-sufficient creature is the only one of all concerned—including audience—who is unaware of his situation. In the hands of an actor of genius this character would be a treat indeed, but would require the most airy and elegant gifts. He is a gentleman, and a pleasant creature; with all his dandyism is interesting, and has our sympathy. It might be thought that even an average actor could not fail in making some crude attempt at presenting some such view. But the American gentleman, who has played it over a hundred nights at the St James's Theatre, has, with a blindness almost amazing, turned the 'agreeable rattle' into a sort of solemn prig, a sort of dull, persecuted gentleman, taking the whole *au grand serieux*.

His advances to the supposed barmaid are in the style of a commercial traveller's. To take a specimen, where the true 'airiness' required by the play is curiously missed, Marlow asks the barmaid, wishing to invent an excuse to detain her, 'Have you got any of—your—a—what-d'-ye-call-it, in the house?' and is answered: 'No, sir, we have been out of that these ten days.' Both question and answer were given off glibly, as learnt by heart, and produced no effect. It really conveyed the idea that some undefined drink was asked for, and could not be supplied. Now, with more refined acting, Marlow would ask in a sort of *distrait* way, showing that he wanted nothing; and was so taken up with the idea of detaining the young lady, that he could not recollect the name of anything to call for. There would be, besides, an element of gaiety and fun, as he had to fall back on the description, 'what-d'-ye-call-it.' The answer, too, would not take the shape of a glib, pert retort, but would be delivered with a sly gravity, and twinkle of enjoyment. It may seem trifling to linger on so small a matter as this; but where such an obvious and necessary reading was missed, it shows that far more serious mistakes are made. Again, too, the gentleman who plays Hastings illustrates but a too common vice of the stage—the getting broad, coarse effect, at the expense of the situation. Thus, in the delightful passage where Hastings is flattering Mrs Hardcastle, the effect produced is of *ill-bred humbugging to her face*. It is needless to say the true effect should be that of *a gentleman*, paying false, but elaborate, compliments, with an extravagant and obsequious courtesy. But this is the coarse colouring of existing stage manners; every player must be in *rapport* with his audience, and these coarse effects, he thinks, impress his merits better on them. That delicate *insinuation* of a point is too difficult and troublesome.

How rich, again, in broad Leslie-like touches of character! Hardcastle instructing Diggory and his fellow-servants, the reception of Marlow and Hastings at the supposed inn, with their contemptuous inattention to the landlord.

'Gentlemen, you are, once more, heartily welcome. Which is Mr Marlow?—Sir, you are heartily welcome. It's not my way, you see, to receive my friends with my back to the fire. I like to give them a hearty reception at the gate; I like to see their horses and trunks taken care of.

Mar. (*aside*). He has got our names from the servants.—We approve your caution and hospitality, sir. (*To Hastings*) I have been thinking, George, of changing our travelling dresses in the morning; I am grown confoundedly ashamed of mine.

Hard. I beg, Mr Marlow, you'll use no ceremony in this house.

Hast. I fancy, Charles, you are right; the first blow is half the battle. I intend opening the campaign with the white-and-gold.

Hard. Mr Marlow, Mr Hastings, gentlemen, pray be under no restraint in this house. This is Liberty Hall, gentlemen; you may do just as you please.

Mar. Yet, George, if we open the campaign too fiercely at first, we may want ammunition. I think to reserve the embroidery, to secure a retreat.

Hard. Your talking of a retreat, Mr Marlow, puts me in mind of the Duke of Marlborough when he went to besiege Denain. He first summoned the garrison—

Mar. Don't you think the *ventre d'or* waistcoat will do with the plain brown?

Hard. He first summoned the garrison,' &c.

Now the contrast between the host's exuberant welcome, his joy at seeing his old friend's son, his vast sense of importance, and the delicious indifference of the two guests, is perfect comedy. The whole is worked out with a wealth of ideas, and a cumulative power that is marvellous.

One could write on and on, in praise of this delicious comedy. What was before Goldsmith's mind was the local colour, as background for Marlow,—the picture of the old country house and its old-fashioned tenants, its regular types of character, as full and round as the portraits on the wall. Then there is the artful contrast of the characters, every figure in it separate, distinct, alive, coloured, round, and to be thought of, positively like people we have known. Young Marlow, and Tony Lumpkin, — old Hardcastle, and Diggory, and Mrs Hardcastle, — these are things to be recalled hereafter, from being framed in an admirable setting at a theatre in this metropolis, where the background, the atmosphere, the scenery, and dress, is like a series of old pictures, and helps us over many shortcomings that strike the eye. With excellent playing in one leading character, Tony, it haunts the memory as something enjoyable; and, to one who goes round the playhouses, it is as though he had been stopping at some cheerful country-house from which he was loth to depart. Never, it must be said, was Goldsmith so honoured before; and this treatment deserves mention, as being a judicious mean between reckless overlaying of decoration and 'mounting,' such as distinguished Mr Kean's revivals, and mere meagre adornment. It is impossible to dismiss from the memory the several pictures in this play—the dresses, so subdued and rich; the furniture, so marked and complete, yet not obtrusive. The village alehouse, a charming interior in sober subdued colours, is scarcely worthy of Wilkie—as is boasted in the bills—but, taken with Goldsmith's animation, is in Wilkie's key. Mr Hardcastle's drawing-room, with its great fireplace, its great deep colouring, its sombre hues, its general air of *oak*, its very original architectural arrangement, is beyond praise. There are episodes, too, and groupings that come back—as, the blaze of the cheerful fire on the two travellers in their riding-coats, sunk down in the great 'Cromwell pattern' chairs, while the owner of the house tries in vain to 'cut in' with his stories. Other plays have been also mounted with the most minute attention; but here it is Goldsmith himself and his genius that supports this embroidery.

What a play! We never tire of it. How rich in situations, each the substance of a whole play! At the very first sentence the stream of humour begins to flow. Mrs Hardcastle's expostulation against being kept in the country, and her husband's grumbling defence; the alehouse, and the contrast of the genteel travellers misdirected; the drilling of the servants by Hardcastle; the matchless scene between Marlow, his friend, and the supposed landlord; the interrupted story of the Duke of Marlborough, unrivalled in any comedy; the scene between the shy Marlow and Miss Hardcastle; Hastings' compliments to Mrs Hardcastle; the episode of the jewels; Marlow's taking Miss Hardcastle for the barmaid; the drunken servant, and Hardcastle's fairly losing all patience; and the delightful and airily delicate complications as to Marlow's denial of having paid any attentions; the puzzle of his father; the enjoyment of the daughter, who shares the secret with the audience,—all this makes up an innumerable series of exquisite situations, yet all flowing from that one simple *motif* of the play, the mistaking a house for an inn!* Matchless piece! with no-

* It is curious that about the beginning of the present century a similar 'mistake of the night' occurred in the case of Lord Oriel, the last Speaker of the Irish Commons. His house was at the end of a village; and some officers on the march, coming by at night, mistook a hatchment over the door for the sign of an inn. They knocked, and were admitted; and the Speaker, familiar with Goldy's then recent play, was not indisposed to carry out the humour of the thing. After dinner the mistake was betrayed through some accident, and they were hurrying away in much confusion. But they were kept for the night. 'Gentlemen,' said Lord Oriel, with the formal politeness

thing forced, nothing strained, everything natural and easy. 'Gay' would be the word to describe it. We regret when it is over, and look back to it with delight.

Again, with this let us compare the most popular piece of the day, 'School.' There a young *ingénue* thinks the moon should be addressed as 'she,' because it is always out so late at nights; a quip that produces the roar of the night. An average English 'swell,' slow, and rather dull, speaks in a dawdling fashion of love. 'Love is the mellow sunshine'—these are nearly the words—'and there is no eclipse . . .' Again: 'Yes; Love's an extra. Love is a species of lunacy of which marriage is the strait waistcoat . . .' He is asked is he married, and answers he was once in quarantine for so many days. 'I am an orphan,' he adds; 'can go in single or in double harness.' Some one makes a remark about not wanting money. 'Not want money! *You should be photographed*,'—which produces a roar. Douglas Jerrold put nearly the same idea in a very different shape. 'My dear friend,' says one of the

which belongs to 'the old school,' ' you came into this house for your own pleasure; and I beg that you will remain for mine.'

characters in 'Bubbles of the Day,' 'you cannot image how much I am in want of a thousand pounds.' The other answers, 'My dear ——, *every man is in want of a thousand pounds.*' This is founded on human nature and human character, and points at the cravings of even the richest : the other frail speech is unmeaning, and falls to pieces when touched. Why should a man be photographed for holding *any* opinion, when everybody is photographed? If it was, indeed, 'you should be engraved and published,' or, your head, like Lofty's, 'stuck in the print-shops,' there would be more sense; but in either shape there is neither wit nor epigram. So that 'go in single or double harness' belongs to a very stale shape of jest that has been uttered over and over again, and which rings the changes on marriage being 'a yoke,' 'wearing the snaffle,' 'a curb rein,' and such like. This gentleman saves some young ladies from a pursuing bull, and they thank him for killing the cow. A roar when he acknowledges their civility, adding, ' *Only the cow was a bull.*' He begs them to say no more : ' A bull is shot—what matters it who shot him, *particularly to the bull?*' The young lady is described as 'artless as moss; fresh as nature.' She is running to get some milk in a jug, and he says he thought that in the country 'they carried the milk about *in cows*.' These may not be the precise words; but the point produced, perhaps, one of the loudest guffaws of the night. So did an allusion to the costume of 'A Life Guardsman in kid boots or breeches, *cool to fight in* and convenient to cross country.'

Now, all this style of remark is not in character, even putting aside the question of its merits. The piece is supposed to be a reflection of the manners of existing society; but any gentleman talking in such a style would be set down as an idiot, or a ridiculous pedant. Let us conceive a gentleman at a dinner party addressing a surprised company with, 'Love is but a species of lunacy,' &c., or making a reply in answer to the question if he was married, 'I was once in quarantine at Malta.' Such a speech would scarcely be made by a gentleman, and might be considered a piece of ill-bred flippancy. The supposition of milk being carried about in the cow is either sheer fatuity if spoken in earnest, or else a 'joke' of a very low sort. But all this comes from a false notion of dramatic effect; the same failing, in short, which is the bane of the existing acting. The actor introduces himself, his fun, his gags, and his vanity into the part, quite regardless of whether any be appropriate to, or at variance with, the character. In the same fashion, the writer only thinks of what he considers 'good things,' that will tell on the audience, never considering whether his 'sparkling epigrams' are suitable to the situation, or ridiculous in the mouth of the particular actor. It is hardly fair thus to put 'School' beside one of the first of comedies—'She Stoops to Conquer,' but the strangest thing is, that we look in vain through the latter piece for anything that at all corresponds to 'epigrammatic' dialogue. That true master and excellent observer of nature knew that men and women did not talk in forced quips, but with 'gaiety' and pleasantry. To give a selection from the 'good things' in that incomparable play would fill sheets. We have only to think of the rare occasions when we have sat by a person full of wit, and at the same time full of spirits, we can recall the indescribable pleasure we had in listening—the ease, the nature of his sallies, their pleasant à propos. They certainly do not take the shape of 'Love is a species of lunacy,' &c.

All 'good things' should come in naturally, and be born of vivacity. It will be seen at once, by an instance or two, how easily Goldsmith's wit fits into its place. Hastings is flattering Mrs Hardcastle, declaring that such a head in a side box at the play-house would draw as many gazers as my Lady Mayoress at a city ball.

Mrs Hard. I vow, *since inoculation began,* there is no such thing to be seen as a plain woman.

Now, this is a 'good thing;' yet it has not the air of the author saying it, and it drops from her lips quite unconsciously. Again, the following may be tested in the same way.

Hast. As you say, we passengers are to be taxed to pay for these fineries. I have often seen a good sideboard, or marble chimney-piece, though not actually put in the bill, inflame it confoundedly.

Mr Hardcastle inveighing against the follies of his time, declared that once they crept slowly amongst us. 'Now they come down not only as inside passengers, but in the very basket.' This speech is not merely by way of 'epigram,' but is simply an old grumbler's way of putting his opinion most forcibly.

Now, the 'epigrammatic' and 'sparkling dialogue' for which some modern playwrights obtain a reputation, is founded on quite a different principle. Again, we may take the most successful dramatist of the day—Mr Robertson—as type of the rest. The epigrammatic writer seems to introduce his 'epigrams' with the same flourishing personality that Joseph Surface does his 'sentiments.'

In one of his latest productions, the following jests are put into the mouth of a maidservant. She can never accept a gentleman for a lover; 'as the pitcher that goes often to the *swell* gets broken at last.' Some one asks why cannot the heroine get back her voice. The maid replies, ' You can't advertise for it as for a lost dog.' Men are always deceivers; 'for, like the dogs in Dr Watts, "'tis their nature to."' Now, to test great principles by such trifles, the first 'jest' about going to the 'swell' must either have been spoken by the maid as an intentional jest, in which case it was forced and at variance with her character; or else it was the author speaking 'an epigram' through her mouth and therefore dramatically false. The advertisement for a voice, as for a lost dog, is unmeaning ; for by no torturing, either by figure, or by way of wit, or metaphor, can advertising be brought in connection with the recovery of a lost voice.

It seems absurd thus to analyze seriously what perhaps never cost the author a thought, but it illustrates the false *principle* on which it is constructed. I am tempted to go on and give specimens of the truer treatment of character as presented in the old comedies. It would be difficult to give reasons for the truth and excellence of these pictures, but his own instinct will convince every reader. The test would be to set the particular situation as a problem for some of our modern writers, and we could almost guess the handling. Should we conceive the case of a much-tried husband remonstrating with a fashionable wife on her late hours and dissipation, it would take the shape of a regular formula. The husband would fret and fume and stamp, the wife talk pertly about her opera-box. There would be much that was 'smart' and of the 'give and take' pattern. In a modern successful piece, 'War to the Knife,' we see how two ladies will talk of an absent gentleman. The dialogue is not dull or heavy, and is certainly far better than what is to be found in the average play of the time.

Mrs H. (R.) You know him, then?

Mrs D. (L., *coquettishly*) Well, yes, I do—I've met him.

Mrs H. Come, now, I can see you know him very well.

Mrs D. Go along, my dear! But don't *you?*

Mrs H. No, I've never seen him.

Mrs D. I met him at Harrogate last year—met him a great deal. You know what watering-places are. Society seems to fling aside its conventional reserve, and people revel for a short season in being natural. Folks get quite friendly and familiar until they come back to town with its gloom and its dismal propriety.

Mrs H. What's he like? handsome, Charley says.

Mrs D. Oh! he's well enough as men go.

Mrs H. Come, now, Madam Quibble, from your manner I suspect—

Mrs D. My dear, never suspect; always be certain, you'll find it'll save a world of trouble.

Mrs H. Then I'm certain you take an interest in Captain Thistleton. He's coming to-night.

Mrs D. I take an interest in him, indeed! how utterly absurd! when do you think he'll come?

Mrs H. Oh, with Charley, no doubt.

Mrs D. (*looking at her watch, impatiently*) How very inconsiderate it is of your husband being so late. All alike!

Mrs H. Are they? was Mr Delacour at all like—

Mrs D. (*quickly*) Dick Thistleton? Not a bit! Delacour wasn't handsome, nor young, nor agreeable, not a good dancer, nor—

Mrs H. Nor everything delightful, which it is evident Captain Thistleton *is*.

Mrs D. Who said so, pray?

Mrs H. Nobody; only I don't suspect, you see; I make certain.

Mrs D. Upon my word, an apt pupil. (*crosses*, R.)

Mrs H. After all you've said I'm quite anxious to see this Admirable Crichton.

Mrs D. (n., *a little offended*) Indeed, my dear! pray, remember you are a married wife.

Mrs H. Now you're jealous! I'm sure you're jealous.

Mrs D. Am I? (*laughing*) Well, perhaps I am just the least bit in the world; but there, it's over now: I've only to look in your eyes, dear, to see that you are as simple and as honest as the light of day. (*They kiss.*)

Now, this seems all 'thin,' and it is merely no more than a bit of narrative broken up and distributed between two people. Indeed, it thus only fairly follows the modern mechanical school of play-joinery, in which the writer chiefly thinks, how he is to bring his crowded incidents before the audience. The figures are used either to narrate or to suffer; the incidents and 'characters' are introduced, quite detached, and solely to show off the 'funny' person of the company. Now, to go back to the buoyant and spirited 'Provoked Husband,' the work of a mere beginner, yet every line in which shows a knowledge of character. There is no one who reads the following short extract but will gather a notion of plot, character, and dramatic interest, which he would fail to do from a whole volume of narrative.

Lord Townly. Going out so soon after dinner, madam?

Lady Townly. Lord, my lord! what can I possibly do at home?
Lord T. What does my sister, Lady Grace, do at home?
Lady T. Why, that to me is amazing. Have you ever any pleasure at home?
Lord T. It might be in your power, madam, I confess, to make it a little more comfortable to me.
Lady T. Comfortable! And so, my good lord, you would really have a woman of my rank and spirit stay at home to comfort her husband. Lord! what notions of life some men have.
Lord T. Don't you think, madam, some ladies' notions are fully as extravagant— In short, madam, the life you lead—
Lady T. —is to me the pleasantest life in the world.
Lord T. Tell me, seriously, why you married me.
Lady T. You insist upon the truth, you say?
Lord T. I think I have a right to it.
Lady T. Why, then, my lord, to give you at once a proof of my sincerity and obedience, I think I married to take off that restraint that lay upon my pleasures while I was a single woman.
Lord T. How, madam? is any woman under less restraint after marriage than before it?

Of itself this extract is rich in story and possibility of story. There is a genuineness and reality in the lady; and we can see there is a certain goodness under the frivolity, which gives us a glimpse as to the plot of the play. True character is in itself story.

For broad humour and humorous situation we may go back also to Morton's pleasant 'Cure for the Heartache.' The two Rapids, father and son, the 'push on, keep moving,' are perfect traditions, with the nabob, who was so unlucky as to get no one to listen to the great speech he was preparing. How agreeably is this *motif*—not a very strong one—worked out.

Rapid. Oh, it would never do for me.

Vortex. But you must learn patience.

Rapid. Then make me Speaker; if that wouldn't teach me patience, nothing would.

Vortex. Do you dislike, sir, parliamentary eloquence?

Old R. Sir, I never heard one of your real downright parliamentary speeches in my life, never. (*Yawns.*)

Rapid. By your yawning, I should think you had heard a great many.

Vortex. Oh, how lucky! At last, I shall get my dear speech spoken. Sir, I am a member, and I mean to—

Rapid. Keep moving.

Vortex. Why, I mean to speak, I assure you; and—

Rapid. Push on, then.

Vortex. What, speak my speech? That I will; I'll speak it.

Rapid. Oh, the devil! Don't yawn so (*to* Old Rapid).

Old R. I never get a comfortable nap, never!

Rapid. You have a dev'lish good chance now. Confound all speeches. Oh!

Vortex. Pray be seated (*they sit on each side* Vortex). Now, we'll suppose that the chair—(*pointing to a chair*, R.)

Old R. *Suppose* it the chair! why it *is* a chair, an't it?

Vortex. (c.) Pshaw! I mean—

Rapid. (L.) He knows what you mean—'tis his humour.

Vortex. Oh, he's witty?

Rapid. Oh, remarkably brilliant, indeed! (*Significantly to his father.*)

Vortex. What, you are a wit, sir!

Old R. A what? Yes, I am; I am a wit.

Vortex. Well, now I'll begin. Oh, what a delicious moment! The house when they approve cry, 'Hear him, hear him!' I only give you a hint, in case anything should strike.

Rapid. Push on. I can never stand it. (*aside.*)

Vortex. Now I shall charm them. (*addresses the chair*) 'Sir, had I met your eye at an earlier hour, I should not have blinked the present question; but having caught what has fallen from the other side, I shall scout the idea of going over the usual ground.' What, no applause yet? (*aside—during this,* Old Rapid *has fallen asleep, and* Rapid, *after showing great fretfulness and impatience, runs to the back scene, throws up the window, and looks out*) ' But I shall proceed, and, I trust, without interruption.' (*Turns round, and sees* Old Rapid *asleep*) Upon my soul, this is—What do you mean, sir? (Old Rapid *awakes.*)

Old R. What's the matter?—Hear him! hear him!

Vortex. Pray, sir, don't you blush? (*Sees* Rapid *at the window*) What the devil!

Rapid. (*looking round*) Hear him! hear him!

Vortex. By the soul of Cicero, 'tis too much.

Old R. O Neddy, for shame of yourself to fall asleep! I mean, to look out of the window. I am very sorry, sir, anything should go across the grain. I say, Ned, smooth him down!

Rapid. I will. What the devil shall I say? The fact is, sir, I heard the cry of fire—upon—the—the—the water, and—

Vortex. Well, well. But do you wish to hear the end of my speech?

Rapid. Upon my honour, I do.

Vortex. Then we'll only suppose this little interruption a message from the lords, or something of that sort. (*They sit,* Rapid *fretful.*)

Vortex. Where did I leave off?

Rapid. Oh! I recollect; at—'I therefore briefly conclude with moving—an adjournment' (*rising*).

Vortex. Nonsense! no such thing (*putting him down in a chair*). Oh! I remember! 'I shall therefore proceed; and, I trust, without interruption—'

Enter John, R.

John. Dinner's on the table, sir.

Vortex. Get out of the room, you villain!—' Without interruption '—

John. I say, sir—

Rapid. Hear him! hear him!

John. Dinner is waiting.

Rapid. (*jumping up*) Dinner waiting! Come along, sir.

Vortex. Never mind the dinner.

Rapid. But I like it smoking.

Old R. So do I. Be it ever so little, let me have it hot.

Vortex. Won't you hear my speech?

Rapid. To be sure we will—but now to dinner. Come, we'll move together. Capital speech! Push on, sir. Come along, dad. Push him on, dad.   [*Exeunt, forcing* Vortex *out*, R.

It is surprising how much English comedy owes to Irishmen; and indeed, if we were to withdraw the contributions of that country from the vivacious shelf, the gaps would be serious. We should lose Farquhar, with his 'dash' and boisterousness, combined with a wit that is never too elaborate and epigrammatic—a rock on which so many witty writers suffer; for they make their characters talk *too* wittily for their situation, and, like Goldsmith in the 'small play,' the author's hands are seen working under the actor's cloak. We should lose Bickerstaff, Macklin, Murphy, Goldsmith, and Sheridan and O'Keefe. In fact, let any one disparage English comedy, and the 'School for Scandal, or 'She Stoops to Conquer,' is at once held up to him. If any one were inclined to refute those sceptics who protest that the excellency of the old acting which entranced the town from the days of Garrick, was the mere grumbling jeremiad of old people, who think that whatever they saw must be better than what younger men saw, it could be done by going to see Macklin's 'Man of the World,' and Mr Phelps in Sir Pertinax. There is little story in that racy comedy; it is more like looking at a dramatic print of Hogarth's. For the whole is Sir Pertinax himself; but still the wonderful vitality, the shifts and turns of his character, are in themselves a whole story. He absorbs us; his advances and his defeats are like so many incidents in an exciting narrative. Everything he says is *genuine*, and in character; but not after the current sense, which means using a catch-word or some funny speech which makes the audience laugh *coûte que coûte*, without regard to appropriateness. There is interest, life, vigour, business, in every line. The 'character' is there—the mean, scheming, grovelling, canny Scotchman—independent of the stage or the actor. We can read it with pleasure. Once see him, and he lingers on the memory for all time; it seems as though we had lived in some house or town with such a man, and can never forget him. For us, there certainly *is* such a being. Much of course is owing to the admirable player whose name is identified with him; but set that admirable player to the stuff now written, and he could make nothing of it. There is the truth—good plays make good actors, and good actors, in their turn, make good plays. But the reform must come with the plays. With a part written on a wrong principle an actor can do nothing; he cannot do, as the admirable old school of actors used to do— study human nature in their own hearts.

Nothing in all comedy is finer than Sir Pertinax's—or perhaps Mr Phelps's—attempts to cajole the clergyman to a degrading office; and, when the latter rejects his offer with scorn, his malignant fury and disgust. He really seems to snarl and whine, like a chained-up dog who cannot get at his assailant.

Sir P. How! what, sir? do you dispute? Are you na my dependant? . . . And do ye hesitate about an ordinary civility which is practised every day by men and women of the first rank?

And on Sidney's making a high-flown invective against faction and venality in high places, he bursts out with—

Oho, oho! vara weel, vara weel! Fine slander upon ministers, fine sedition against government! *O ye villain!* *You—you—*you are a black sheep, and *I'll mark you!* I'm glad you show yourself. Yes, yes, ye have taken off the mask: you have been in my service for many years, and I never knew your preenciples before.

Sidney. Sir, you never affronted them before. . . .

Sir P. It is vara weel. I have done with you. Ay, ay, now I can account for my son's conduct : his aversions till courts, till ministers, levees, public business, and his disobedience till my commands. Ah, you are a Judas, a perfeedious fellow ! *You have ruined the morals of my son, ye villain!* But I have done with you. However, this I will prophesy at our parting for your comfort, that sin' you are so very squeamish about bringing a lad and a lass together, or about doing sic an' a harmless innocent job for your patron, you will never rise in the Church.

This is wonderful for truth and spirit, for the mixed spite and rage and wretched contempt; and the passages in italics seem like sudden snarls, new discoveries bursting on him. The account he gives of his own rise, and the arts by which it was accomplished, including 'booin',' is well known. Better still is his serious chiding of his son for his childish strait-laced notions as to political morality. By the modern canons of so-called comedy, this would have been all utterly exaggerated, and some very 'funny' notions exhibited. Something to extort a laugh, some audacious and 'comic' principles of political action, would have been addressed to the pit, and caused the conventional roar. Here would be something in the shape of the modern style:

Sir P. Conscience! a little bit of gutta-percha, my dear boy, is better; you can pull it out the length of the street. The worst is, you raise so little money on it. One of block-tin would be better.

Eger. But would not that attract attention by the flash?

Sir P. And you be like a dog rushing down the street with a tin kettle tied to his tail; all the wicked boys would shy stones after you.

This—or something like it—would be called 'epigrammatic.' Yet it will be seen that the writer, as it were, leaves his characters, and speaks, in his own person, something that is quite inappropriate. But the real Sir Pertinax is not thinking of the audience, nor is his creator—he wishes to get his son to *do* something, and is alarmed at, and full of contempt for, his highflown notions.

Conscience! why, you are mad. Did ye ever hear any man talk o' conscience in poleetical matters? Conscience, quotha! I have ben in Parliament these three-and-thrnty years, and never heard the term made use of before. Sir, it is au unparliamentary word, and you will be laughed at for it.

Egerton launching into an inflated tirade on what a true patriot should do—talking of those who plunder their country, and their 'black infamy,' and of 'a Roman spirit,' his father replies:

> Why, are ye mad, sir? Ye have certainly been bit by some mad Whig or other. Oh, you are young, vary young, in these matters!

What can be better than this—more natural, more exactly like the mixture of reasoning and reproach that an 'old schemer' of this pattern would compound on such an occasion? 'I'll just humour you with an explanation,' he would say; but the thing must be done. When the son, grown desperate, at last tells him the secret of his private marriage, his 'aversion' to the proposed match, the father, not believing him, breaks in hastily and even wildly—

> Your aversion, sir! *How dare you use sic language to me?*

The son goes on, and tells him 'his heart is another woman's.' Every one will remember Mr Phelps's 'reel' here, as if he was receiving physical blow after blow—his shriek at 'What other woman?'

> How, anither woman? And—you—you—*villain*—how dare you love anither woman without my leave? But what other woman—what is she? Speak, sir, speak!

Egerton breaking out most naturally in raptures about her perfections, he is cut short:—

> Haud your jabbering, you villain! haud your jabbering! Nane o' your romance nor refinement till me. I have but one question to ask you—but one question—and then I have done with you for ever, for ever.

The whole is a perfect study; there are no more *words* here, but flesh, and blood, and life. The good actor has matter to work on—something that repays and adorns his labour, that sets *him* off; while, in its turn, the part is set off by a good actor. In the ragged stuff that makes up the material and dialogue of a modern play, there is neither character, nor nature, nor life. What can the actor do? He has to supplement these deficiencies with things not in keeping, that have nothing to do with the piece. Whenever the 'Man of the World' is played, there is an enjoyment—a zest and relish; even the laughter has a different and heartier note from the artificial cachinnation produced by the feeble quiddities of a burlesque.

An essay might be written on Goldsmith's two delightful comedies. 'She Stoops to Conquer' is the more popular; yet it may be questioned if the 'Good-natured Man' has not a more delicate treatment of characters. In each of these two incomparable plays is illustrated a different fashion of treatment: we might take any half-dozen sen-

tences, and each passage would illustrate *character*
—the parties would speak as real persons would,
not as actors. Take the first scene of the 'Good-
natured Man,' where Jarvis, the steward, is remonstrating with Honeywood, and showing him
his growing difficulties. He says :

> A broker has been at a great deal of trouble to get back the money you borrowed.
> *Hon.* That I don't know ; but I am sure we were at a great deal of trouble to get him to lend it.
> *Jar.* He has lost all patience.
> *Hon.* Then he has lost a very good thing.
> *Jar.* There's that ten guineas you were sending to the poor gentleman and his children in the Fleet. I believe that would stop his mouth for a while at least.
> *Hon.* Ay, Jarvis ; but what will fill their mouths in the mean time ? Must I be cruel because he happens to be importunate ; and, to relieve his avarice, leave them to insupportable distress ?
> *Jar.* S'death ! sir, the question now is, how to relieve yourself—yourself. Haven't I reason to be out of my senses when I see things going at sixes and sevens ?

Now the modern actor or modern author to
whom the idea of such a passage occurred, and
even that detailed treatment, would make Honeywood's answers a series of pert repartees. But they
are not so meant. Thus, the speech of the stupid
but tranquil and *poco curante* Honeywood—who is
really gently expostulating with a follower whom

he thinks mistaken—' Ay, Jarvis; but what will fill their mouths in the mean time?' is exquisite comedy in itself; for it implies an air of infinite superiority retained on high logical and moral grounds, with a something of pity underneath.

Croaker, too, is excellent—quite beyond the clumsy brush of modern artists. The Jesuits are swarming everywhere. ' But,' says Mr Honeywood, 'they will scarcely pervert you or me, I should hope.' 'Maybe not. Indeed, *what signifies what they pervert*, in a country that has scarcely any religion to lose?' The *conception* of Lofty might readily occur to a writer of our time—a fussy, false fellow, pretending intimacies and acquaintances and power, and quoting the names of noble persons he did not know. Yet the idea would be treated in a conventional way: it would be repeated *ad nauseam*. What *finesse* in the witty Goldy's treatment! How good the passages in italics!—the artful depreciation of the great, which is self-exaltation all the time:

Lofty (to his servant). And if the Venetian ambassador, or that teasing creature the marquis, should call, I'm not at home. *Damme, I'll be pack-horse to none of them!*—My dear madam, I have just snatched a moment—and if the expresses to his Grace be ready, let them be sent off: they're of importance. Madam, I ask ten thousand pardons.

Mrs Croak. Sir, this honour—

Lofty. And, Dubardieu, if the person calls about the commission, let him know it is made out. *As for Lord Cumbescourt's stale request, it can keep cold: you understand me.*—Madam, I ask ten thousand pardons.

Mrs C. Sir, this honour—

Lofty. And, Dubardieu, if the man comes from the Cornish borough, you must do him—*you must do him, I say.*—My dear madam, &c.

Mrs Croaker then complimenting him obsequiously on his being so *répandu,* he says:

I vow to gad, madam, you make me blush! I'm nothing, nothing, nothing in the world: a mere obscure gentleman. To be sure, indeed, one or two of the present ministers are pleased to represent me as a formidable man. *I know they are pleased to bespatter me at all their little dirty levees.*

How admirable that! An average hand, to convey the idea of being sought by the great, would have told a story. 'Do you know Lord Manniken? He said to me at the last levee,' &c.; or, 'When I dined with the Duke of A——.'

Again, when pretending to be advancing Miss Richland's cause at court:

Lofty. Apropos, I have just been mentioning her case to a certain personage—we must name no names. When I ask, I'm not to be put off, madam. No, no; I take my friend by the button. 'A fine girl, sir: great justice in her case. A friend of mine. Borough interest. Business must be done, Mr Secretary. I say, Mr Secretary, her business must be done, sir.'

Mrs C. Bless me! you said all this to the Secretary of State, did you?

Lofty. I did not say the Secretary, did I? Well, curse it! since you have found me out, I will not deny it. It was to the Secretary.

How lively, rather, full of life, this is! We feel that such a character must speak in exactly some such way. There is nothing forced. Put it beside some of Mr Robertson's agreeable pieces, and it is like the grass of a lawn beside a painted bit of canvas. What is so praised as 'epigrammatic' writing is forced and unnatural near it, when the players seem to be trying to trip each other up with smart 'sayings.'

It is all simply delightful. What is remarkable about it and other such pieces is, that they are *packed* so full of matter—and there is nothing slight or sketchy. A comedy in that day was a work like a piece of sculpture; it often took years to write, and whole months to correct. It was the work of many heads and hands; it had as many readers as it had hearers; and when printed, was as much in demand as the last new novel. We need only read Garrick and Colman's letters, when the 'Clandestine Marriage' was being written, to see what consultation there was over the writing of a play. How it was mapped out again and again, rewritten, altered, condemned; anxiously weighed as to whether it would be 'safe;' and perhaps finally laid aside. The managers, it would seem, knew their business; and indeed, like all other persons engaged in a business, they themselves chose the article they were about to offer to the public. Would it do? could it be made to do? were the questions asked. They were play-writers themselves *because* they were managers; and did not, as is often the case now, become managers because they were play-writers or actors. Colman, Garrick, Macklin, and Foote were remarkable instances of the manager, writer, and actor combined. Now, unhappily, a manager goes on the strength of a name, and 'commissions' a writer, or else accepts what the author has ready. In the great lumbering quartos which hold the Garrick correspondence, printed as it were by the pound, is set out the whole of the painful stages of the elaboration of a good comedy —the secret councils and debatings—which, in reality, was founded on a wholesome terror not of the paying, but of the *critical, public.*

The correspondence of any living manager would exhibit a very different story; and, indeed, those directors would naturally be amused, or bewildered, by such anxious consideration for a judgment which they hold cheaply enough. 'The pit think *that* a little overdrawn; that too forced; that character not enough to do with the action; the wit too forced in that scene!' They would laugh loudly at such qualms. Some of ⸺'s friends might, indeed, make a noise on the first night. But would the 'great engine-room scene' draw? Well, if so, all that was wanting was a little 'smart' dialogue thrown in here and there, and it will run its hundred or two hundred nights: if he be a manager of some theatrical reading, will ask if the most successful piece of Garrick's time 'ran' beyond a dozen nights. This might seem a fair test of popularity; and it is a truth, that nine nights was then considered a success. But then compare the future destiny of the pieces! The older play, carefully written, and of real good stuff, was entered on the stock list of the theatre: it was sacred to its own special circle of players, who alone were associated with its merits. They and it were called for at short intervals—say once a fortnight, or oftener; and many of the successful comedies of old Drury-lane enjoyed this real 'run' during a period of some twenty or thirty years.

Whereas late pieces, of the Jackson-and-Graham sort, become, like the painted furniture and effects that have set them off, faded, rickety, tottering, unsubstantial. They have served their turn. Send for one to the theatrical bookseller's, and a duller quarter of an hour's reading never was. But for an inconsistency in the situation, the parts in the dialogue might be shifted, changed to different mouths, to different names—for there is little attempt at character—without much confusion. It is all meagre; and indeed the author might reasonably complain of being tried by this test, and in fairness demand his stage, his 'explosion in the mine,' 'ship' or 'house on fire,' or whatever else was the true strength of his piece. On the contrary, take down from the library shelf a volume of the 'British Theatre,' and we shall find plenty of real entertainment; and with a good reader, who has seen them acted, and has a turn for mimicry, genuine enjoyment will result.

There is a dramatist whose name is associated with some of the triumphs of our great actors, whose pieces can well afford to stand by themselves, but who suffers from undeserved neglect. If the name of Morton were mentioned as an honourable

British dramatist, it would be assumed to be that of Mr Madison Morton, the ready farce-writer, or rather ingenious remodeller of French vaudevilles. But there was a Thomas Morton once very popular; and though his pieces were spoiled by the gloomy and lurid German tone which was then fashionable, he possessed a true spirit of humour, and showed a great variety in his many characters. Some of his plays still keep the stage, that is to say, are revived occasionally when a sacrifice is to be made —that is, a compliment is to be paid—to legitimacy. Their characters are all *distinct* from each other, well marked, borne forward by a singular vivacity, which redeems a great deal of exaggeration and helps on the piece. The 'Cure for the Heartache,' 'Speed the Plough,' and the 'Heir-at Law' are really enjoyable pieces, and when fairly acted, leave a pleasant sense behind. Bob Handy and Sir Abel never flag; with Farmer Ashfield, and the countryman who there, for the first time, quotes the imperishable Mrs Grundy. Even the depressing Sir Philip Blandford—one of the earliest wicked baronets of the stage, who soothes his remorse by taking out a 'knife and bloody cloth' to look at—evidences of his crime—becomes a foil for the rattling gaiety of the rest. Old play-goers were never tired of extolling their favourites in these admirable parts, and characters and the players acted and reacted on each other.

There is one piece which, well played by a first-rate corps of actors, could leave no second impression as to the merits of George Colman the younger. Under such conditions, it would deserve all the praise of being 'a good comedy,' and, what is no mean test, would send the hearer home pleased, smiling to himself, eager to talk it over, and recurring to it at intervals the next day, as though he had been in the refreshing company of real characters and real humorists. There are few more satisfactory comedies than the 'Poor Gentleman;' and though it is hopeless to think of seeing it well 'cast' now, the play and its characters carry the audience on. That delightful bit of extravagance, Dr Ollapod, overdrawn as it is, in Mr Compton's hands, shows what must have been the effect when the other parts all good found representatives to correspond. The variety of his different attitudes, the unceasing novelty of his remarks, are wonderful; and though he uses a catchword, 'Thank you, good sir; I owe you one,' it is a mere accident and eccentricity of manner that accompanies other and newer eccentricities. In a modern play that single oddity would have formed the leading, and perhaps the only, humour of the character. Taking this one play, so rich is it found in characters of an unconventional sort, that a modern playwright might lift his hands in wonder at such prodigality. There is this militia doctor, comic in every way, and yet with a serious side in his meanness, toadyism, and even cowardice; the old country Squire, Sir Robert Bramble; and his man, a servant of the blunt old school, that tells truth in the rudest way; Miss McTab the spinster, with nothing but old-maidism and 'the blood of the McTabs' to go upon; Corporal Foss; and the ploughman bitten with military ardour, who picks up military knowledge from him. There is the eager young nephew from Russia, whose impetuosity in doing good and trying to relieve distress makes him forget that he has no purse. It is, in short, a most agreeable piece, and, with a little pruning and shaping, which all old pieces require—for the old audiences, with all these treasures of vivacity set before them, put up unaccountably with some singularly heavy scenes

—would always delight and entertain. Over this play, and over others like it, there is a gaiety and a pleasantness of aspect that is very inviting. But it will be called 'a wearisome five-act play that no one could sit out;' and it conveys the idea that one is commencing a long and heavy theatrical journey quite tedious. There is truth in this; and five acts do produce a sense of repulsion. But we must call up the old conditions: the house crowded to the ceiling, and filled with eager play-goers—not with persons who have gone, as for fashion's sake, to an opera; the early dinner long over; the really great actors all stars, and all in a band, acting together. It is as with old music, whose *shape* alone is old-fashioned; and these pieces a judicious hand might readily turn into the more suitable modern shape. I cannot resist giving a short specimen of this good comedy.

Miss Lucretia McTab. Provoking! a stupid, technical, old—— But what can a woman of birth expect, when the ducks waddle into her drawing-room, and her groom of the chambers is a lame soldier of foot?

Re-enter Corporal Foss, L.

Foss (crossing to R.) There is one Mr Ollapod at the gate, an please your Ladyship's honour, come to pay a visit to the family.

Miss L. Ollapod? What is the gentleman?

Foss. He says he's a cornet in the Galen's Head. 'Tis the first time I ever heard of the corps.

Miss L. Ha! some new-raised regiment. Show the gentleman in. (*Exit* Foss, R.) The country, then, has heard of my arrival at last. A woman of condition in a family can never long conceal her retreat. Ollapod! that sounds like an ancient name. If I am not mistaken, he is nobly descended.

Enter Ollapod, R.

Ollapod. Madam, I have the honour of paying my respects! Sweet spot here, among the cows; good for consumptions. Charming woods hereabouts! Pheasants flourish—so do agues. Sorry not to see the good lieutenant—admire his room—hope soon to have his company. Do you take, good madam? do you take?

Miss L. I beg, sir, you will be seated.

Ollapod. (*places chairs and sits down,* R. C.) Oh, dear madam! (*aside*) A charming chair to bleed in?

Miss L. I am sorry Mr Worthington is not at home to receive you, sir.

Ollapod. You are a relation of the lieutenant, madam?

Miss L. I! only by his marriage, I assure you, sir. Aunt to his deceased wife. But I am not surprised at your question. My friends in town would wonder to see the Honourable Miss Lucretia McTab, sister to the late Lord Lofty, cooped up in a farm-house.

Ollapod. (*aside*) The Honourable! Humph! a bit of quality tumbled into decay. The sister of a dead peer in a pig-stye!

Miss L. You are of the military, I am informed, sir.

Ollapod. He! he! yes, madam. Cornet Ollapod, of our volunteers—a fine healthy troop, ready to give the enemy a dose, whenever they dare to attack us.

Miss L. I was always prodigiously partial to the military. My great-grandfather, Marmaduke, Baron Lofty, commanded a troop of horse, under the Duke of Marlborough, that famous general of his age.

Ollapod. Marlborough was a hero of a man, madam, and lived at

Woodstock—a sweet sporting country, where Rosamond perished by poison—arsenic, as like as anything.

Miss L. And have you served much, Mr Ollapod?

Ollapod. He! he! Yes, madam—served all the nobility and gentry for miles round.

Miss L. Sir!

Ollapod. And shall be happy to serve the good lieutenant, and his family. (*Bows.*)

Miss L. We shall be proud of your acquaintance, sir. A gentleman of the army is always an acquisition among the Goths and Vandals of the country, where every sheepish squire has the air of an apothecary.

Ollapod. Madam! An apothe——Zounds!—hum!—He! he! I——You must know, I——(*sheepishly*) I deal a little in Galenicals, myself.

Miss L. Galenicals! Oh, they are for operations, I suppose, among the military.

Ollapod. Operations! He! he! Come, that's very well, very well, indeed! Thank you, good madam, I owe you one. Galenicals, madam, are medicines.

Miss L. Medicines.

Ollapod. Yes, physic: buckthorn, senna, and so forth.

Miss L. (*rising*) Why, then, you are an apothecary!

Ollapod. (*rising and bowing*) And man-midwife, at your service, madam!

Miss L. At my service, indeed!

Ollapod. Yes, madam: Cornet Ollapod, at the gilt Galen's Head —of the Volunteer Association Corps of Cavalry; as ready for the foe as a customer—always willing to charge them both. Do you take, good madam, do you take?

Miss L. And has the Honourable Miss Lucretia McTab been talking all this while to a petty dealer in drugs?

Ollapod. Drugs! (*aside*) D—— me! she turns up her honourable nose, as if she was going to swallow them!—(*aloud*) No man more respected than myself, madam ;—courted by the corps—idolized by invalids ; and, for a shot—ask my friend, Sir Charles Cropland.

Miss L. Is Sir Charles Cropland a friend of yours, sir?

But at the wonderful humorist whom Johnson called 'incompressible,' the modern dramatist may well throw up his hands. The collection which contains his comedies and farces is an amazing treasury of gaiety, vivacity, boisterous 'fun,' and wit. The procession of characters is long drawn out, and each, as he talks, never seems to flag. A single scene there has spirit and variety enough to bear being beaten out into a dozen modern pieces. A single character has such colour, roundness, breadth, and distinctness, as would carry through any modern play. Mr Forster has given an admirable analysis of Foote's pieces, with sketches of the characters, which show inexhaustible imagination, and whose talk is the talk of living persons, and of living persons with souls, natures, and peculiarities. As we read, it is like sitting in an ante-room and listening to the spirited conversation of real men and women. They tell their stories, retort, utter their exuberant jests and quips, as though these were provoked by the occasion.

What these pieces must have been, with Foote himself playing a leading part and inspiring the others, may be well imagined. And here, it may be remarked, it was well known that the chief fount of inspiration from which Foote drew was personality: he brought on real persons, and their tempting peculiarities and tempers. Superficially this may seem a faithful carrying out that holding the mirror up to Nature, one of the inculcated elements of dramatic instruction; and vulgar workmen often think, that a true and exact copy of what amuses in life must have the same effect. An artist like Foote knew better, as artists possessed of the same tact know very well also; and will 'abstract' the essentials of such a character as distinguished from the accidentals, or at least what are on the surface. Such a student, who is studying Nature with a view to find out the most effective angle at which to hold up his mirror, will not merely reproduce singularities of speech and gesture, but will put the character in a good and new situation, and make it act and speak as the original would probably do under such circumstances. Following out this high principle, Yates, one of the true old school of players, when he received a new part, would fix on some living person tolerably akin to the part, for assiduous study; and striving always to view the written sentiments as he imagined such a one would view them, thus reached to an extraordinary vitality. And this is the great secret of the real dramatist—the putting himself within the shell of his characters, and learning by keen study and keen observation how such should speak and act.

But to introduce Foote and his humour is to introduce something as utterly different from the dramatic humour of the time, as the Birmingham jewellery sold at fairs is from the contents of one of Mr Hancock's cases. We know the conventional touches necessary to put in the stage-character of a miser—stingy, 'would skin a flint'—gets young heirs into his clutches—is called 'old Shylock'—with other points which the reader can supply for himself. Foote's comedy miser is a knight and gentleman, whose shoes are made *out of the leather of his grandfather's coach;* while the barber shaves him every fortnight, and is paid with the annual shearings of the knight's and his daughter's heads. There are a hundred touches of this sort: but let us see how much deeper Foote could go. His miser scrapes all he can from every one; and as Elwes picked up old wigs and shoes out of the street, so this man is intellectually covetous, and picks up greedily a slang story, any anecdote he can, which his stupidity mangles and destroys in the telling. There was the master and there the man who had studied character, that gives us a picture of avarice from the very pretensions that accompanied it. Foote's pieces, be it remembered, are delightful *reading;* and the effect of such characters on the stage must have been doubled.

This radical difference in the treatment of the drama can fortunately be illustrated in a very curious way by setting two pieces on the same subject side by side, but with an interval of about one hundred and ten years between their production. One was 'High Life below Stairs;' the other, 'Our Domestics,' a 'Strand' adaptation of a little French piece. There is one scene common to both; but the subject—the airs of servants—is treated on false principles in the modern play, on true in the old one. Now, it may be repeated, mere habits and *outside* behaviour have no dramatic significance, unless as illustrative of inner workings.

The mere contemplation of servants' hall life, 'the ways' of such a place, would be a mean subject of study after all. The bare exhibition of their plundering their masters, wearing their clothes, and affecting to call each other by their masters' names, is in itself nothing amusing, beyond the impudence of the thing. But show them so spoiled and arrogant, that they actually *believe* themselves as fine as their masters—that, say, a nobleman's servant should be so pampered as to take *his* position relative to the other servants, be accepted as such by them, this genuineness and thorough sincerity is quite a different thing. A comparison between the two pieces will show their different spirit. First, for the modern one: the master and mistress have gone out, and the servants have a party, dress in their mistress's clothes, &c.

All. Bravo! capital!

Joseph. Ankor! ankor! (*to* Francis) Don't my get up alarm you?

Franc. It's rather short in the waist.

Joseph. That's master's fault. I shall speak to him about it. If I'm going to wear his clothes I can't have my figure spoilt.

Julia. Suppose we have supper.

Franc. Excellent. (*addressing* Benjamin *and* Adolphus *in grand tone*) Chairs! (*They all place chairs round table.*)

* * * * *

Julia. Now then, let us begin.

Joseph. (*giving* Sarah *wine*) Your health, my dear!
Sarah. Yours! (*All drink.*)
Franc. (*taking out watch*) Plenty of time, it's only eight.
Joseph. That's a nice watch! Meeks?
Franc. No, mine, bought it out of the Christmas tips.
Adol. The devil you did—mine only came to five pounds.
All. (*with indignation*) Five pounds!
Joseph. Disgusting.
Ben. It's low.
Franc. I should have presented them to the porter.
Julia. Ladies and gentlemen, I recommend this wine (*they fill the ladies' glasses—to* Adolphus) and you actually remain in such a place? Come, we are acting as mean as our masters with the wine. Don't I see them talking and gammoning the guests instead of passing the bottle. (*She drinks.*)
All. (*stand and drink*) Yours!—yours!—yours!
Franc. (*knocking*) Silence, if you please. Ladies and gentlemen, I consider this the moment when a blow should be struck for the liberty of the British livery.
All. Hear! hear!
Joseph. Ankor! ankor!
Franc. The domestics of Great Britain are a persecuted people.
All. Hear! hear!
Joseph. Ankor! ankor!
Franc. Speaking figuratively, the shine has been taken out of our buttons. Why ain't we represented? Are we represented in the Peers?
All. No! no!
Franc. Are we represented in the Commons? No! Are we represented anywhere except on the stage? No! but in the words of the immortal Higginbotham, author of 'Tight Thoughts.' Many a rose is born to *plush* unseen, which is corroborated by that distinguished poet Lord Bacon in his Don *June,* when he says, 'There is a tide in the affairs of men, which taken at the "Flying Scud" leads on to-to—'

All. Go it—try back.

Franc. To-to the-the Antipodes. Ladies and gentlemen, I can't finish the quotation because I don't know it, but I ask why are we trampled on, and our calves gored by John Bull and Punch, when we're in the rumble—their *rumble* servant, I might say, except there's a wheel within a wheel. I don't pretend to be a horator like Mr Nature Groans, but I have attended the Hyde Park meetings in uniform, and I'm on terms of intimacy with a groom at Buckingham Palace ; and I say our talents ain't recognized. Haven't we contributed to the British Literature ? Who wrote 'Sally Brass ? ' wasn't it a Butler—one of our cloth ? Who wrote ' Black-Eyed Susan ? ' wasn't it a Cook ? another of our cloth. I repeat—for positively the last time—are we to be dumb, in fact, are we to be dumb waiters—ain't we uniform in the matter ?

All. Hear! hear!

Franc. Don't the *mews* descend on us ? Ain't the stable commodity of this country, livery ? Then let our war-cry be blazoned on every napkin, 'Delivery us.' Why is there a difference between the *hymenial* and the *low* menial ! why ? Echo answers—why ?

Joseph. We'll halter it.

All. We will, we will.

Franc. I shall conclude in the words of the immortal bard of Stratford-le-Bow, and the unpublished and rejected manuscript of literary members of the St Jeames Club. Meetings must be horganized ! Trafalgar Square must be taken ! Hyde Park must be hoccupied. The man that dares to raise his hand, to raise, to raise—— Ladies and gentleman, I can't finish the squotation because I don't know it, but I ask you to drink to the destruction of our tyrant—the master.

Joseph. Ankor! ankor! (*aside*) Ain't he giving it to 'em ?

Franc. We've been trampled on, ridden over, our rights have been encroached upon, and a fearful retribution must be visited on our masters—a great Livery Union must be established.

All. Hear! hear!

Joseph. Ankor! ankor! Go it.

Franc. I ask you to drink to their downfall.

All. (*with enthusiasm—drinking*) Here's to our emancipation. Let us give a general strike and down with the tyrants!

Julia. Let me add, Justice to the British lady's-maid. Why should not females have a voice? Why should not *young* women, as well as *old* ones, be heard in the house?

All. Hear! hear! Bravo! Ankor! (*Rattling of glasses.*)

Now, the dramatic fault of this is, that it is prosaic, and without any touch of character. But worse than that, it is all untrue to nature. From the burlesque speech no doubt was got a great deal of fun, especially in the hands of the 'premier comique' of the Strand; but it was addressed to the audience, not to fellow-servants: 'Many a rose born to *plush* unseen'—such jests are mere buffooneries of the author, and have nothing appropriate. Again, the allusion to 'tips,' &c., are all shown to be false by the study of human nature. There would be too much dignity and self-respect.

Now let us look at the older writer. It must have been a treat to see King, Palmer, Mrs Abington, and Mrs Clive, as 'My Lord Duke,' 'Sir Harry,' 'Lady Bab,' and 'Kitty.' The gentlemen, too, wore the most gorgeous and sumptuous liveries, cocked hats, gold, silk stocks, and *bouquets*, in which they might take a just pride, as in splendid regimentals. They would not condescend to dress up in the master's cast-off clothes.

Enter Sir Harry's Servant, L.

How have you done these thousand years? (*Shakes hand with fingers.*)
  Sir H. My lord duke!—your Grace's most obedient servant.
  Duke. Well, baronet, where have you been?
  Sir H. At Doncaster, my lord. We have had devilish fine sport.
  Duke. And a good appearance, I hear. The devil take it! I should have been there; but our hold duchess died, and we were hobliged to keep ouse, for the decency of the thing.
  Sir H. I picked up fifteen pieces.
  Duke. Psha! A trifle!
  Sir H. The viscount's people have been demnibly taken in this meeting.
  Duke. Credit me, baronet, they know nothing of the turf.
  Sir H. I assure you, my lord, they lost every match; for Crab was beat hollow, Careless threw his rider, and Miss Slammerkin had the distemper.
  Duke. Ha, ha, ha! I'm glad on't. Take this snuff, Sir Harry. (*Offers his box.*)
  Sir H. Rappee?
  Duke. Right, Strasburg, I assure you, and of my own importing.
  Sir H. No! no!
  Duke. 'Tis, I assure you!
  Sir H. Oh no!

And again:

Duke. Heigho. I am quite hout of spirits. I ad a dem'd debauch last night, baronet.
  Sir H. I advise your Grace to take a wapour bath or get shampoodled.
  Duke. Lord Francis, Bob the Bishop, and I tipt off four bottles of Burgundy a-piece.

Comedy.

This last stroke of 'Bob the Bishop' is exquisite. The passages marked in italics are equally good.

Duke *and* Sir Harry *come forward.*

Duke. (L.) They certainly saw us, and are gone off laughing at us; —I must follow. (*Crosses*, R.)

Sir H. (L.) No, no.

Duke. I must; I must have a party of raillery with them—a bong mot or so. Sir Harry, you'll exquese me. Ajew! I'll be with you in the evening, hif possible; though, hark ye, there is a bill depending in our ouse, which the ministry make a point of our hattending; and so, you know, mum! *We must mind the stops of the great fiddle.*— Ajew! [*Exit*, R.

Sir H. What a coxcomb this is!—and the fellow can't read. It was but the other day that he was cow-boy in the country, then was bound prentice to a hair-dresser, got into my lord duke's family, and now sets up for a fine gentleman. *O Tempora! O Mores!*

Re-enter Duke's Servant, R.

Duke. Sir Harry, pr'ythee, what are we to do at Lovel's, when we come there?

Sir H. We shall have the fiddles, I suppose.

Duke. The fiddles! I have done with dancing ever since the last fit of the gout. I'll tell you what, my dear boy, *I positively cannot be with them, unless we have a little*——(*makes a motion as if with the dice box*).

It should be borne in mind that this piece was not consigned to the 'funny' players of the house, as it would be now, but to the first comedians of the day, who did not disdain to throw their whole genius into it. Only such could impart the true delicacy, and real earnestness, and the dignity necessary. It would be vain to expect to see it well played now.

For tragedy and tragedians the age seems to have but little sympathy. At the present moment there is virtually no prominent tragic actor before the public, with the exception of Mr Barry Sullivan. But he, with those of inferior degree, only represent the loud declamatory school—the player we associate with the fighting Richard and Macbeth, with Virginius and togas, and long speaking; but we have long lost the tender, passionate tragedian—victim of despair and of love—and well used to the melting mood, such as was Barry in the last century. Disguise the truth as we will, our hearts do not go with these official mouthings in five acts. Let us but lay such out for an evening's entertainment, and it hangs round our necks like a log for the whole day before. Tedious, too, is the cold and slow process by which the interest in the earlier scenes is evolved or protracted. The meaning of this existing repulsion to tragedy, and to the old shapes of tragedy, is that it does not reflect the spirit of the time. We are now so educated in the processes of thought and emotion, and are so familiar with the conventional commonplaces of such dramas, that we anticipate their slow evolution of hackneyed sentiment. Moreover, from the peculiarly practical tone of the day, we have lost sympathy with those heroic delineations: and the vulgar taste goes heart and soul with that species of sensation case which actually overflows the columns of a journal, and craves something which will correspond to the mere mechanical flow of events. Such 'newspaper cases' are indeed in possession of the stage. But the sort of tragedy suited to the time would be a reflection of our domestic life, the incidents refined and purified by art and genius. That suffering, and mental conflict, and splendid victories of good passions over evil, are going on about us, is conceded: and we can learn from the French, who get the interest of tragedy out of their own bad manners and morals, how to make the stage nicely reflect the tone of its age. And if we were asked to point to a class of drama which should be a model for the treatment of the passions of romantic life, we might name the well-known 'Gamester.' Overdone as it is, piled up as it is with horrors, it is written on principles which Balzac would have approved, and the overpowering interest worked out, not from mechanical events, but from the conflict of passions. With its old-fashioned subject, its crude, coarse villainy, its needless protraction of horror, that play remains a work of intense power, and unequalled for its attraction in absorbing the whole interest and sympathy of the hearer. It comes home to the lowest; and all hearts go with the miserable wife, sitting alone night after night, waiting till the return of the husband shall bring her some new horror. The day of being ruined by 'Hazard' on a green cloth has, of course, passed, but there are chords still touched by the passion of gambling which have only taken another direction and other shapes. The worst of it is, this play —and so with other plays like it — is brought forward with old-fashioned traditions, and accompaniments which are not of our time, and, as far as they go, remove it from our sympathies. There is the ancient stilted mannerism, and hoarse declamation, scarcely the fashion after which suffering is expressed in our day. There is that dawdling circumlocution and protraction before alluded to. When such plays are revived, a man of tact and nice skill should take it in hand; and, setting himself in place of the author, should not rudely compress, as the fashion is, merely using the knife, but should consider *what was substantial, and what was mere accident;* what was mere fashion of the moment, and what permanent and essential. But of course there is the vanity of the player, and his foolish traditions, in the way—some piece of fustian which he must roar and roar again—or, in the slang of the profession, some morsel of 'fat,' too precious to be sacrificed.

The Gamester, with its fierce passion, recalls a curious controversy on the stage, in which no less a person than the great Bishop of Meaux figured. It arose in the year 1694, when 'a certain abbé Caffaro published a very injudicious apology for the French stage of his day. Among other strange arguments he urged, that our Saviour had never condemned stage plays, and that various Fathers of the Church had approved them. The eagle of Meaux came swooping down, and tore this pleading into shreds. Every word of this masterly and sarcastic exposure applies to the French stage at this present moment, and cannot be refuted. Frenchman as well as ecclesiastic, he is *spirituel* as well as logical. He deals with the morality of the question, and dwells not merely on the undeniable outrage done to religion and morals by exhibiting positive vice on the stage, but hits off the true distinction as if he was arguing with the author of ' Formosa,' instead of with the well-meaning abbé. The whole, he said, turned on the interest and sympathy excited by such pictures, and he indirectly paid a compliment to the wit and genius of his countrymen, which their dramatists deserve at this moment. If, he said, scenes and pictures are presented which do not touch the hearts and sympathies of the spectators,—scenes of sober virtue and morality,—he of course can make no complaint of the stage. But then arises the unpardonable sin of *stupidity*, of which he cannot convict a Frenchman. They must therefore be artistic and logical, must exhibit on the stage what can alone be interesting to them— the vices of the age, which had their heartiest sympathies, and which, as a picture of the manners of the time, was the dramatic shape they might fairly take. Hence his utter condemnation of it. And he quotes St Augustine, who had acutely remembered the ' We see ourselves upon the stage : we become a secret and unperceived actor in the piece. And there is there acted before us our own special passion.' Who will say that this would not apply to pieces of the 'Paul Forrestier' and 'Dame aux Camelias' class, where shame, virtue, compassion, sympathy, and the tenderest passions, are woven round the coarsest vices? The great bishop went further, and with justice protested against the enfeebling effort of doses of the mimicry of violent and extravagant passions, undue sympathy with such was unwholesome for a strong mind; and in this view a great English mind unconsciously supported him. Bishop Butler, in a remarkable passage of the 'Analogy,' has admirably pointed out the damaging effect of the exertion of mere sympathy, not followed by action, on the formation of active habits of any kind. Bossuet's argument applied equally to the comedy of his day, which, like the modern French comedy, turned entirely on ridicule of topics of conjugal morality and domestic virtue of any kind; and certainly religious teaching could have no such fatal enemy. For the spirit of comedy, set off by airy native wit, would have invested such lapses with an air of good-natured harmlessness and indulgence. But this could not apply to a pleasant English comedy and manners, which, after a legitimate way, made vice absurd, and virtue agreeable.

This question, however, is intimately connected with another; and if the spectacle of violent mimetic passion enfeebles all moral action, the senseless ridicule of things long respected, the presenting of what is refined and venerated in connection with low and degrading associations, must go far to corrupt public taste, and to brutalize, rather than elevate. This brings us to the consideration of modern BURLESQUE, and the corrupt principles on which it is founded.

PART III.

BURLESQUE.

WHENEVER a question of patent or license is brought before a court of law, we are often entertained with the spectacle of divers professors and gentlemen of the stage, leaders of the orchestra, authors, and managers, being examined as to the definition of the point in dispute. It is amusing to hear the wild theories and explanations vouched on such occasions; the vague expoundings and hazy mystifications of what is simple in itself. The question often turns on whether the interdicted performance amounts to 'a burletta,'—the shape of entertainment to which the terms of their patent allows managers to object. The whole tribe of artists is put into the box in succession; but no one can logically define a burletta. When pushed to the metaphorical wall in cross-examination, they invariably catch at the old-fashioned and now 'exploded' ' "Midas." "Midas" is a burletta.' 'What is a burletta?' ' "Midas." '

'What is "Midas?"' 'A burletta.' The utmost that is usually obtained is that it is a something with songs interspersed,—in short, like 'Midas.' But if there should arise a question of patent or privilege as to burlesque, there would be a far greater difficulty. It may be doubted whether a single one of the managers who 'command' a burlesque, of the authors who write it, of the players who play it,—though no one would dream of asking anything from them,—or of the vapid groundlings who take stalls, and, with vacant mind, 'guffaw' over the poor antics they come to see,—could offer a definition of, much less describe, a burlesque. The swell of our day, according to his lights, will have before his eyes,—and before nothing more intellectual,—a mixture of low dresses, comic songs, and break-downs. 'But why burlesque?' he is asked. 'Well, you know,' he will answer, 'a fellow dressed up as a woman, and Polly Melville doing Prince Arthur,—hang it! what more fun could you have?' If we ask the ingenious punster who furnished the programme for the night, and the agile and exhausted artists who each night, by sheer wind and limb, carry all through, to tell us the point at which they are straining, the answer would be the same: 'Oh, a thing made up of dancing and jokes and an old story.' The greater public scarcely asks more.

Yet through being content with such husks and such shams, it little dreams what chances of real fun and enjoyment it throws away. It accepts what appeals to the mere senses, instead of what appeals to the intellect and brain. Frequent appeals to the former only end in monotony, and at last find no answer; while appeals to the latter find a growing and steadily increasing response. Writers, actors, and audiences of burlesque, are all on an utterly wrong tact, and act and react on each other so as to produce stupidity. Our modern burlesques merely tickle the ear, not the brain. These 'Polly Melvilles' or 'Nelly Beauchamps'— such names do as well as any others invented by the actresses,—acting Hector and Achilles, only delight the eye. It is the same, too, with their refined jigs, poor elocution, and feeble coquetries. Already are to be seen signs of exhaustion; the meagre well of invention has been drained dry; there is nothing more to be pumped up but the old mud of 'break-downs,' slang songs, and puns, which has been drunk again and again. Real burlesque is the clearest pellucid stream, flowing abundantly from the rock, delicious, always welcome, and always to be drunk with enjoyment. Let us see what may be accepted as the true principle of burlesque, or at least as something truer than that lack of principle to which is due the wretched stuff which is now palmed off as burlesque upon the public.

It has been often repeated that every subject has its serious and its comic side; or, at least, may be so handled as to have its comic side. The lowest manner of producing this last effect is by dress or distortion of face. A man comes on in an absurd dress, and the surprise to the eye produces a laugh. A large nose in a pantomime makes the children scream with enjoyment. But see the dress or large nose half-a-dozen times and the effect is gone; nay, rather, there is produced a sense of weariness and depression. There was something highly comic in the Æthiopian serenaders when they first appeared; now no one smiles at their high linen collars and blackened faces. What is wanting is the intellectual element, an underlying earnestness. Thus, could we suppose Mr Mill— and we ask his pardon for such a supposition—to

be so eager, in justification of the negroes and of
their state, as to come forward and identify himself with their cause by lecturing in the popular
Ethiopian dress,—triangular collar, blackened face,
woolly hair, &c.,—and were he to impress his
views earnestly, argumentatively, and passionately,
the effect would be irresistibly ludicrous, especially
as he grew more earnest and more passionate. This
would discover an elementary principle: and the
example reveals one of the secrets of true burlesque,—an unconsciousness that it is burlesque.

Every one remembers that exquisite bit of fooling, 'The Rejected Addresses;' and a criticism,
made on the imitation of Crabbe, really touched
the true key-note of burlesque. It was said that
if this poet had been set to write a poem on the
fire at Drury-lane, he would have written it much
in the same style as the caricaturist did. The
latter had placed himself in the position of the
former, and had viewed the matter as he thought
the other would have done. The supposition is
that Crabbe would have gravely set himself to the
trifling theme, and if he had condescended at all to
describe the fall and rescue of Tom Jennings' hat,
and the check-taker 'who gives the check he

takes,' he would have used the same strain as his imitator. Here is the real humour of the thing; the hypothesis of the poet taking this new attitude, and his belief that he was as dignified as before. So at an electro-biological séance,—to come lower down,—the sight of a grave professor dancing away or singing is really ludicrous.

To turn to instances more familiar to the public mind, it may be asked, how is our test to be applied to a burlesque on some mythological or historical story? Here, again, a transposition of the subject matter into, or its contrast with, some inappropriate time or condition, produces mirth. Thus, how droll is it to see one of Shakespeare's plays done at country theatres by inferior actors,—with their inferior shifts and pretences at dignity and grandeur. The effect is proportioned to the earnestness of the actors; let them but show they are conscious of the ridiculous situation in which they are, or rather, let them wish to show it to the audience, and the 'fun' disappears. The contrast too of togas, &c., with the face, bearing, and speech of the present time, has something comic. But a yet truer test is this. The real humorist knows that human nature must be the same materially in all times, and he will try and reproduce his old Romans and Greeks as nearly as possible with the weaknesses and conditions of our every-day life; showing that it is only the dress that makes the difference. And this task he will carry out with perfect earnestness and gravity. Again, knowing how inconsistent such old manners and customs are with our present habits, he will exaggerate the former so as to make the discordance more startling. The consummate art of Cervantes has invested Don Quixote with a pathetic interest. He is a gallant and sincere, though crack-brained, gentleman. Otherwise he had been a sublime type of burlesque from his very earnestness, and we can laugh with safety at the minor incidents which his ridiculous craze brings about.

A good illustration of the utter misapprehension of the true principles of burlesque is to be found in some recently published college squibs of Mr G. O. Trevelyan, and which are strangely described by the generally discriminating *Spectator* 'as singularly good specimens of modern burlesque.' The 'fun' lies in investing Horace, during his known stay at the University of Athens, with the attributes and associations of a modern Cambridge student. This is done on an old common trick, which is purely mechanical, and consisting in fitting modern offices and modern characters and manners to old names. For instance:

> 'Don't you know him?
> The same that got the Chancellor's Prize Poem;
> Who wears six rings, and curly as a maid is;
> Who's always humming songs about the ladies;
> Who never comes inside the gates till four;
> Who painted green the Senior Tutor's door.'

Taking these six lines, it is plain that the process is merely mechanical; that is, rhyme in the incidents of modern college life, and substitute Latin names and allusions. So with the battle of Philippi, where a 'Times' correspondent is introduced, Quintus Russellus Maximus, though there is a touch of humour in the name 'Maximus':

> 'What means this most discreditable bustle?
> I am the correspondent, Quintus Russell.
> Describe the enemy, that I may draw him.
> *Sol.* We can't describe him, for we never saw him.
> *Rus.* You never saw the foe! This is indeed
> A most confused, unsoldierlike stampede;
> I never met with such a shameful scene,
> As daily correspondent, though I've been
> (At least, I doubt if you will find a dailyer)
> In every fight from Munda to Pharsalia.'

All this is simply *English* talk, not Roman.

Now, what would be the true principle? To try and project oneself into the mind of a Roman, who was inclined to be satiric on the subjects of the time; or better still, go back again to that masterpiece of burlesque, the imitator of Scott, in the 'Rejected Addresses.' That was supposed to be written by a friend and admirer of the lost Higginbotham, who believed himself a poet, and wished to write with as much feeling *upon a subject he considered as full of dignity as Marmion.* The result is something exquisitely ludicrous. He did not take Scott's thoughts and allusions, and parody them, substituting firemen's slang; but he *wrote* as a poetical *fireman would do* on such a subject.

We are accustomed to invest these old scenes with an unfamiliar air and almost heroic grandeur; and the surprise at finding that their heroes are inspired by our own earthly motives and inclinations produces a comic effect. What the true tone of this sort of ridicule should be, could be well shown by another illustration not drawn from the stage. One of the happiest satires of nearly two generations ago was a novel called ' Little Peddlington,' and which, though forgotten as a story, has been preserved by name in the commonplace book of literature. There is far more real humour in it than in M. Sardou's 'Nos Bons Villageois,' which is founded on the same notion, and its purpose is to show, that in the most rural little corners there is as much meanness and pettiness as in greater communities. The gem of the whole is 'The Guide-Book' of the place, a delicious parody of the unconscious vauntings and vanities of such chronicles. Now, an inferior satirist of our time, who had got hold of the same idea, would do with it as the burlesque writers do with *their* ideas, and in falling into raptures over the beauties of the town, would pitch on absurd far-fetched things, such as no real guide-book maker would choose. At every turn we should see the comic writer *himself* behind what he was writing. Not so that superior artist, John Poole, who is perfectly in earnest all through, and writes his guide-book as if he were the real guide-book writer of Little Peddlington, proud of the new cast-iron pump which replaced the wooden one, of the 'portion of the old stocks' preserved in the museum, the beauties of the crescent, 'Yawkins' Library,' &c. We are told that but a footstep separates the sublime from the ridiculous; but our present funny writers seem to think it is a yawning crevasse, and use proportionate exertion. The true humorist, knowing that every highly-strained emotion and incident verges on this peril, chooses only the most prominent points whereon to dwell; a slight exaggeration disturbs the balance, and without further exertion on his part, produces the effect for him.

But it is hard—as it was in the old discussion on the definition of wit—to define nicely what a burlesque should be. It is easy to show what it has been, and also to show that its present shape is utterly faulty, flat and insipid. That we have reached a sort of finality is certain; the old common forms are used up; they have been interchanged, compounded together with something like desperation. What the state of burlesque now is, whether it corresponds, not to the reasonable canons of burlesque, but even to the lower standard of buffoonery, may be illustrated by a piece lately played at the Royal Strand Theatre, and which purports to be a burlesque history of Joan of Arc. Now, at the outset it may be doubted whether there was tact in the choice of such a subject, owing to the dignity and purity of that famous heroine; indeed, a glance at the familiar little statue, the bent head, and the sword clasped devoutly, would seem to forbid ridicule. Burlesque, abashed, might pass on. But the true comic view,—if one was to be taken,—would seem to be drawn from the position of a modern lady of our day in some similar attitude. The practical tone of our times would jar at every turn upon such a conception. But, in truth, the task would be difficult,—in fact, impossible; for the sincerity and gallantry of the maid must interpose at every turn, and check the attempt to ridicule.

Another gross mistake is in choosing subjects for burlesque that are but little familiar, or with which the public mind has made but recent acquaintance. The idea of burlesquing a play is a false one. The object of a burlesque should be something existing in the mind of the public, part of the common stock of popular knowledge, not something that has been seen by mere eyes, heard by mere ears, and that by the eyes and ears of but a few. In this 'Joan of Arc' a good deal is made to turn on the historic character of a Prince of Burgundy, utterly unknown to pit and galleries, and the lowest depth of mimetic fun is reached as he exhibits on his cuirass a painted bottle and two wine-glasses filled with Burgundy. This is *labelling* fun with a vengeance: and the author might nearly as well take his stand in front, a wand in his hand, and point, and explain the meaning of his characters, as in a wax-work.

But, indeed, this utter want of intelligibility is a special feature of the existing burlesque. Scenes and antics succeed each other, song follows song, in a sort of dreary monotony, till we wonder what is going on. We hear, certainly, laughter about us, but laughter is not a certain sign of enjoyment. So simple and cheap a movement as a wink has convulsed many an audience: and, stranger still, the proposing, or taking of, a kiss never fails to excite roars. With a little judicious compounding of these certain elements, a laugh may be generally counted on to cheer the player's efforts.

How many dreary, weary hours have we to lay to the account of what is called so complimentarily 'a capital burlesque;' or, to quote the hoardings, 'The last glorious burlesque; 400th night.' The elements are familiar enough: and the following is no exaggeration of the modern fashion of putting a bill of fare before a childish public:

ROYAL THAMES THEATRE!

GLORIOUS AND UNEQUIVOCAL SUCCESS!

CHARLES THE FIRST; OR, THE ROYAL BLOCKHEAD.
Sculptured by NOLL-EKINS.

THE GREAT TOPICAL SONG,
Encored six times every evening.

Miss POLLY BUXOM as KING CHARLES.
PRINCE RUPERT .. MISS BESSIE GREEN.

MR D. JACKS as OLD NOLL.
NOLL'S DAUGHTER .. MR TOMS.

A HOUSE OF COMMONS DEBATE.
THE SPEAKER .. MISS NELLY GRACE.

'TAKE THAT BAUBLE AWAY!'
Encored six times nightly.

Roars of laughter at the ROUNDHEADS' DANCE.

DOUBLE BREAK-DOWN.

We are enticed in, and enter with a certain alacrity, as believing that a delightful night is before us, yet not without misgivings. What follows we all know. We can read it in the faces of the departing audience about eleven o'clock. The feeling experienced by the listeners is very much akin to that felt after sitting out a long service in a church; it cannot compare to the absorbed interest with which we pass a whole day following a trial, or 'a severe cross-examination;' or the little sense we have of the progress of minutes and hours passing by unappreciated, in a real dialogue, or struggle, between a cross-examiner and his witnesses. This is, indeed, the fault of our modern acting; all has become so conventional that we have actually now the spectacle of actors imitating other actors; and the tricks and gags of a leading tragedian, or funny man, are copied with veneration by his provincial brothers. The simple result of all this is repetition, monotony, and fatigue. The 'screaming' new burlesque at the Royal Thames is the screaming old one of six years ago, with its cards shuffled. The rival 'Nellys' and 'Pollys' in the pink satin or blue satin 'tights' go through their little dances as before, and the funny man wears a higher false forehead and a more startling shape of moustache, say five inches longer than his last pair. The 'great topical song' which this artist favours us with is usually a feeble doggerel of this nature:—

> 'Once more has Rachel been refused
> To be let out on bail;
> Enough to make the ladies all
> Become so very pale.
> *Burden, to a facetious air.*
> What it means—
> What it screens—
> I'm sure I cannot tell.'

The 'encoring ten times' is contrived by the singer retiring at the end of each verse, as if he had quite finished, and reappearing, as if much to his own annoyance. This takes in the simple stranger at first; but more amazing still is it to hear the fanatic applause with which rhyme and sentiment far inferior to the above are welcomed. At one of our leading funny theatres, the other night, a perfect hurricane of applause greeted something worse than the following extract from 'the great topical song:'—

> 'And so the cabman's fare, at last,
> Is settled, nearly quite;
> I'm sure there's no one here will grudge
> Poor Cabby all that's right.
> *Burden.* What it means—
> What it screens—
> I'm sure I cannot tell.'

But who can blame the 'funny' writers who supply this stuff? Better would not, perhaps, extort even a reluctant guffaw. At houses of this sort it is a fact that the players actually encore themselves; and when an indifferently comic trio, 'My airy love blooms in the airy,' obtains a faint flutter of applause, the singers often wait, half bowing acknowledgment, half asking for more, until the groundlings—always delighted to be allowed to take part in anything going on—respond to the challenge faintly.

'Ixion' seemed to give our conventional notions of mythology quite a modern turn. Yet, as will be seen by-and-by, this is a very ancient idea, and has been tried very often, from the days of 'Midas' downwards. 'Black-Eyed Susan,' too, was a happy thought, and the old story, including the conventional licentious captain of the British navy, held the elements of burlesque. But still, though the result was 'funny,' somehow the piece had no relation to the original story, and formed a mere diverting spectacle. Such was enough, it will be said, and all that the manager asked. But it would seem that there are elements of yet deeper fun to be evoked, which would have provoked more intense enjoyment. How utterly astray public criticism was as to the true key-note to be touched, was shown by a representation of 'The Admiral of the Black,' represented as a negro in naval uniform, and which was loudly commended and called attention to by the press, as a device of true humour. This jest, in truth, bore the same relation to real burlesque as a bad pun or verbal quibble would do to real humour. There could be no chord of humour touched,—indeed, there was no real meaning,—in having 'William' played by a young girl in blue satin trousers. One would have fancied that the weak point in 'William's' character, and its suitability for ridicule, would have been found in his heroic sentiments, and the high-flown splendour of his diction, which our own experience tells us are not the common characteristics of the British tar. This feature of the original drama has often amused the spectator, notwithstanding its interest and popularity. But, surely, to have a young girl in blue satin trousers dancing break-downs and singing comic songs is no way of bringing ridicule on the gentle William. Captain Crosstree, with his spyglass and its exercise, it must be owned, did verge on the humorous. But, if we look across the water, we must own that the French are in possession of the secret, as in the 'Belle Hélène,' or in a character or two of that piece. A leading figure is Calchas, the high priest. Under English treatment the point would be to extract as much 'fun' from him as possible, by giving him artificial corpulence, an artificial nose, and vast spectacles. In fact, on such principles a heathen clergyman was thus dealt with not long ago on the stage. A vast umbrella was placed under his arm, from which he never parted, and by whose aid he performed the most grotesque dances. But the French Calchas drew laughter from deeper but more inexhaustible wells. With true native profanity, he transformed the heathen priest into the modern clergyman: at every turn came out the French ideal—for such it is—of modern sacerdotalism. A thousand little touches pointed at this. Above all, there was worked out a smug air of comfortable imposture, such as the heathen priest would have borne to a sharp-eyed sneering Greek, who saw through the trickery. The exquisite reality of the whole,—the character of Calchas, his snuffiness,—the snuff not being taken in that noisy conspicuous way which belongs to the English stage, but in a corner, as it were, in a greasy comfortable enjoyment, — his stoop and walk, and his inimitably sly revelations of disbelief in the imposture he was carrying on,—the contrast of this vivid every-day portrait to the old heathen accessories and dresses,—the under-current of hints conveyed, that these old pagans were mumming and theatrical, even in their helmets and dresses,—all these refined touchings made up an idea of burlesque exquisitely mirthful.

The working out of English burlesque has got to be inconceivably poor and trivial. We have not even 'mere buffoonery,' which is often amusing. The following, which seem the mere 'rinsings' of the 'funny' mind, are taken from one of our later burlesques :—

> 'Let's fly, love, we ne'er shall, if we elope
> To *Gretna Green*, be e'er *regrettin' a slope*.'
> 'Who 'cross the Tweed, weds folks for trifling sums,
> Oh, do leave off a-*tweedling* your thumbs.'
> 'Give me the *bag :* now all of you stand *bag*.' *

---

* The following is more elaborate, and the reader will note the labour and the number of lines required to bring in the poor, high, much-prized conceit :—

This sort of jesting is almost effrontery, and clever writers are obliged to furnish such an article. But whether these puns be bad or good, there arises another question :—What amusement or

> 'My detested enemy
> Shall find his threats, his hatred low and trickey,
> His deep-toned vows of vengeance, are all—dickey.
>   [*Brings a dickey from the bag.*
> Don't be so sharp—
> K.   Folks mostly say I'm blunt.
> A . Don't in that snappish manner take *a front.*'

But here are more flowers of fun :—

> ' How I should like to hocus him—*ho-cuss* him ! '
> ' His skill they all then questioned—each bold prancer
> Got for his question a sharp little *l'ancer.*'

And for fear this conceit should not have strength to carry itself through, a stage direction is added,—

>   [' *Makes a motion of thrusting.*']

But this is not enough, and it is pushed further :—

> 'My fish I landed with one little *l'ook.*'
> ' Making one cry when he the street is haunting.
> Pray cease ! Troubadour! *end—chanting.*'

The following specimen is literally unintelligible :—

> ' My love is not return'd, my letters *are,*
> Under which circumstances, *ha! ha! ha !* '

Or,—

> 'Oh, he's come ! Yes, *mum,*
> That's why I feel all *froth*, because he's *come.*'
> ' On his feet *high lows.*
> —Oh, why should *hi lose* him ? '

entertainment can there be in such quibbling? Any person in private life, persistently troubling us with such remarks, we should think impertinent, or should form a very low opinion of the mind that could find enjoyment in such tricks. But when we have such jokes learnt, studied, set off with dress and scenery, and officially brought forward under the dignified influence of 'the stage,' their thin, poor, frail character, seen in all its barrenness, is revealed; and their unsubstantial framework seems to creak lamentably under the load of dressed, and too often undressed, figures, which are stuck upon it. As well keep one's eye fixed all the day to a peep-showman's box, and see repeated again and again the daubed battles, and the triumphant processions, and the crowned heads. Again and again must it be repeated that there is nothing dramatic in what appeals merely to the eyes and ears. Something else must be stirred. Our senses are unintelligent, and, like country bumpkins, when the first stupid stare of surprise is over, show astonishment at nothing. To rouse this dull languor there is but one method by the framers of the so-called burlesques of the day,— the method by which the dram-drinker must rouse himself,—namely, by repeated doses and more fiery draughts. These the manager must supply to a sated and querulous public, and, as there is nothing known more fiery than cayenne, the term of such stimulants is soon reached.

Some twenty or thirty years ago a very different species of humour was offered to the public,— which might then without compliment be called a discriminating one. The rabble of dancing girls then found no encouragement, or were confined to their proper regions at the opera-house. The antics of a Polly This, or Patty That, would have been reckoned an insufferable familiarity, and the humorists of those days would have laughed contemptuously had they been called on to supply situations, the whole point of which turned on a fast young king being played by a girl, and a severe-looking woman by a man. Some of the pleasant pieces of these more fortunate days were delightful scenes of fun, conceived in the happiest spirit of true burlesque, the best of which we owe to that excellent artist, Mr Planché. His name is more popularly associated with pieces of what the French call 'féerie,'—a kind of dreamy and spiritualized version of one of our fairy tales, done with a certain seriousness, very much as it would appear to a child's eye. His name recalls the 'Sleeping Beauty in the Wood,' 'King Charming,' 'Invisible Prince,' and many other pieces associated with the Vestris triumphs. Not so familiar are his truly humorous satires and pieces of pure burlesque on the old stories of mythology, where the doings of the gods and goddesses are ridiculed with a quiet gravity. His treatment of a single classical story, 'The Golden Fleece,' is an excellent example, and may recall to a forgetful public the true principles of the art of raising laughter. In some instances he has followed less respectable models, and repeated the common jingles and puns, which disguise other works. Few play-goers will forget Mr Charles Mathews in his representation of that odd portion of the Greek dramatis personæ, the Chorus,—that tedious body of moralizers and incessant interrupters of the business, who have perplexed and wearied so many a schoolboy with their Jeremiads and explanations. Any reader of Euripides or Sophocles will recollect the dismal commentaries of 'the Chorus.' The terrible grandeur of the Greek plays made such an adjunct quite in keeping, and lifted it above the possible bathos of a dangerous familiarity. But to the scoffing Greek we can quite conceive the utterances of these supernumeraries furnishing a subject for inextinguishable ridicule; and, indeed, no more legitimate subject for burlesque could have been supplied to a Planché living at Athens. But there is this peculiarity in real burlesque, as distinguished from the false, that even those unacquainted with the subject that is satirized can see there is something ridiculous in what is satirized.

Fancy a body of old men sitting where the musicians now play, and after each situation, or at the end of each scene, turning to the audience with some such remark as this: 'Ah, the unhappy Lady Clara!!! What is to become of her now? How is she to escape from that bold, bad baronet? Surely she is overwhelmed with more wretchedness than she deserves. Is there no Providence? Where are the good men? Ah! what is to become of her?' Or, again, when the bold, bad baronet is unexpectedly killed by his own pistol going off as he is scaling the wall to Lady Clara's window, the commentators in the orchestra, if the drama were conducted on Grecian dramatic principles, would turn to the audience and say: 'See there! Such is the consequence of indulging our own unbridled passions. He lies there, that unfortunate baronet, a bleeding corpse. Punishment, though slow, hath o'ertaken him. Ah! what will happen now?—what will become of us all? Wonderful are the decrees of fate! Not one of us can escape them!'

The story of the 'Golden Fleece' is, of course, familiar to all,—at least in its broad outline. There is the arrival of Jason, the labours appointed for him before he can win his bride, his desertion of her for Glaucé, her fury, and her sacrifice of their children. There would be a regular recipe for dealing with this tale by the workmen of our day, which our experience can supply.*

* The leading funny man would be the King of Colchis,—with a red nose, an enormous artificial forehead, &c., and a reasonable wager might be accepted that he would be described in the play-bills after this fashion :—

 Æetes, King of Colchis (so gluttonous that he would *eat-us*,
  and possibly fond of *cold cheese*).

 Jason would, of course, belong by right to one of the pert and familiar young ladies of the establishment, who would appear in small satin 'tights,' with an eye-glass and moustache and whip; would talk with a drawl, and use 'demmes' and 'bay Jove's,' sing slang songs, and, like Mr Fezziwig in the 'Carol,' appear 'to wink with her legs.' The bill would, of course, run :—

How very different and even artistic is Mr Planché's treatment! The real gravity and earnestness becoming to burlesque are not lost sight of. The image of the Greek theatre is retained, and the Chorus sits in front. How pleasant and natural the flow of the introduction!—

> *Chorus.* Friends, countrymen, lovers, first listen to me:
> I'm the Chorus; whatever you hear or you see,
> That you don't understand, I shall rise to explain—
> It's a famous old fashion that's come up again,
> And will be of great service to many fine plays,
> That nobody can understand now-a-days;
> And think what a blessing, if found intervening,
> When the author himself scarcely knows his own meaning.
> You may reap from it, too, an advantage still further,
> When an actor is bent on marriage or murther,
> To the Chorus his scheme he, in confidence, mentions,
> 'Stead of telling the pit all his secret intentions;
> A wondrous improvement you all will admit,
> And the secret is just as well heard by the pit.
> Verbum sap—To the wise, I'll not put one more word in,

JASON (a young swell from an a-*jasont* country), Miss POLLY LIGHTLEG.

Medea would, as a matter of course, and without discussion, be done by the well-known comic gentleman of the house, who has done queens, and countesses, and washerwomen, and governesses, and Minervas. There would be the captain of the 'Argo,' like the captain of a steamer; policemen, as a matter of course; in short, any play-goer could sketch out the framework. The effect on the mind would be the usual one,—nothing distinct or special, a general sense of 'break-downs,' romping, and bad puns, and the great 'topical' song as before.

> Or instead of a Chorus they'll think me a burden;
> But just say, this is Colchis, and that's King Æetes,
> And this is young Jason, he coming to meet is.
> And there are the forty odd friends of young Jason,
> And that's their ship Argo, just entering the basin.
> At the end of each scene I shall sing you some history,
> Or clear up whatever is in it of mystery.

Compare, too, the song in which the Chorus—and Mr Mathews as the Chorus—tells the story of the Fleece, with the average common form of a burlesque song. The easy, natural way in which he converses with the audience, without the common gagging and familiarity with which such communication is generally carried on, on the stage, is inexpressibly amusing :—

> However, my business at present is merely
> To tell what may not have appear'd quite so clearly,
> The cause of the voyage, which in the ship Argo
> Young Jason has taken; and why this embargo
> Is laid on the fleece, which lies here on the shelf;
> And as I'm the Chorus, I'll sing it myself.
>
> SONG.—*Chorus.*—'The Tight Little Island.'
>
> There reigned once on a time, o'er Bœotia's clime
>   A King (Athamas he's known by name as);
> He packed off his first wife, and thought her the worst wife,
>   Till the second the first proved the same as.
> The second was Ino, who, you know,
>   Was very displeasing to Juno,
> And a shocking step-mother the children of t'other
>   Found her, to their cost, pretty soon, oh !

She threaten'd with slaughter her step-son and daughter,
    But a ram with a fine golden fleece, sir,
Flew up thro' the sky, with them so very high,
    They could not see the least spot of Greece, sir!
They got in a deuce of a fright, sir,
    Poor Helle, she couldn't hold tight, sir!
She fell in the sea, but the young fellow he
    Came over to Colchis all right, sir!
What do you think this nice man did, as soon as he landed
    And found himself safe, the young sinner?
He saw the king's daughter, made love to, and caught her,
    And had the poor ram kill'd for dinner.
'Twas very ungrateful you'll say, sir,
    But, alas! of the world it's the way, sir,
When all a friend can, you have done for a man,
    He'll cut you quite dead the next day, sir.

The rhymes here, and even the puns, are all witty and flowing; and the very source and spring of the story is something like that a facetious Greek, bent on ridiculing one of the legends of his country, would have conceived.

Now, beside this versified narrative let us put one taken from the introduction to a modern burlesque :—

    SONG.—*Fernando.* Air, ' Cork Leg.'
    The late count had a brace of sons,
    Extremely plump and handsome ones,
    As like as two new Enfield guns,
    Or as a couple of hot cross buns.
      Quite true, all true, ritooral, &c.
        Chorus. Quite true, &c.

A gipsy's son, of poaching fond,
The count sent o'er the herring pond.
The very day he went away
Our master's younger brother—
All.   Eh ?
Ferr. Was lost, right tooral, though the rural policeman did search.
            Chorus. Right tooral, &c.

'Twas thought the poacher's mother did
Feloniously prig the kid.
Wherever could young *master be ?*
Has always been a Mister *E.*
            Right tooral, &c.

If ever that misguided gal
Should be by master caught, my pal,
Her life will not be of much *val-*
—ue, ritooral, ritoo-*ral.*
            Chorus. Ritooral, &c.

For years a morbid man lived Count di Luna,
Till he saw Lady Leonora—sooner
Than you could say 'Jack Robinson,' plump fell
Into love's meshes that Italian swell.
Nightly to love him here he has brought her,
And though they empty on him jugs of water,
And heavy boxes, too, of mignonette,
Hoping by such means some repose to get,
He sings his *solo,* though him they *do wet ;*
And though they hope to vex him, past a doubt,
It doesn't quench love's flame, or *put him out ;*
But soft ! his idol comes ; it's very clear
That we must not be caught thus idling here.

What inferior stuff this is beside the other! On the other hand, how truly humorous, especially to one recalling his weary hours of hammering over the Greek plays, is the appeal of the Queen to the Chorus:—

> He's gone! and yet his god-like form before us
> [*Chorus advances.*
> Appears to hover. Ah, my gentle Chorus—
> You the impartial confidant of all—
> You, to whom every Colchian, great or small,
> Imparts his hope or fear on this sad stage,
> Have I done wrong with Jason to engage
> In this great struggle 'gainst my royal sire?
> *Chorus.* It's rather—
> *Medea.*   Silence, sir, I don't require
> To be told that, whatever it may be
> You were about to say: but answer me,
> Have I done wrong?
> *Chorus.*   You—
> *Medea.*   Interrupt me not.
> Have I done wrong, I ask? if so, in what?
> *Chorus.* I—
> *Medea.*   Ah! your silence answers me too plainly.
> *Chorus.* But —
> *Medea.*   And you offer consolation vainly.
> 'Gainst Fate's decree to strive, who has the brass?
> For what must be, comes usually to pass.
> So let me haste and pack up my portmanteau—
> I've got that horrid dragon to enchant, too!
> *Chorus.* If I might ask—
> *Medea.*   Now what I mean to do?
> In confidence, I don't mind telling you.

The humour of this situation lies in the possibility of the *working* of the chorus, actually leading to such a painful discussion from the anger of the august person they presumed to advise. The weakness of human nature is pretty much the same in all eyes: and with all the sanctity and august prerogatives of this band of advisers, they were exposed to such a rebuff.

Excellent, too, for its gravity and earnestness, is the conclusion of the first act, where the Chorus again interferes in a soothing way, and where there are quips our modern burlesquewrights might envy.

Enter Æetes.

Æetes. My mind misgives me—wherefore was that shout?
What, ho! my slaves within—my guards without!

Enter Guards and Sages.

We are betray'd! robb'd! murder'd! See—oh, treason!
Yonder he goes, that young son of—old Æson.
Chorus (advancing). *Be calm, great king—'tis destiny's decree.*
Æetes. *How dare you talk of destiny to me?*
What right have you with such advice to bore us?
Chorus. *Sir, I'm the Chorus.*
Æetes. *Sir, you're indecorous.*

There is something truly humorous in the verses which we have printed in italics,—and, as was before remarked, though few in the pit and galleries may have known how the great tragedy kings and queens of the Greek stage turn angrily on the expostulating Chorus,—still the effect of true burlesque should be humorous in itself, quite independently of ridiculous absurdity. For those acquainted with the Greek stage there is, of course, a double enjoyment.

At the end of the piece Medea sends Glaucé the fatal garment which is to destroy her, and prepares to kill her children. Many will recall the late Mr Robson in this scene, but in another version, constructed on the modern principles, and which are dull enough; above all from the Medea being played by a man. For there is this principle also in burlesque which will surprise not a few,— that there is a loss of 'fun' by such inversion, and that there is a far greater and more humorous contrast in the conception of a Medea as played by a woman. When played by a man, this perversion is always intruding—it takes the whole thing out of the range of possibility. We know that the personage we see could not be a ridiculously angry and fiercely jealous woman,—a kind of troublesome Xantippe, worrying her husband; but is merely a disguised man, going through grotesque antics.

Medea.   Tell me all—how do they fit her?
Nurse. Fit her: she's frying in them like a fritter.
Medea. She stole my flame, and now in flames she lingers,
     And, with my wedding ring, she's burnt her fingers.
     The tyrant, Creon, too, does he not frizzle?
Nurse. He does—and so will you, unless you mizzle.
Medea. Fly—save thyself; I've still a deed to do,
     No mortal eye may see, save my own two.
                                            [*Exit* Nurse, L.
     Yes, my poor children—yes, it must be done,
     Your fate it is impossible to shun.
Chorus. What would you do to them? Say, I implore.
Medea. (*drawing a rod from out the sheath of a dagger*)—
     That which I never did to them before.
Chorus. Whip 'em? Oh, wherefore? Is the woman mad?
     What is their crime?
Medea.   They are too like their dad!
               [*Snatches up children and exit* R. U. E.
Chorus. 'Tis plain her wrongs have driven her wild, or will.
     Help, Jason, help!
                    Enter Jason, L.
Jason.   How now? What more of ill
     Has Jason now to dread? The king's a cinder;
     My match is broken off—my bride is tinder;
     And I am left, a poor, unhappy spark,
     To go out miserably in the dark.
     Where is the wicked worker of these woes?
Chorus. Inflicting, now, the heaviest blows
     Upon thy children.
Jason.   On my children—where?
Chorus. Behind, of course.
Children. (*within* R.)   Oh, mother, mother!
Chorus.   There!
     You hear them?

Jason. (*rushes to door*) Paralyzed with awe I stand—
Medea, hold, oh, hold thy barbarous hand:
The door is fast, where shall I find a crow?
Chorus. You have one—
Jason. Where?
Chorus. To pluck with her, you know.
Jason. I mean an iron crow, to force the gate
Which she has bolted.
Medea. (*within* R.) Fool, thou art too late!
Jason. Too late, by Jove! She's bolted, too—despair;
Nurse. Gone in a dragon-fly, no soul knows where.
Jason. A dragon-fly! How dare she so presume!
A *witch's carriage ought to be a broom.*
Chorus. I said that she was flighty, and she's fled.
[*Thunder, &c. The palace sinks, and* Medea *is seen in a chariot drawn by two fiery dragons, amidst the clouds.*
The palace sinks—behold her there instead.
Jason. Thou wicked sorceress—thou vile magician!
Come out, I say, and meet thy just punition.
Medea. I told you I would play the very devil,
If to another you should dare be civil;
I've done the deed—didst thou not hear a noise?
Jason. Barbarian, I heard you flog the boys.
Medea. I didn't flog 'em—I but made believe.
Chorus. Oh, shame! *the very Chorus to deceive.*

The last line is admirable. But, indeed, a whole homily could be delivered on this text, and on this excellent bit of fooling.

It is hardly fair to judge a burlesque of the day by the strict rules of burlesque, which it does not claim to follow. Such are entertainments of a special kind—a blaze of rich dresses—a flashing of many twinkling feet — dancing of tremendous energy—with songs and rhymes strung together. This medley is addressed to a particular class of the community, who require it, and enjoy it. How obscure in its meaning, how incomprehensible, how tedious, how disconnected a thing is a modern burlesque, has been pointed out even to weariness. It is a show—a piece of fooling; but it has no pretensions whatever to the name it bears, any more than grinning through a horse-collar, which used to be popular at fairs, is a burlesque. Indeed, the principles by which this species of composition are guided seem to defy apprehension. It might be fancied that the story selected as the object to be 'burlesqued' would be followed as a guide, and absurdly distorted. But the theory defies even this elementary rule, and staggers on, a wild succession of disconnected pranks—each player trying to make 'fun' for himself out of his voice, dress, mouth, gestures, and, above all, legs. The French, always exact and logical, have a name for such an unmeaning piece, and call it a 'Buffoonery.' This might be worthy of importation, and be added to the list of other felonious takings from the French. Now, besides the inherent dulness of such performances—for the whole gamut of grins, breakdowns, and grotesque dresses, &c., is soon run out, and can only be repeated—they have the bad effect on public taste of leading it astray from the richer pastures and laughing meads of true humour. We are content to accept these husks, without thinking of the vast hoards of delicious truffles which a little searching will find. Genuine burlesque would be infinitely more diverting; and its principle a very simple one. Men in heroic situations, when the foolish spirit of conceit and affectation overpowers them, take a fatal step— often only an inch or two—and become ridiculous. A very happy coincidence allows of these two principles—that of the false burlesque and of the real burlesque, being placed side by side; so that any one with a sense of humour can see for himself which principle has the fairest claim to the title. At the pretty theatre of St James's, which looks as if it was the private theatre of the Grand Monarque himself, with its blue and gold decorations, is now playing a burlesque on the convential model, drawn from the story of 'Pocahontas,' the Indian princess, who was married to Smith the

Englishman. This has been treated as might be expected. The Indian Chiefs sit in council, and parody the proceedings of the British Parliament, talking of 'Mr Speaker,' and the like; the leading Chief sings comic songs, and dances comic dances. The young princess is seen at an Indian school, under the direction of a squaw governess; and there is a kind of parody introduced, of a popular comedy now playing at a little theatre. Smith is dressed in a fantastic old-fashioned garb, and buffoons, and dances and sings with his Indian mistress in all sorts of wild fashions. In short, the subject would seem to have been chosen as a good peg, or a series of pegs, on which to hang contrasted buffoonery. It was Indian, and there might be Indian dresses, tomahawks, &c. The scenery is good, the dresses rich, the dancing abundant, but it is unmeaning as a whole, though taken in detached bits it may amuse.

Yet the story, properly treated, contains the elements of true burlesque; and one with the same elements, though not the same names, was many years ago put into the old-fashioned shape of burlesque by one Kenney, and caused more tears of genuine laughter than a bushel of modern so-called burlesques. This was the farce of 'The Illustrious Stranger,' a conception of true humour, and rarely acted now, through the want of an actor with the broad racy tone which it requires. The story is that of Benjamin Bowbell, an English Cockney, wrecked on some fabulous island, the daughter of whose barbaric king, the god of the country has declared, must marry an 'illustrious stranger.' He is found by the natives, carried to Court, and informed of the glorious destiny intended for him. In the treatment of these incidents, everything is worked out seriously. The rich dresses, procession, &c., all circulating round the bewildered Cockney, who exhibits his selfishness, and almost incredulity as to his good fortune; his chuckling over every fresh homage; his unconcealed laughter at the formal bowings of the 'foreigners' in this strange country; his grotesque imitation and return of their salutations; and, above all, the grand procession to barbaric music, when he is placed in a splendid seat and borne on men's shoulders to the temple,—this becomes a spectacle that the most iron muscles could not resist. A finer and more delicate portion of the treatment is the vulgar arrogance of the man gradually developing under this prosperity. Then comes a more grotesque situation still, when the princess grows ill suddenly, and the courtiers come to congratulate him on *the glorious privilege* of being allowed to die with the princess; the half alarm, half incredulity of the man at this news; his 'Go along now!' and when the news of her death arrives, his being solemnly congratulated by the courtiers on the glorious privilege he will have, in being burnt on the same funeral pile, according to the custom of the country,—all these are elements of true humour. All this, too, is in a spirit of perfect gravity, and the whole is one of those situations which belong to the broad humour of all countries and all ages, and would be effective in any language.

But we should send our writers to France to learn the true spirit of burlesque. They never forget that first principle—the being in earnest—which is also helped by a certain exaggerated splendour. In English historical burlesque, for instance, from Henry the Eighth to Guy Fawkes, the whole is as familiar and boisterous as an Ethiopian serenader's buffoonery, or the blackened

Christy Minstrels' performance of 'Norma.' From the outset there is no attempt at realizing the character of the time or the situation. The figures are, as it were, ticketed with names, and dressed a little after their models, and a faint outline of history follows; but there the likeness ends; the rest is wild and irregular tumbling, fooling, singing, punning, dancing. Any diligent frequenter of say the Strand Theatre, will find it difficult to point in the performances of that facetious pair, Messrs James and Thomas Thorne, any special character belonging to the long series of pieces they have played in. They each expend an extravagant, untiring energy, that shows them to be conscientious performers, bent on producing what seems absurd. Further, many historical personages themselves must have been conscious that they were lending themselves to a farce; and at times may have been inclined to be merry under their functions and prerogatives, and to have gone through them in a grotesque sense. This, a little exaggerated, should be the foundation of burlesque; and there are very few of the French school that will not bear this test.

Thus 'Chilpéric,' which a single clever Frenchman has written, composed, brought to London, and acted, is another specimen of the tone of legitimate burlesque. It is impossible for any one, unfamiliar with the days of that monarch, not to catch from this piece the tone and flavour of the time and social order it burlesques. To look at the bill and read Chilpéric, Fredigonde, Druids, and such names and officers, the prospect seemed to speak of the dry bones of mediævalism; but the author, instead of following the precedent of our English writers, seizing on the meagre names and some meagre legend, then putting English dresses on the characters, and putting English allusions into their mouths, has followed a more true and philosophical course. Take one portion of his legend, the dismissal of Fredigonde from the palace for fear of being an 'inconvenience,' in respect of the marriage with the Spanish princess. There the skilful Frenchman looks around him, sees what *has* happened, and may happen, in royal families, or in great houses, at a similar, and developes a comic, situation, which his instinct tells him *must* be common to all ages, whether mediæval or even more remote. Even the 'romp' of an umbrella-dance has a *vraisemblance* from the way it is done. We could fancy a Court thus surprised in a forest by a shower: and the variegated colours of the umbrellas gave the dignity of the situation. But in the hands of an English workman we should have Mrs Gamp's umbrella in every shape and form.

We have also the means of furnishing a contrast between English and French treatment, in a burlesque of the same author, which, after a great success in Paris, was literally 'hewn' into shape for the English market. This was the famous 'Little Faust.' It came to the Charing Cross Theatre under the witty title of 'Little Faust and More Mephistopheles,' and was transformed into one of those unmeaning English burlesques, the meaning of which it is hopeless to follow. Later, this clever M. Hervé brought out an almost literal translation at the Lyceum, and tried to teach the English players some of the airy fun which makes the charm of French pieces. The result is brilliant, intelligible, and charming. Again, we have Offenbach's 'Princesse de Trebizonde,' at the Gaiety, with such good players as Mr Toole and Miss Farren—a piece founded on the most perfectly humorous subject, the sudden change of a family of mountebanks from this profession to affluence. The exquisite treatment of this idea by French artists is not to be described. The sudden breaking out of spinning of plates on sticks—the old Adam—in the midst of finery, the striking of attitudes,—all this was easily copied by the English players; but there, and in repetitions of these simple symptoms, it all ended. Not so the French, who in every look, motion, and general uneasiness, showed the recollection of their old calling. In short, it is not by '*doing things*' that the actor enforces his part on the audience, but by a bearing, a demeanour, a glance, a struggle between his nature and what he assumes.

There is one, perhaps most familiar of all to the public, whose merits as a composition have been overpowered by the extraordinary popularity of its music. No one will be at a loss to guess the name of 'La Grande Duchesse,' associated with the triumphs of the free, and too familiar, Schneider. A word might be said for the piquant and nicely-suited character of the music; but the story itself is admirably done, and still more admirably entangled with the musical pieces, which seem to come in without violence. Going a little back, it will be seen how the burlesque notion of this plot might have been evolved. It came to England, was, of course, hewn and chopped by the adapter's adze to fit English players and audiences, and it will be seen how the former imparted to it *their* notion of burlesque.

The picture of the tiny German court, with its exaggerated etiquette, needless abundance of state officers, armies of thirty men, &c., has often made the traveller smile. Some, too, in their descriptions might use the phrase, 'burlesque of a Court.' If they were asked why they used such a phrase, a man like Thackeray might answer with those few most amusing pages in 'Vanity Fair,' where the Court of Pumpernickel is described gravely and without any straining at comic effect—the cabal about the dancer, the intrigues of the little officers of the Court, &c.—and yet the effect is that of exquisite burlesque. It arises from the contrast between the grand machinery properly belonging to great kings and courts being applied to some petty matter. The best part of the whole is, the actors themselves being utterly unconscious of their producing this effect, and being firmly persuaded of their being equally important with those who play on greater stages.

In this view those two consummate French artists and collaborators, MM. Meilhac and Halévy, pp roached their subject. Everything in that story is burlesque, yet a burlesque regulated by probability and seriousness. The very story was chosen with a view to contrast such elements, and was only what might have taken place at such a Court. Thus the mere framework, a young spoiled princess, newly come to power — such power as it was — surrounded with intriguing ministers no higher than valets de chambre in mind and intellect, taking fancies to men in the ranks and giving way to other extravagances, was quite in keeping. So with the intrigue for the foreign alliance with Prince Paul, his tutor and diplomatist Baron Grog; in fact, the whole has quite the flavour of the old 'Mémoires Secrets,' or the 'Lettres Galantes,' written from Spa or some other hotbed of intrigue. All who have been at the Variétés will recall the wonderful ensemble, the surprising delicacy with which it was played by the original corps; and though the piece abounded with *cancans* and other extravagances that seemed not in keeping with probability, there was this to be remembered, that all seemed the possibly unnatural ebullition of absurd people, giving way to violent and insane bursts of spirits; with a sort of *arrière pensée* for the audience, that they were trying obsequiously to court favour with their wild young mistress, and imitate her in all her pranks. Indeed, it was easy to see, from those capital and round characters—*Boum, Prince Paul, Fritz,* and the *Duchess* herself—that the writers had powers far above libretto writing—a belief since justified by that exquisite little drama of 'Frou-Frou,' now the success of the day.

But when this burlesque came, in due course, to England, to be adapted, translated, and acted, the transformation was marvellous. The most instructive part was really to see the different view of the whole taken by the English players. It seems to explain quite clearly what is called the present decay. Their object, it was evident, was not to set off the piece, but to get 'fun' and business for themselves out of each part. It was assumed that if the *Prince Paul* was played as a mere imbecile, *unconscious* of his own folly, an audience would assume that *this was the imbecility of the actor*, a common actor's delusion. At all events, 'that sort of thing would not tell.' The actor would make it tell, 'by business.' It was astonishing how unmeaning the whole became by the adoption of such a principle—how stupid, and what a gross and clumsy joke the whole seemed! The ignorance began with the manager who placed the scene on the great stage at Covent Garden, with *spectacle* and a vast Covent Garden army, disposed with all a stage-manager's art. We think of the little cabinet pictures at the Variétés—small as Thackeray's little chapter—and see at once how a pleasant garden of burlesque is utterly choked by this vast, clumsy tree, with its large branches. It was at once lifted from burlesque into serious grandeur: for there was nothing ridiculous in so sumptuous a Court, with its grand army and dresses.

This was the first blunder. Next, every character, in detail, was mistaken, and played according to the glorious tradition of English burlesque. First, the lady who acted the *Grand Duchess* gave her fantastic orders, carried out her curious whims, with an air of despotic stage grandeur worthy of the Italian opera. She was called the English Schneider; but that artist, with all her shortcomings, was at least the character she played. The *Prince Paul* at the Variétés was an

exquisite specimen of the character known as
niais — that *unconscious* imbecility which betrays
its own folly at every turn—excellently revealed
in the scene where he reads the passage from the
Gazette D'Hollande — the complacent and idiotic
enjoyment in which, and ignorance of its ridicule, was exquisitely done. In London, this
was put into the hands of Mr Stoyle, a trained
burlesque actor, who proceeded to make a 'funny'
part out of the materials. First giving it a lisp,
talking of the 'wight wing' of the castle, he proceeded to turn it into an *active* and energetic
'funny' man, now speaking in a deep bass key,
now running up a sort of gamut of odd gutturals,
now simulating grotesque terror, now skipping
about with odd steps; in short, making the whole
raw, coarse, and without any distinct character
whatever. There was a great deal of laughter at
these antics—funny enough in their way; but all
reference to the piece was lost. The spectator
thought fondly of the subdued, graduated, delicate,
and infinitely more droll *Prince Paul* at Paris.
More lamentable was the contrast in that character of true comedy *Fritz*, the low soldier, shy, yet
familiar, coarse, impudent, amusing. All this was

delicately conveyed by Dupuis, contriving to interest us by a hundred little touches. In England, a stiff player, and tolerable singing, made the usual conventional 'rough soldier' out of the part, of coarse and strong flavour; but with 'business,' and therefore acceptable to the groundlings.

In the condition of the English drama there are one or two symptoms of wretched decay, which, strange to say, offer some reasonable hope for the future. Out of the miserable decomposition about us, a blooming fungus, as Dr Solomon might put it, has shot up in the night. In a recent bill, which the flagging audience peruses so vacantly, is the following singular announcement: '*The furniture by Mr Nosotti, of Oxford Street.*' That is, some gilt 'occasional' chairs, an ottoman and cabinet in a nobleman's mansion, were from the atelier of that well-known upholsterer. This brought to mind a late pantomime in which the dresses of a set of gay ladies were announced as being from the millinery warerooms of 'Messrs Stagg and Mantle, Leicester Square.' This sort of thing is a healthy sign, because it puts matters on an intelligible footing. We know whither we are moving. It is right that the drama, having become a reproduction of railway trains, steam-boats, and houses on fire, should boldly glory in their humble aspirations, and call whatever spade it uses, a spade. Thus in the same play the practicable 'Putney Bridge' might surely have been made more effective had the assistance of a professional gentleman been sought, and his service acknowledged by a line,—

'The Bridge constructed under the superintendence of Mr Foreman, of the Messrs Cubitt.'

By-and-by we shall come to this. A garden scene by moonlight might be rendered doubly attractive by applying the same principle:

'The Garden laid out by Mr McWhirter, Head-gardener to his Grace the Duke of ——.'

This wretched system would at least be honest; and let the drama enjoy, what it is at present, though it will not take the name of, an Exhibition.

PART IV.

THE FRENCH STAGE.

BUT it will be said, is not the *drama*, pure and simple, flourishing as the drama never was? We look to the Eastern and Western Theatres, and see them brimming over. Are there not Mr Robertson's 'sparkling' comedies with their 'epigrammatic' dialogue, supposed to quite restore the old 'palmy' days of the drama. People who deny that sterling English comedy exists are bidden triumphantly to look at the astounding success of that little cabinet piece, now playing at a little cabinet theatre, and called 'School;' look at the same author's 'Home,' 'Progress,' 'David Garrick,' 'Breach of Promise,' and other pieces. Stalls have to be taken so many nights in advance; and even a *blasé* and bloated aristocracy are convulsed at the 'epigrams' with which these pieces abound. Most of these are shaped from French sources, according to an easy formula, as readily as a publican can doctor his spirits, beers, and wine—according to a printed book of receipts, or just as an ingenious man will see a patent invention, and fit it, say, to a velocipede. After all it must be some solace to the French artists who are pillaged in this way, and exceeding pride, to think that but for them the British Drama must go out altogether; and though they be furious at this systematic highway robbery, still they must have many a sneer and joke at these poor devils of English, who can't write plays, and are like 'the purchasers of ladies and gentlemen's second-hand wardrobes for exportation,' and which are trimmed, shaped, and patched before being exhibited for sale. Not only that, but they seem to be content with 'misfits,' ugly, uncomfortable garments, which suit neither their climate nor their habits, as any one would find who took the trouble to sit out 'Escaped from Portland' or 'A Life Chase.'

Translation and adaptation, i. e. the exportation or alteration of 'used wearing apparel,' is destroying the drama. Such things do not entertain. They are looked at more with expectancy and curiosity than with amusement: they do not suit the soil—nor the air. The playgoer will point to the various great 'hits' of the last ten or fifteen years—the 'Ticket-of-Leave Man,' 'Still Waters run Deep,' 'The Game of Speculation,' 'The Leap for Honour,' 'The Streets of London,' with a whole tribe of successes which have brought money into the manager's treasury. All belong to another country, to other manners, other associates, and other wits. We have to import characters, and lively dialogues, and, above all, stories. It is scarcely consistent with dignity to be in this state of dramatic destitution, and to be so dependent on the aid of others. That we should be anxious to see a good piece, which has been successful abroad, upon our own stage, is as natural as that we should like to read a good novel through the medium of a translation. Such becomes almost a duty. But there is a further want of dignity, something that in the case of a common social obligation would be called meanness, in striving to disguise any sense of such aid by the arts of adaptation. It was seriously contended, not long since, that this process actually amounted to original treatment, and that the adapter exhibited quite as much genius as the inventor. The evil, however, remains, that the more this help is sought, the more helpless we become; and, like a person learning to swim with corks, or one raising his spirits with brandy, it is at last found impossible to break off the habit. Every new French piece is watched for, pounced on by the dramatic body-snatchers, turned over— to see if it can, in any way, be made to 'do' for the English anatomists. There is a vast amount of clever 'knack'—but nothing higher—in the English adapting trade.

The British stage is still the garden of transplanted plants and translated shrubs. So long as this system continues we shall have no true stage relish or enjoyment, which is the real point of the drama as regards the audience. We shall only be looking at maimed French plays acted in England, just as a stranger would go to a French theatre in Paris. For, as has been often shown, the drama is a reflection of the manners and sentiments, the special follies and humours, the essential story of the life, of those who are looking on; and this single reflection will show how faithless for such an end must any French play be to a British audience. And this is the more inevitable, as the French are notoriously fond of viewing everything from a French point of view, and of dealing with such things only as take a local French shape. Of course, a broad story of sympathy and passion is common to all the world. But there are only a few of these, and the more general they are, the fewer points of interest they contain; while a special story, that draws its interest from local colour and character, though it appeals to a smaller circle, obtains, in proportion, a more intense appreciation. We may form a notion of how remote our sympathy is from incidents founded on such special points, by the feeling with which we regard an historical drama of some very early period, where the figures and story seem about as real and vital as one of David's Roman pictures in the Louvre. But between us and French stories and characters there is a specially wide chasm, as will be seen by a little consideration of the character and morals of that nation. Their dramas are *interesting* because logically reflecting that character and those morals. First, there is that cloud of intrigue in which the Parisian lives, moves, and has his being—that striving after *bonnes fortunes*, that questionable species of *chasse* which gives the zest to his life. It is notorious how disorganized

is Paris social life—not, be it observed, after a
guilty or forbidden fashion, but as an accepted
and approved rule of life, encouraged, and almost
necessary. The stage, therefore, duly and duti-
fully—in the hands of accomplished and nicely
logical writers—is made to reflect what is before
it; and it is certain that every piece of merit and
success has this 'ground coat' under much wit
and character. The first step of the adapter,
therefore, must be to maul, bend, and twist this
immoral curve with violence into a straight back-
bone, that will suit British morals. This was duly
done with that wonderful piece of Victor Hugo's,
Ruy Blas—Mr Fechter's masterpiece—the whole
power of which lay in a secret *liaison* between a
woman of rank and a man of low birth, which at
every turn was on the point of precipitating horror
and confusion, and culminated in a guilty and
tragic end. Such was not to be tolerated—as it
was indeed repugnant to an English audience;
and the objectional relation was 'watered' down
into the conventional respectful but hopeless passion. This was worse even than leaving out
Hamlet; and yet such was the artistic treatment,
the consummate dramatic force of the author, that

this emasculation escaped notice, and the lavish wealth of the piece carried it through triumphantly—those only who reflected and who knew the original, feeling how absurd and artificial was the present arrangement. Again, the French character has a vast deal of melodrama in it; and a certain amount of high-strung declamation and exaggeration is made to *envisager* most situations in life. The nation, through its books, journals, speakers, and soldiers, is always willing to work up any incident into something semi-romantic. This, too, is reflected in the plays, which are therefore pitched in too warm a key for the wondering British Pittite, and are founded on a fashion of viewing things which seems to us exploded. Hence a real French romantic drama loses its whole bloom, its chivalrous air, when transferred, and we seem to be dealing with unnatural people, and with acts which belong to an era as romantic as King Arthur's; or else the usual process must be employed, and the whole made coarse and strong. There is a delicacy, too, in working out the finer emotions and characters, which requires an audience accustomed to the daily exhibition of such things, even in an artificial way, and which 'seems Greek' to an audience without such a habit, or else mere childish refining.

The charming 'Roman d'un Jeune Homme Pauvre' illustrates this excellently. A young tutor, consumed with a passion for a lady above him, and who, besides, exhibits all the mean associations which destitution brings with it—hunger, &c.—would not be a character of dignity on the English stage; our notions of tutors and music-masters being rather 'antiphathetic' to romance. We should be inclined to look with a pitying derision on the sickly young men who figure in French ballads, looking after flight of birds, or on a flowing stream. But a young French tutor in real life may lawfully look on his profession as advantageous for prosecuting 'amours' either with his master's wife or daughter. This theory being accepted by the audience, and perhaps approved, sympathy follows his stage career, and all the struggles of the 'beau jeune homme, si gracieux, si charmant,' are watched and commiserated—even his proud starvation, which a good-natured landlady relieves with a timely bowl of soup. All this, on English boards, would be pronounced 'unmanly' and sickly, and the young man a poor whining creature. The eye of the British adapter wisely settled on the 'situation' of the piece—the leap from the castle window to save the honour of the lady; the knife and brush were used, entirely with a view to lead up to that, and, with that stout centre-piece, a tolerable British drama was tacked together out of the *débris*. Wonderful French work!—that bears so much hacking, and still cannot be spoiled.

But coming to the lighter pieces, the exquisite trifles, which are like expanded epigrams, or flashes of wit drawn out—the farces, in short—it is here that we find the fatal mistake that is destroying the humorous side of the English stage. As is well known, we draw our *entire* supply from this source, and have done so for many years. Let us see how this works. The English and French characters are totally unlike in this lighter direction. Their lives are utterly different. First, the French are more of a *community*, and live more together. In the country, the great families live together in clans, and married children live in the same château with their parents. In Paris, as we know, every house contains a whole colony distributed on different floors, with a common stair,

&c. Thus, people are going up and down, meeting on a common thoroughfare, mistaking rooms, wilfully or otherwise. Most people dine at cafés; most people sit out on chairs on the Boulevards, taking coffee, ice, &c. Again, as to persons and characters; with their notorious laxity as to conjugal relationship, a good husband is popularly looked on as being always on the defence, and a sort of marital policeman; and, having to live under the conditions described—common stair, &c. —is at a fatal disadvantage. Further, the foolish, stupid husband—bourgeois—stout, and in trade, actively provokes attack. With all these elements duly mixed together, the list of 'comic' situations becomes endless—situations that are highly probable and do occur. Now, if we look at all our so-called English farces, from the English pens of Messrs Morton, Williams, Charles Mathews, and others, taking them with their adaptation, we shall see that they all reflect a situation arising out of these very French conditions, and a situation that could never arise on British ground. Set the original piece beside its adapted shape, and it will be seen that the 'jokes,' story, and figures all turn on those French attributes above described — that living so much in public, in the open air, and in a common house. With the characters it is the same. There is a favourite character of an English farce, one which actually furnishes a distinct 'line' for leading 'funny' comedians—that of a dapper, smart Cockney, who talks with extraordinary glibness — like Mr Charles Mathews, using a sort of epigrammatic terseness, and falling into odd mistakes; as, for instance, 'Imagine my rapture, when I discovered it to be a one-horse woman in a fly—I mean, a fly in a one-horse woman—no, I mean,' &c. Or, 'What was my joy in finding she was a sky-blue creature in a sweet young bonnet.' To his persecutors, such a person replies with rapid utterances and quaint, flippant repartee—a style, in short, that is quite familiar to us. But this is all, as regards England, purely conventional. We have no such characters, and no one who would behave in such a way. The Frenchman, on the contrary, gay, in good spirits under any difficulty, ready to extract something *spirituel* out of his inconveniences, is exactly such a character. He belongs to them and reflects them. We have grown to imagine there is some prototype for such extravagance. So with that free-and-easy relation of his story to the audience, when a chair is taken and brought down to the footlights. This freedom requires to be touched airily, and, under the hands of our British actors, becomes coarse and broad, and insufferably familiar —it destroys the illusion of the scene; but in a clever French actor's hands is conveyed the notion of talking to himself in lively soliloquy. Indeed, that sort of airy explanation, half-serious, half-bantering, is precisely what a light-hearted Frenchman is fond of delivering to any audience that he can get together, and on the stage he will take care to address it—not, as our English actors do, to the real audience, thus breaking down the barrier which should exist between the real and the unreal mimetic world—but to fanciful hearers. He will be still unconscious of the audience, and they will have a more exquisite pleasure, being, as it were, in the attitude of listeners overhearing something. How absurd, too, and far-fetched the incidents as presented in their English dress, and at which we laugh! That 'Cup of Tea,' in which Mademoiselle Beatrice acted so pleasantly, exhibited a gentleman who had been brought home from a ball in the wrong carriage and to the wrong house, a thing which could not have happened in England; but which in France, through the system of floors, and also through the easy code of manners, is not improbable. The discreet servants of that nation will allow many to come and go. These scenes make us laugh, as in the country itself we would laugh. But there would be an essential want of sympathy to overcome. How, then, is it that interest is actually excited on our stage, and hearty laughter provoked? First, for the reason given, that through lack of other entertainment, we have been forced to make ourselves relish these exotics. Again, they are received on our boards subject, of course, to material alteration, or 'adaptation,' being converted, as it were; and the foreign character, which we know not, is shaped into a more congenial and intelligible figure, with glaring reds, blues, and yellows thickly daubed on. It is so daubed for the benefit of the actor, and he does his best with it, so as to create a 'funny part,' without regard to probability or plot. This is the true *rationale* and the regular treatment by which French pieces are made acceptable.

The question will now be reasonably asked,

What is proposed, and what remedy is offered? As to rival the French in their neat sparkling pieces, their vivacious march of thoughts and events, their lively dialogue, *that* is simply hopeless. We might as well bid a hesitating, bashful man speak as finely as a practised orator. The French are a people of *finesse;* they require *finesse* in their amusement, and they get it. We have no *finesse*—at least, it is not a national characteristic. We cannot bid it leave the pit and go upon the stage. We must only cast about carefully, take stock of what we have, see what and where our strength is, and transfer that to the stage. It would be idle now to condemn the handing over of the stage to engineers, mechanicians, or to Messrs Jackson and Graham; for by this time it has been discovered that there is nothing dramatic in the exhibition of imitation steamers, race-courses, houses, work-shops, &c., and, what is worse, nothing entertaining. It is a low shape of amusement, which is certainly akin to the 'clown' department, as seen at circuses and pantomimes—that prevailing 'gagging' in look, and speech, and gesture. We have been appealing to that for ages. It has a certain result and success in its way, if we can trust the loud and boisterous guffaws that circle round the theatres. Yet laughter is no test. On a fair green, the Cheap Jack and mountebank brings *his* house down, and by careful training an audience can gradually be brought to laugh at anything. To laugh at a grotesque gesture, a comic leer, a sudden verbal 'sell,' at an absurd mask even, this is the very lowest A B C of humour. It may tickle a refined mid-rib acutely, but only for once or twice. What is the remedy, or where to look for it, is another question. The *roué* who has impaired his health by dissipation cannot blame the doctor who tells him, 'This is your own doing. Such and such a sickness is what is the matter with you. If you are to get well, it is only after a great many years of patient care and abstinence.' The beginning of a cure would be to return to the first principles of the drama, and let clever writers study to make it the reflection of the humours, manners, oddities, follies, and life-histories of the varied crowd who are looking on, sitting in pit, boxes, and gallery.

In France the theatrical ground seems to bloom with verdure, to flower with new and ever-varying shapes of flowers and plants, with tropical luxuriance of leaves, plants, and greenery; and though the abundance is almost rank, the prospect is delightful to the eye. In our poor histrionic ground a few dried shrubs enjoy a sickly and stunted growth; the foliage is as meagre as that of a Dutch garden, with its stagnant little canal and plaster temples. The inferiority is wonderful.

To sit on one night, as the writer did lately, in a stall of a Parisian theatre, and on the next in that of a London one, furnishes the most curious contrast conceivable. We pass at once into a new order of things; and the interval is so short, we seem to travel straight from one playhouse to the other. The general superiority of the French stage is usually conceded; but it is hardly credible that the superiority could be so marked,—a superiority extending to theatre, scenery, and actors; the chief and most striking feature of the English playhouse being a certain meanness, poorness, and even squalor, in all things appertaining to the theatre. This observation may lead us to consider a few of the influences which seem to promote the superior tone of the French stage. In matters of the stage these influences act wholly apart from the important elements of plays and of acting. The drama, entering as it does so largely into the life of the Frenchman,—that is, of the Parisian,—the plays even being *read* by a public as large as the one that listens and looks on,—it is felt that this important element in life should be treated handsomely. It is well known that the State does this officially. The people are invited to recognize and respect the stage as a great profession, and can scarcely help doing so. The very buildings preach this recognition. The British play-goer generally makes his way to his favourite house through some mean back street, and reaches at last a shabby, barn-like edifice that seems to skulk away from public notice. If it be in some more respectable street, its individuality is lost,—it is absorbed into the houses adjoining, or squeezed in between its bourgeois-like neighbours. It seems as though some remnant of persecution attached to the builders of theatres, and that, like the professors of proscribed faiths, they dared not challenge public attention by the ostentatious erection of a building for their worship, but were obliged to adapt and alter, unobtrusively, whatever structure they could get. In this shame-faced, half-apologetic fashion many of our London theatres seem to ask toleration. In the provinces they almost invariably lurk and loiter in the very ghettos of the town. Above all, but too mean, is the poor and sometimes noisome alley of access by which the players have to creep into their building. All this is but some half-remnant of the old squirearchical or magisterial theory that players were rogues and 'vagabones,' and were to be dealt with as such; and perhaps, too, from an impression, that the profession of a player, in a broad view, belongs to an inferior caste; and again, partly from the feeling that a play-house is like any other venture in business, in which all æsthetic feeling or dignity is mere surplusage. It is not too much to say, that a great deal of this sense is owing to the mean housing of the drama,—to these shabby buildings and poor quarters,—and to this hiding away out of sight.

Abroad, on the contrary, what does the State do? It pitches on some open *Place* with a commanding position, and raises thereon a solid, handsome, spacious, showy, architectural pile. It is a Temple. We can walk round it; every side has features of its own. We ascend to it by steps. It is an object,—a landmark, as it were,—that has been built by the town, and has cost about as much as a Royal Palace. In France there is actually a style of architecture for the theatres, and, side by side with all the new Parisian improvements, there have risen noble theatrical structures, vast and massive outside, whose name the stranger is sure to ask. On the Quai, the great houses of the Châtelet and the Lyrique face each other—a wide, open space between, each with a handsome façade, and that honest, self-asserting air of *being* a theatre, which foreign houses display. Our theatres, when they make any architectural pretence at all, try something in the shape of a poor sham portico or a scenic front, which, architecturally, is neither fish, flesh, nor fowl. Round some of the French playhouses, on the lower story, runs the bright café, crowded between the acts, where the bell from the stage rings to give notice that the play is about to begin. There, too, is the bright door, labelled 'Entrance for the artists,'— not in a mean alley, but opening on the broad street. And artists,—the invariable title,—is a much more complimentary name than stage-players, as actors used to be contemptuously termed with us. Even about the older French playhouses there is a stately palatial air, a little old-fashioned and rusted, but not in the least wanting dignity, as, for example, in the theatre at Marseilles, and in the French Opéra Comique, and the Français, that model of a stately theatre. But even in the last century the rules that should guide the building and arrangements of a theatre had been carefully studied by the French architects, and, turning over the wonderful volumes of the Encyclopedia, we find elaborate plans, drawn to scale, for all the different kinds of theatre. But the most perfect homage to the dignity of the stage is found in the new French Opera,—the most gorgeous temple in the world, vast, enormous in its proportions, almost barbaric in its magnificence,—rich in gold and bronze, and crusted over with precious marbles. This enormous pile, placed on the most precious spot in the capital, where every inch of ground might be covered with napoleons, is an almost monumental proof by which our gay neighbours wish to proclaim to the world their respect for the dignity of the great art. And the artists who are attached to the service of such splendid temples must be proportionably ennobled. This public recognition, then, seems to be an important reason for the superiority of the French stage; a recognition much more substantial than our old, poor title of his Majesty's Servants, which was in reality intended for anything but a compliment. In France the comedians of the king, or of the emperor, or of the republic, are in the service of the State, as much as the soldier and the sailor; and when their term is complete, the State takes care of them with a substantial pension.

It must be said that such a sense of dignity prepares the play-going mind, and makes it respect the drama it is going to witness. Thus as we enter Drury Lane Theatre, and pass along its spacious halls, its noble staircases, and fine corridors, and see its old-fashioned stucco and decorations, it is impossible not to have this feeling. But there is no other theatre so magnificently laid out for space. That huge mass, its colonnades, and its standing by itself, makes it an important object: and in all the purlieus, slums, and back streets which stretch away from it, the great establishment is spoken of with respect and awe.

Latterly there has been a vast improvement in the style of the London theatres, and some of the new theatres show great advances in comfort and decoration. Yet it would seem that the architects have not yet arrived at any fixed principles in the construction of theatres. With the exception of the *Gaiety*, built on a true French model, the interior presents nothing more than a succession of light galleries under each other, which is a false principle. Galleries are fitting in a church as a species of extra accommodation, where the floor is the *main* feature; but 'the house' in a theatre is as essentially constituted by the boxes, &c., as by the pit. The artist, therefore, should exhibit these as substantial parts of the house. But a miserable economy interferes. The manager wishes that his pit should stretch away far *under* the boxes, which are thus obliged to be all hung in the air, as it were. The architect, however, to give his theatre a rich look, loads the panels of boxes and galleries with a solid sort of decoration; and yet the whole, supported on thin iron pillars, wears an insecure and unsubstantial look. The French have the true theory, and have held it always. This system of throwing back the pit into a place whence the house cannot be seen, is owing to the stalls, which are so close to the stage, and sunk down so low, as to interfere with all pleasurable stage effect. The French, on the contrary, build their circle from the ground upwards—with a row of boxes on the pit tier, which hold the occupants of our stalls—and in front of the first tier throw out the charming balcony only so far, as to act as a sort of shade from the glare for those under it. The house is thus fairly enclosed, and is far better for sight and sound, which latter does not go travelling away under the boxes. The 'Gaiety,' in its decoration and construction and general air, is quite a French theatre; but Covent Garden Opera House, with its vast space and fine proportion, is truly English in stiffness and formality. The boxes seem, indeed, a number of boxes piled on each other, and look as if made of card-board. Its stiff lines, its strange shape, its yawning amphitheatre, are all in harmony: the boxes, too, are more like little windows, and do not reveal the tenants, which give so dark and brilliant an air to foreign houses. Some of the older theatres, like Drury Lane and the Haymarket, want remodelling in the steep slope of each gallery and the sharp corners, which prevent the spectators seeing well.

Another substantial reason for the superiority of the Gallic stage is to be found in the national character, which is eminently histrionic. In a French conversation, a French speech, a French sermon even, there is always present an eternal vivacity, a gay helping out of the thought with other aids besides that of the voice,—aids which are quite as potent, namely, gesture, expressions of the eyes and face, and even of the shoulders. Then, too, there is the pleasant *esprit*,—wit almost, —the constant lurking insinuation, in lieu of plain statement, which lies at the bottom of true acting. The half undomestic life of the Frenchman, which sends him so much abroad of nights, renders him more exigeant as to the character of the pastime on which his entertainment so seriously depends.

Again, too, it must be said that the French artists are a superior class to the English players; superior in tastes and accomplishments. Their tastes, habits, mode of life, everything, are superior. Their pastimes and accomplishments would amaze our English players, and perhaps excite their contempt. Many are collectors, and what are called in France 'amateurs.' Grivot, of the Vaudeville, is fond of etching, and is curious in bronzes. St Germain collects rare books. Desrieaux delights in pottery, and people go to see his old specimens of old faïence ware. The more famous Doche has an exquisite little museum of rare Dresden and dainty curiosities. Kopp, one of the droll coterie who play in the Grande Duchesse, has a collection of pictures worth 80,000 francs. Lassouche, of the Palais Royal, gathers china. One actor has a collection of clocks of Louis XIV.; another, a choice little cabinet of Meissonier works; a third is a good sculptor; a dozen paint landscapes, nearly all are musicians, and many play on the violin. As for the actresses, it is not too much to say that every second one sings skilfully, and plays the pianoforte as a matter of course. Many French actors write elegant and lively verses, — 'proverbes' sometimes, which they act for their own amusement. All this betokens a refined tone of thought. The directors of the theatres are generally skilled and successful dramatists, and, more often still, trained and refined critics, who have served an apprenticeship on influential papers. The green rooms are not like ours, bare, unfurnished apartments, but noble *salons*, full of busts of great

The French Stage. 225

players and dramatic authors, covered with pictures of scenes from great plays, by great artists, and furnished with presents from the kings of France. As we look up from the street between the acts, we see the attractive rooms of the Français lit up and glittering, looking like the rooms of a palace, and know that the artists who are entertained therein cannot but respect themselves, and have their profession respected.

But, above all, the French stage is superior, because its plays are superior. French playwriters are artists, with a most delicate touch, and a skill in construction that is almost instinct. They give their actors *characters* to act; the actors give them in return a rich store of spirit, vivacity, and abundant details of humour; and player and writer act, and re-act, upon each other. How firm the touch, how elegant the treatment; nothing is ponderous, nothing laborious. And this, too, is the secret of their success: they hold up the mirror to their own curious social life; at night the Frenchman in his stall sees reflected to him the oddities of the day, all that might have happened, and has happened. We adapt these trifles, and the result is a burlesque exaggeration,—not founded on reality, and unsuited to an English audience, who have no social standard to measure it by. Long ago, when the English dramatist took a simple and original course, and despised his neighbours too much to borrow or adapt from them, his pieces were real, living, and, what was better, amusing and entertaining. It is surprising that the incompatibility of these French plots, or more properly French equivoques, to English customs and manners, should not be perceived. Take, for instance, a well-known little sketch of five or six young ladies expecting a gentleman visitor, of whom they have great hopes, and who at last arrives, with rather showy dress and manners. Later comes the piano-tuner, a retiring, quiet gentleman, who remains in the background, as suits his supposed position, and of whom only the amiable girl of the party takes any notice. After an extravagant display of devotion to the showy gentleman, and a corresponding contempt for the other, it comes out at last that the tuner is the real gentleman, and the showy one the tuner. This little trifle will, of course, find its way to the English boards, but we can conceive under what disguise, and in what heavy native buckram. It

will not bear transplanting; for the situation is
French, and might occur in any of those Parisian
'flats,' where there is a common staircase, and
people are going up and down constantly. But,
when the piece comes to our boards, the tuner will
enter as Twingles; the gentleman as Mr Fitz-
poppet. We shall have a bevy of the boisterous
young ladies attached to the 'burlesque,' and an
additional Betty or Mary as a comical household
housemaid to rush in, and cause fright, and introduce comic 'concealing business'—in the piano
perhaps—by the news that ' Missus is comin'!'

That there is a difference between French and
English playing will be conceded, and that the
superiority lies with the French, will likewise be
admitted by all, save, perhaps, by the members of
the British branch of the profession. The reason
is because we are, in familiar phrase, moving on
another tack. There is as great a difference between a greatly successful French play and an
English one, as between the players in both. The
last famous Français piece, Paul Forrestier, which
has the conventional French immorality, at least
shows us the admirable Favart, perhaps rather
passée now, but full of repressed passion, and who,

when she gives way to a burst, shows that she is struggling to keep back as much passion as she expresses. This is the true theatrical art,—indicating, rather than expressing, emotion. Our actresses might learn from her this disciplined fury, this suppressed agitation, half revealed in eyes, mouth, figure, attitude—in short, in the way in which injured and outraged mothers and wives might display their feelings in an ordinary drawing-room or parlour. With her black dress and pale face she gives us the look of shrinking terror—the torrent of words stumbling, and tripping over each other; the unconscious retreating and cowering—not the stage stride; the tying and twisting of the handkerchief—in short, the lifelike air which must come from the fact of the actress dismissing all conventional stage associations, and fancying she is in some real situation. Happy is the Français in its young lover, Delaunay, handsomest of adorers, who looks about twenty, and whose cheeks are not 'blue' from excessive shaving; who walks like a gentleman, and is exquisitely dressed. So with the no less admirable Gôt, his rough honest friend, who is in love with the same lady. Never did stage lover play rejection so admirably. The look of perplexity and distress, the not knowing what to say—the attempt to speak and make a last appeal, the going to the door, the general uncertainty—were points new, and drawn from the great volume of human nature. Why that volume, so cheap, accessible, and translated into every language, should not be in the hands of our English players is incomprehensible.

The French romantic melodramas — where love, passion, fighting, adventure, hair-breadth 'scapes, handsome men and women, and fine dresses and scenery, all flash before us—have a certain spell and fascination; but they have a charm in their own country which they lose when transported to us. When deformed and adapted to the English stage, they want the link of sympathy; for they are wholly French—in character, manners, epoch, and adventure itself. They reflect the romantic sentiment of the country, which has a corner in the breasts of the most practical and mercantile among Frenchmen. The French public, like the gallery of a transpontine theatre, admires and weeps over representations of self-devotion, self-sacrifice, the rescue of unhappy ladies, and the satisfactory punishment of aristocratic and heartless assailants of female virtue. In this class of piece the story is usually drawn from French history or romance, and the mirror is, as it were, held up to French nature, in the house. There is, therefore, a true *rapport* between actor and audience such as we in England have not. Again, we have not the true hero of romance—the noble melodramatic lover and fighter, with a handsome face, a good figure, and an interesting and heroic carriage and demeanour—and, above all, with a melodious voice, and that demi-chant, musical and melancholy, which is almost 'de rigueur.' Over French melodramatic pieces— extravagant, far-fetched as they are too often— there is spread a charm which always interests. But it is grievous to think that even this *spécialité* is beginning to disappear. We think of the old Porte St Martin and its glories—that wonderful playhouse run up, some forty years ago, in a few weeks, to serve as a temporary booth until a new and more enduring structure should be got ready, and which has flourished ever since—and of its long line of glories. No theatre could boast of such an important series of plays, which have left their mark on the French drama. The 'Tour de Nesle,' the 'Chiffonnier,' 'Belphégor,' the charming 'Victorine,' 'Le Bossu'—our 'Duke's Motto'—the 'Vautrin' of Balzac, and 'Richard Darlington,' are only a few among the list. But the mantle— if a theatre has a mantle—of the old Porte St Martin has been contemptuously thrown off, and picked up by a newer and more gorgeous house — the Châtelet. There we can see the villain's career worked out steadily, with dignity and due magnificence. This noble building is noted for its perfect arrangements, its enormous coulisses, where the mechanical resources stretch over a vast deal of ground, and where the joke runs that the stage-manager rides about on horseback to give his orders. The house is famous for having the best theatrical orchestra in Paris, directed by one of the Chéri family; and let it be said that, for a stately and pathetic melodrama, a full orchestra—rich in melodious airs, that can give out broad and flesh-creeping chords—is absolutely essential. A vast amount of really good orchestral music may be noted as one of the many strong points of the French stage.

At the Châtelet was lately given the 'Vengeur,' of which so much was talked before it was ready, and which was considered a fiasco when it did appear. It scarcely deserved such a condemnation, and seemed an interesting and romantic piece, catching happily enough the tone of the period described. On the London stage we fancy ourselves tolerably familiar with the Revolution, and there is no period which the regular costumier could mount so readily. Yet something more is needed than tricoloured sashes, and top-boots, and high-collared coats, and allusions to 'Mussier Roberspear' and 'Darntong.' In the 'Vengeur' a tone of heroic sacrifice is present throughout, and the characters were played in a natural, unstagey way, which imparts an air of perfect reality. The piece turns on the nautical side of the Revolution. A young sea-captain, pursued by a vindictive rival, and separated from his sweetheart, finally sacrifices himself for her sake, and goes down on board the 'Vengeur' in the fashion in which the original vessel did *not* go down. This hero was played by a handsome man, with a musical voice, in whose bearing and face it was impossible not to feel an interest. He seemed at home, also, in his dress,—one of the points in which our native actors are deficient; and indeed I find it noted, by an acute critic, to the praise of the famous Bressant, that 'he seemed to carry every suit of clothes he put on, as if it was his ordinary dress.' We, who have seen artists in our own land in Louis Quatorze dress, or, worse, in a dress evening suit of the day, know what a divorce seems to exist between the clothes and their wearers, and that an amount of buckram is present for which no tailor is responsible.

The scenery of this piece, too, suggests a reflection. It is commonly said that in that department, at least, 'we beat the French,' and proof is instanced in the scenes of Alhambra transformation pieces, which have been sold to French theatres. But this is altogether a mistake. In a landscape, —in effects with the lime-light, in transformation devices, in mechanical changes, in colour, our superiority may be admitted; but in purely picturesque effect—in the tone of a scene and the conception—the French artists show they are becoming masters. They have the true touch. Thus, at the beginning of the 'Vengeur' there was a scene in old Paris,—a lonely street, admirably broken up with Gothic houses and porches and effects of shadow; and over all there was a tone of tranquil mystery thrown, as though the times were those of danger and plots. The red cap business and sabot-clattering was not overdone, as it would have been near home. The colours were all subdued. There was a pleasant comic underplot turning on the embarrassments of a portly barber. One scene in this piece shows in a small way how perfectly the French understand the true principles of fun. The barber has been induced to let his shop for a few hours to a stranger, who affects to have some eccentric aim, but in reality is a Royalist conspirator who wants the place as a rendezvous. The barber has no business himself, and chuckles over having taken in the stranger. Almost at once a customer arrives and wishes to be shaved. Then another, and another,—in short, a legion of conspirators. The amazement of the barber at this sudden influx of custom was admirable; but not less admirable was the bearing, the supremely natural manner, of the strangers, mere supernumeraries, with only a sentence to say, but who actually seemed to be what they represented,— people coming in from the street.

Later in the piece came a scene representing the deck of a man-of-war of the old pattern, which to those accustomed to our theatrical decks, to 'Black-eyed Susan,' and even to the 'Africaine' at Covent Garden, must have been startling,—so picturesque, so really original, was the whole conception. Instead of going straight back, the ship ran diagonally across the stage. There were sails, masts, cannon, portholes, cabins, all indicated with that touch which is so much more valuable and effective than the mere servile reproduction, or fac-simile making, which seems to be the fashion on our stage. Then followed a *Chant du Vengeur*,—a fine and spirited scene, grouped with surprising taste and effect, and with a middies' dance,—wonderful in spirit and originality. The last scene—the sinking of the vessel—was a surprising triumph; and though vessels rolling on a practicable sea are familiar enough now, even this was done in an original way, and on true stage principles. At a certain London theatre in one of Mr Robertson's pieces, there was given two or three years ago, a piece in which there was a ship also, on whose deck the characters were to talk and move about. The vessel had to strike a rock and go down slowly with all hands, the soldiers standing gallantly to their post, refusing to save themselves, before the ladies. The after-deck and fore-deck were both brought in. There was a sail set, and the whole was considered a triumph of mechanical skill. Yet nothing more journeyman-like, or untheatrical, could have been conceived. The vessel, as it stood on the canvas waters, was about the size of a small yacht. The figures of the actors were about three times the height of the hull of this large troop ship; and though the heroine came up — with difficulty — through a little hutch that was called a cabin, and was made love to by the lover, the helmsman, who was turning a practicable wheel about a foot off, heard every syllable, there being no room for him to get farther away. Such is the result of realism. The true principle of theatrical effect is to convey the idea of size, which will make a deeper impression than size itself. Now this 'Vengeur' ship illustrated the difference. They only brought on a portion of the vessel. One half was under the rolling waves,— the half nearest the spectator. We saw the whole width of the deck; at the stern, high in the air, a huge stump of a mast banged to and fro, the hull itself rolling, and getting deeper in the water every moment. There was very little more superficial space used in this vessel than in the English yacht before described. Yet the effect was overpowering.

So, too, on the comparatively little stage of the Olympic, in 'Little Emily' was given the hull of an emigrant ship, little more than seven or eight feet long, and yet by adroit indication made to convey the idea of a huge vessel. But, in truth, scene constructers generally only study to reproduce or imitate, instead of laying their minds to the theory of *delusion*.

There are a few other things we might copy with advantage from the French as regards their theatres. That gathering together of all the play 'posters' on one large sheet, at several fixed points, in the same type, livery, and colour, commends itself at once. Charles Lamb would have been delighted to read the eager pondering faces, wistful yet doubtful, drawn to this piece by inclination, distracted by so many other pole stars, and who are gazing at these radiant and glorified proclamations through all hours of the day. Such a *coup d'œil* is vastly convenient for the playgoer, and very necessary; for the theatres are not rigorous in enforcing a long run of a successful piece, and of a Sunday night a popular play is often withdrawn to make room for the re-entry of a favourite actor and another piece; so that this fatal upas, 'the run' for two hundred and three hundred nights, is not always spreading dark and blighting branches over the stage. But with a bit of scenic show, one of those costly 'women-pieces,' where all is '*decors*' and dresses and procession, it is of course impossible to suspend a run, from the bands of supernumeraries engaged, and who are paid by the week. The sumptuous appointments, too, cannot be allowed to lie fallow, or rust even, for a single night, and the manager must realize as fast as he can. But in the more reasonable cases, the manager wisely thinks he has another class of clients, whose interests he must consult, namely, those who have *seen* the successful play that is running; and the performance of so prodigiously successful a play as 'The Grande Duchesse' is frequently interrupted and alternated with something less familiar. It is curious, indeed, to think of the philosophy under this influence of a 'run,' and that the actual *success* and popularity of particular pieces should be one of the reasons that is hurrying the stage to decay. For there can be no question but that to be acting a single piece for a year or longer must dwarf the powers of the actors, and give them no field for variety. Further, too, the same system shuts out a large section of play lovers from their favourite enjoyment; since, like Mr Swiveller, in his credit difficulties, he finds various streets and shops 'blocked up' and cut off from a too fatal familiarity. In the old 'palmy' days of the drama there was a delightful variety, and at Drury Lane, under Garrick's management, the playgoer could have a fresh play and a fresh set of actors at least every second night.

The universal box-offices, of which there are some half-a-dozen in Paris, are another most convenient and agreeable feature in Parisian theatrical arrangements. They are not on the select and rather costly system that prevails with us, which some music-sellers and libraries turn to a means of speculation and profit. They are little halls, as it were, open to the street, into which the playgoer walks. Running round the sides are open models three or four feet high, of every theatre in Paris. The name of each class of seat is visible, the number of every seat is marked, and the play for the night is pasted up over-head. The gandin and his friend discuss the place they would like, and for all purposes might be in the theatre they have chosen, —select their numbers, and call over the 'administration' to announce it. The charm of this admirable plan is, besides its convenience, that a common bourgeois can walk in, and take even his one franc pit-ticket. Every information is given, the officials of these places are posted up even in future theatrical arrangements; they are most civil and communicative. These places are open till 'all hours,' and it is characteristic to find the playgoers busily engaged peering into the miniature playhouses, and eagerly taking places, even at midnight.

There are things, however, about the French theatres that one would gladly see abolished; notably, the three violent knocks of the mallet which causes such a thrill of delight to run through the audience. This savours of barbarism, seems to grow more noisy every year, and is supplemented at some houses by a final disorderly thundering of the same instrument on the boards. To one accustomed to the more familiar 'ting' of

English houses, the effect disturbs the nerves, and coming at such a moment—always welcome—this savage prelude routs everything dramatic. But we may suppose the French to be attached to this odious relic. Again, the women box-openers—one of the few rapacious classes in the country—with their footstools and worryings about cloaks, and hats, and bills—are a serious drawback. It is surprising how the audience endures their tyranny. With the new theatres a crop of these plagues has started up ready made. But the 'Figaro Programme,' sold between the acts, is welcome; and the invitation to 'Ask for the photographs of the artists' is more tolerable. For twopence-halfpenny to acquire the faces of all the actors on a card, with their names and characters in the piece underneath, is a not unacceptable shape of souvenir.

The system of having the prompter's box in the centre of the stage, as at the opera, may have its advantages. It may, however, be open to the objection that it would make the actor less inclined to rely on his own resources, who is thus secure of support in every possible way. It is characteristic, however, that it should be rendered necessary by those great spectacular pieces, where it is more requisite to *see* the prompter, his motions, and directions, than to hear the text. It might be introduced in the case of veteran actors who are not well up in their parts, as in the instance of Frederic Lemaître, the very lees and dregs of whose acting are more precious than the choice runnings of the best existing histrionics. This wonderful genius, for all his decay, his haltings, his failing memory and powers, still left the impression on one who had never seen him before, of great and unconventional gifts, and of a round and distinct *character*, which remains present to the mind long after. With that exquisite art which is French, and French only, he had been nicely and accurately fitted with a part that suited him exactly; an old schoolmaster, gentle and pastoral, and whose whole life has been coloured by the memory of a loved wife, who died years before. This bereavement has given a gentle and childish tone to his mind; but later he discovers suddenly that she had been unfaithful to him. This shock unsettles his reason, and at the scene where he makes the discovery, and begins to wander, singing snatches of an old song, and then suddenly turning to fury, it was possible to form a perfect notion of what the old Frederic was. Further on, when his little scholars gather round him, and ask him if he did not remember them, one of our conventional players would have had his regular round of business ready,—an immense deal of passing hands over the face, of tossing back his hair, of looking up at the clouds, of rolling the eye, finishing perhaps with a grin and much shaking of the head. Not so this great actor. He gave a little start as he was addressed, looked eagerly but naturally at the questioners with a puzzled air, and then said, with an indescribable half-sad, half-vexed tone, 'No, dears, *I do not know you.*'

In this piece was a new scenic device which may be commended heartily to the professors and mechanicians of sensation carpentry. The programme was that a gentleman was to pay a farewell visit to a lady whom he admired, at midnight, and was then to be assassinated as he came away by an outside gallery and stairs which led down into the garden. It is scarcely necessary to add that the lady was not single. The lover was, indeed, a tall man, of a vast girth round the waist, which, as he came to pay his addresses in a scarlet tightly-buttoned hunting-coat and buckskins, had an almost ludicrous effect. But, to use the French idiom, 'That does not hinder'—sentiment fines down even exaggerated corpulence, and on all sides was heard, 'O mon Dieu, qu'il est charmant! Comme il est noble!' &c. The room in which he took this midnight farewell was semi-circular, and filled the whole stage! but when he had passed out it all began to glide away slowly to the right, the prostrate lady lying overwhelmed with grief; and then the outside front gallery, flight of stairs, and garden itself began to come into view, and the next moment, when the room had finally disappeared, the escaping lover made his appearance on the outside stairs, descended in the usual guilty fashion, and was duly shot. This striking effect produced a hurricane of applause, and was talked of everywhere as the 'chambre à roulettes'—the room on castors.

PART V.

ACTORS PAST AND PRESENT.

THE most disastrous part of this general decay is, that at the present moment there can be found in the ranks of the Profession excellent sterling actors—some of the first quality, many with genius, —only wanting material and opportunity to display their abilities. Yet the line is meagre enough. With the twenty theatres *in esse* and four *in posse*, the list of notable players extends but to eighteen or twenty,—not one for each. In fact, one or two actors virtually represents each house, and bears the leading business on his shoulders,—a meagre promise for the audience, and fatal result of the economic star system. And it is curious that the question in society now always takes the shape of, 'Have you seen A—, or B—?' the individual rather than the piece, a sure sign of corrupt taste. When there are glimpses of a more correct taste, we ask, 'Have you seen *School?*' But this allowance of an actor or two to each theatre speaks for the pieces as well as for the player, which are all written to bring out the centre figure, and which is in itself a want of art, and a bad reflection of nature. In social life this general interest is always desirable. We look back to Drury Lane even after Garrick's retirement, and in the first caste of a famous comedy, find King, 'Gentleman Smith,' 'Jack Palmer,' Yates, Parsons, Dodd, Farren, Mrs Abington, Miss Pope, and Mrs Hopkins,—*ten* artists of the first class, in a single piece! But the Drury Lane list was often far stronger than this, and at one time comprised as many excellent artists as there are now at the twenty London theatres. But these were the 'palmy' days of the drama.

There are some curious phenomena in the actor's constitution. Often in some obscure provincial theatre we are struck by an inferior character played with such singular tact and propriety, so *perfectly*, in short, that we wonder at the hard fate which places the artist in such a position. But the confusion which reigns in the profession explains it. An eminent living writer was so struck by an instance of this sort, that he called on the player and offered to use his influence with one of the leading London managers. An engagement was accordingly offered, but a demand was made for parts of the very foremost order, for Hamlet, and characters of the same calibre! And this is the misfortune of there being no great theatre, or school for acting, as in the last century. This ambitious player, seen perhaps by Mr Garrick in his travels, would have been brought to Drury Lane, and fitted with parts, strictly of the class in which he had so distinguished himself. There every one had his own department. Now an actor has some success, and he strikes at the first place exorbitant salary, and must at least manage a theatre. But there is another shape of punishment which is overtaking the actors of our day, in the shape of a sort of competition from without. When it is found so easy a thing to be an actor, it is not surprising that any number of outsiders should carelessly step forward and compete, and this free-and-easy fashion of taking up a great profession has had its share in vulgarizing the stage.

There is another vulgarity which in itself helps to degrade the stage. As we walk the streets the eye is now and again attracted by some coarse and gigantic picture representing an actor in some part now the rage. It is made as exaggerated, as grotesque, as showily coloured as possible. That a manager should 'work' the advertising part of his performance is only natural, and that, as far as print goes, should puff his wares, may be a necessity of excessive competition. But an actor who had regard for his own dignity would not allow a caricature of himself to disfigure the public hoardings side by side with the pink and yellow and blue manœuvres of horsemanship and the daring riders. And positively there is a dignity in the latter not in the former. The horse-riding is addressed to the eye,—it is a daring, dashing show, and those exaggerated pictures of leaping through hoops, and flying round the arena, are done in a romantic way which may once or twice betray us into stopping and looking. But the actor's 'make up' is but incident to his part; his real glories cannot be painted. To see that clever artist, Mr Toole, in Wat Tyler, the modern 'low' radical, put back centuries, is a pleasant night's entertainment. There is a grotesqueness in his dress that, taken with what he burlesques in the play, is fairly legitimate. But such a figure set by itself in a poster might as wellbe the picture of a buffoon or a tumbler. It really shocks us as we go by, and helps to lead public opinion to feel contempt for a profession which could invite us to admire it, by such means. Not long ago people walking through the streets were met by men carrying placards, on the top of which were fixed a pair of boots, cut out in wood, 'in profile,' as the property-man's phrase runs. This was an advertisement of the astounding success of an American player in some buffoonery part, named 'Wellington de Boots!' The belief was, that the public were drawn by this low conceit. A compliment indeed to the kind 'patrons.' But by-and-by the fruits of all this will be manifest. The jesters and buffoons of the music halls have the same modes of invitation open to them; they are not so much imitating the ways of actors, as actors are following and imitating them. Very soon the public, too contemptuous to take the trouble of discriminating, will class all together,—tumblers and singers, dancers and joke-makers. And this was the class of 'scurræ,' 'buffoons,' which the classic writers, and even the Fathers, were so loud in condemning,—a condemnation accompanied with the bitterest contempt. Their object was to extort the laugh anyhow and everyhow, no matter what the means. They were the slaves of a wanton master. Everything is preparing the way for this lamentable fusion, and confusion also. There are even certain signs in the lamentable and suicidal abandonment by players of that dignified privacy, which gave a sort of veneration, as Hazlitt says, to the actor's profession. We see this self-exhibition and fooling at fancy fairs, where, so far from carrying out any condescending mimicry of Merry Andrews, they are only playing the Merry Andrew after a most inferior fashion. We see it in free and familiar speech-making, from the stage, and from other places, justly offensive to any audience that has respect for itself or for the profession. Again, that prim figure of Garrick, which postures in Westminster Abbey, might well shudder as he would be told that now-a-days a play is interrupted, while an audience actually *encores* five times the reading of a letter. All this is the worse now, on account of what may follow; and in ordinary life we know what the beginnings of an undue familiarity usually lead to. And can we wonder if actors now find themselves hustled and shouldered by 'artists' from the music halls,—competed with by persons who leave them behind in the gifts of audacious familiarity, who can 'gag,' wink at the audience, sing their slang songs, buffoon with every limb, and make speeches! Already we hear it stated gravely that 'the music halls are excellent training for the stage,' and managers, who must look to their treasury when they find their own players inferior in such gifts (gifts which are well appreciated by their audiences), will naturally seek to recruit their ranks from those who really excel in this sort of genius. This is what we are hurrying to: and we must thank Burlesque for bridging over the old yawning gap between the Drama, and what it is not too disrespectful to call Tom Foolery.

Indeed, the actor's position is becoming a critical one. The new theatres of the present taste have, indeed, created a demand, and the high salaries for a few are tempting. But by-and-by the ease with which an actor can be manufactured will draw crowds into the profession: the competition will be enormous; the regulars will be 'pushed hard' by the untrained, the incapable, and music hall gentry, who have a certain fertility in devices, never wanting to the '*scurra*,' and will be unable to compete with them at such struggle. It is as in society. Let the man of refined satire enter into competition with some rude, social jester, and he will be worsted; let him keep to his own weapons, and his own dignity will be a defence.

It is always a pleasant study, setting long-established conventional usages at a distance, looking at them as if we were strangers, and demanding what they mean. Thus, the great aim and struggle of life would seem to be what is elegantly and vaguely called Fame, but which in broader phrase is publicity; to be the centre of a crowd, to be talked of, stared at. There are only a certain number of pedestals to be occupied, and possession is to be obtained only by thrusting down some one else. It is like a seat in the House, or a bishopric. The fact remains that this honour of having an audience, or a crowd, is at the present time above all the prizes of the age.

Now, men of genius follow this ambition as a means to an end, because the command of a crowd gives them power. But meaner and cheaper natures, the poor creatures of society, whose souls, in stage phrase, are only 'in profile,' take the means for the end. All they ask is, not the grand and permanent audience, which a great man

always has, and which never breaks up; but a
crowd ever so little, to be got together anyhow—
bribed to sit by and look on while they exhibit
themselves. Vanity is at the bottom of all, and
will spare no expense to gratify itself. This is
what begets the *amateur* player or singer.

The race is increasing hourly, so much so that
dramatic amateur performers are a nuisance. The
common mistake that brings this alarming mob
to invade the boards is, the mistaking an easy
effrontery for gifts. Some free soldier who would
stand up and buffoon before the Queen and Royal
family, finds himself so much at home before the
foot-lights, so ready with an extemporized joke,
that he assumes himself to be a born actor. Why
histrionic gifts are supposed to be convertible with
wearing a red coat, has always seemed a mystery,
but it seems to be accepted as a sort of gospel
truth. At every little town or watering-place the
regular proclamation greets us, 'The officers of
the —th will have the honour of giving a dramatic
performance;' while, between the two pieces, we
may certainly count on the Yorick of the regiment—the side-splitting captain, who has graduated at the music halls, who knows and treats the

facetious Codlin, and 'The Great' somebody, and is supposed to give 'Captain Jinks of the horse-marines' with far more real power than those great artists.

This eruption of amateurs is really making itself felt on the profession. These importunate postulants, bursting in among the side-scenes, craving some sort of employment, any office, so that the foot-lights blaze on their faces, are causing a sort of demoralization. It is as with a well-known club, once a free-and-easy and delightful haunt, a mixture of players, artists, humorists, but which in a fatal hour gave in to the allurements of a Circe, called Fashion. The result was that the club became fine, the 'swells' and others began to 'bean' the eccentric element, which had been the charm of the place; and it now stands a thing of the conventional pattern, but warped from its old original model. So with the stage. It is hard for players to resist this pressure of amateurs, this 'treating,' as it were, or acquaintanceship with swells, who require something substantial for payment. And yet, between the amateurs and the players, what a broad trench! Kean's or Kemble's remark sums the whole up; who, invited to an amateur performance, called out aloud when some gave a message, 'Ah! *there's* an actor!' This was really some poor professional supernumerary. An amateur cannot import weight to the most trivial sentence. He knows not the secret of that measured exaggeration, which is like the coarse strokes of the scene painter.*

Another great actor once protested that he never saw an amateur who was worth eighteen shillings a week. The truth is, no amateur is worth

---

* The writer once saw a performance at which, as a bait for the public at a popular actor's benefit, it was announced that 'Mr ———, the distinguished amateur, had promised his valuable services.' The beneficiaire took a secondary part. He was a favourite. In vain the distinguished amateur ranted and raved,—his audience affected not to perceive; but when their idol made some insignificant remark in a level tone even, they all but cheered him,—a constant rebuke to the intruder. On another occasion, an amateur, who had adopted the stage as a profession, came on in a burlesque of the usual pattern, as a ballet-girl in *tulle*. He had the whole 'fat,' as it is termed; all the business and funny speeches. It was rumoured that he had given 'a gratification' to be allowed this exhibition. Yet, with these advantages, he could not hold his own; the smaller characters, whenever in contact with him, took the wind out of his sails in the most mortifying manner. Some poor fourth-rate jester, but who knew stage business, would utter his quips with a point and energy that raised him to first rank, especially as he had such a good foil. The audience soon entered into the situation; indeed, there was a ludicrous incompatibility between the grandeur of the part,—the displayed type in the bill, and the overpowered performer.

much more to 'draw.' The amateur who takes to the profession resolutely declines to begin in the ranks, and must do his Romeo or Claude Melnotte. The profession naturally refuses him such suspension of the usual training; the amateur will not give way, so the only course for him is to open his purse and purchase the step; either to subsidize a manager, or hire a theatre for himself, as seems to have been recently done in this metropolis, with a rather disastrous effect. The amateur resents his being thus heavily weighted in the race, and puts forward a claim as a 'gentleman,' having tact or elegance, which must make itself felt upon the stage. But this is a great fallacy. It no more follows that a born gentleman must appear a gentleman upon the stage, with better effect, one who imitates a gentleman, than that a real scenic spectacle is more effective there than an imitation one.

The profession of acting hovers between two positions, according as it is understood and interpreted. It may be the most degraded and contemptible calling that men or women can take up, or it may rise to a dignity beyond that of any other profession. At the outset there are some perilous associations, some serious disabilities to get over; and the public might fairly be inclined to treat as an inferior caste those who had to dress in strange clothes, fix on false hair, cover themselves with smirches of paint, sham the characters that they are, and exhibit themselves, their weakness and excellence, for money before vast crowds. It was no wonder in old days that *Jongleurs*, tumblers, delineators, jesters, buffoons, and players were all classed together; and even now, if we would realize the feeling, we have only to visit a flourishing music hall, and see 'The Great Some-one' singing idiot songs, followed by his idiot dance, to the vociferous bidding of the crowd. We may laugh, but we feel the degradation of human nature. The bare suggestion of ourselves or others, reduced to such a position, makes us blush for shame, and we almost pardon the harshness of the statute of Elizabeth which classed such with rogues and vagrants, *unless* they were servants of some great baron. Yet actors, with all the accompaniments of a theatre, the scene behind, the professional clothes, the paint and patches, reduce themselves to this level, when the intellectual part is forgotten. But one thing alone can lift them above the livery, the smirching, and this abdicating of all independence from being placed at the mercy of perhaps an ignorant mob; and that is the power of *real* acting. Let them be *actors*, show us human nature, human character, the delightful science of motive, mental strength or weakness—fields and pastures boundless, inexhaustible, and ever new— and they rise at once to a commanding place; they become associated with the glories of the fine old art. Then there is dignity, command, power; they are kings, and we come to listen respectfully. It was with some such feeling as this that Hazlitt, more than fifty years ago, speaks of the delight and interest with which actors were then regarded; even off the stage they were attended by a mysterious sympathy and regard. Now, the highest standard of playing is to hit the public quickly, and strongly, while novelty without propriety is all that is asked for. Now, we feel that the actor who exerts himself so much to entertain us, with his grimacing, his antics, and his ready fertility of verbal and corporal tricks, is only a very *clever* fellow, but whom fifty others, with the same opportunities, might excel in cleverness. We see them in the street, but feel only the curiosity of a moment, not the old respect and even veneration. The profession cannot fairly protest against the intrusive rage for amateur acting, which their own mediocrity is the cause of; for when playing is reduced to such elements as readiness, buffoonery, and versatility in outward tricks, of course, with a knowledge of stage-business, there is no reason why outsiders should not enter into competition and acquit themselves quite as well.

The mere exhibition of themselves by men or women, with their various physical qualities or gifts, has always been held by the world as something degrading; and by the Church as something immoral, or leading to what is immoral and degrading. And this is hardly surprising: for the nice sense of retirement and modesty is outraged, and the function of amusing a crowd, or gratifying curiosity, by dancing, tumbling, low comic singing, or grotesque feats, leads to a just contempt. A barrister has indeed been compared to an actor; but the ostensible aim of his business is intellectual, to help the innocent, or secure their rights for the injured. But simple *self-exhibition* remains, and always will remain, a degraded calling. Dancing-girls in savage countries, the lower class of jugglers down to the old professional jester, have always been an inferior caste. For those whose profession it is to amuse our eyes, we feel an indifference or contempt. To follow the matter further, a mere beautiful face, when intelligence is wanting, scarcely affects us. Now, *real* acting is not self-exhibition; it is an appeal to our intellect and our passions. It raises a mimic world before us: the actor is a man, one of ourselves, and we are with him in his struggles. His self-exhibition is but a means to an end. The most grim ascetic, who has witnessed a good play throughout, would not, with the deepest antipathy, feel anything that was not respect. There is something noble in it, when followed on its true principles. But the more it verges towards mere physical performance, the more the actor runs the risk of falling under the contempt that follows the other calling.

It might indeed be guessed that there was something unsound and decayed in the drama at present, from a mere superficial glance at the criticisms of old times. We wonder as we read the little volumes in which Leigh Hunt, and Hazlitt, and Lamb expatiated with love and discrimination on the actors and acting of their time; we rub our eyes and wonder what sort of stuff that was upon which they expended so much loving judgment, sagacity, and wit: what pleasant and acute unfolding of these odd humours, the unbounded treasures, and fitful motions of the human soul, seized on and interpreted with infinite delicacy through the medium of the tones, looks, gestures of the great actors. As we read we find we are getting hints of some forgotten art, some mystery long since lost to us, certainly not in the least corresponding with what we see to-day. The idea of a man of wit and taste devoting a volume to delicate analysis of acting; to elaborate expatiation on the beauties of certain players, would seem incomprehensible at the present time. Who could imagine a whole poem in praise, like 'The Actor,' or satirical, like Churchill's 'Rosciad,' and Croker's 'Familiar Epistles,' or essays, like those of Hazlitt and Hunt, being written on the ladies and gentlemen of the Queen's Theatre, or of the Globe, or Charing Cross, Strand, or indeed any of the existing Houses? The most laborious and painstaking would be amazed at finding his honest attempts, directed merely to the study of good business, and the end of making the audience laugh, his uncertain and haphazard effects, treated as the inspiration of genius, and made the subject of admiring analysis. They would feel surprised, as the late Mr Turner was said to have done, at the profound meanings which an admiring artcritic professed to see hidden in his paintings. Even now the critic, who would be discriminating, and re-open the choked-up wells of dramatic refinement, finds that there is no material to his hand; that what he would grasp is mere dust and decay. He cannot make his critical bricks, wanting both clay and straw. There is nothing to criticise; all that remains is to tell the story of the play at length, and say that Mr —— acted 'with com mendable praise,' that Miss —— 'threw much spirit' into her part, and Mr —— 'played with much care and conscientiousness.' A mere glance at a page of one of the older criticisms would show that the fine sytem of acting which then prevailed is quite lost to our players. Rather, in a happy complacency, they believe that their faith includes everything that could be necessary. Here is a little test. The 'School for Scandal' was lately played at one of the theatres, and we might fairly conceive a consultation being held, before its production, as to the 'view' to be taken of each character. Lady Teazle, for instance; granting that all her speeches were to be made to tell on the audience—all the 'points' and traditions to be well brought out, as they no doubt were by the clever lady who played it—what would be the general tone and complexion given to her character? Such a question put to an average actor and actress of the day, who was skilful in the detailed business of his part, would seem unintelligible, or perhaps childish. Yet this was a matter on which the audience of fifty years ago were critical,—the delicate colouring of a character; and proficient critics looked to this as a matter of course. To a trained audience such difference was as marked as the 'manner' and bearing of their own friends; and the skilfully-trained actor was able to convey artificially, what a person in real life did by instinct. Thus, when Miss O'Neill came out in Lady Teazle she was severely judged by Hazlitt, who incidentally shows that there were three or four views to be taken of the character, either 'the complete finished air of fashionable indifference,' which was Miss Farren's way of playing it; or the mixture of artificial refinement and natural vivacity, which appears the true idea of the character; while Miss

O'Neill gave the idea of the lady 'being thrust into a situation for which she was fitted neither by nature nor education:' and besides her mistaken reading, there was 'a perpetual affectation of the wit and airs of the fine lady, with an evident consciousness of effect, or desire to please, without the sense of pleasure.' An admirable distinction. And this idea of colouring a part is hopeless to look for among our players. They cannot grasp the notion. They can make this speech and that 'tell,' and produce its laugh: they can make the part a 'good' one: they can supply this 'colour' to their notions by a good 'make-up,' and a never-flagging grotesqueness of gesture, or some cant word; but can do no more. And it is not their fault. For this bloom is to be secured not by long training, but only in the school of tradition, and at best by profound study and observation. In these old criticisms there are a hundred points like this, glanced at as things of course, but which might be about Chaldaic to our existing actor. If ever there was an actor of that old school, furnished with the most delightful store of rare gifts, it was that light and airy comedian who was fondly called 'Jack Palmer.' Critics of such quality as

Lamb, Hunt, and Hazlitt, were always looking wistfully back to his light and elegant comedy; and as we glance at the spirited little etchings they have left of him, we look round vainly, and see that nothing of the same quality and species, even in the lowest degree, is with us. At what London theatre can we find any player who acts on such principles as the following? As we read these passages let us have in our eye any Mr ——, of any theatre, who will boldly—the very best of them—lay sacrilegious hands on such sacred arks as 'The School for Scandal,' and, being a quick study, get the whole 'up' in an incredibly short time. 'Amidst the mortifying circumstances attendant upon growing old,' says Elia, 'it is something to have seen the 'School for Scandal' in its glory.... It is impossible that it should be now *acted*, though it continues at long intervals to be announced in the bills. Its hero, when Palmer played it at least, was Joseph Surface. When I remember the gay boldness, the graceful solemn plausibility, the measured step, the insinuating voice,—to express it in a word, the downright acted villainy of the part, so different from the pressure of conscious actual wickedness,—the hypocritical assumption of hypocrisy, which made Jack so deservedly a favourite in that character, I must conclude the present generation of play-goers more virtuous than myself, or more dense. Not but there are passages, like that, for instance, where Joseph is made to refuse a pittance to a poor relation . . . . but over these obstructions Jack's manner floated him so lightly, that a refusal from him no more shocked you than the easy compliance of Charles gave you, in reality, any pleasure.' Hazlitt took the same view. 'No one,' he said, 'ever came so near the idea of what the women call "a fine man."' And he then speaks of another demeanour as lost, even to that day, 'a great deal of assumed decorum, and a stateliness of manner.' Lamb almost forecasts the fashion in which Joseph Surface would be played in our time. 'To go down now he must be a downright revolting villain, no compromise—' . . . 'his specious plausibilities must inspire a cold and killing aversion. . . He would instinctively avoid every turn which might tend to unrealize the character.' He follows the same notion through the other characters of the play. Sir Peter Teazle must be 'no longer the comic idea of a fretful old bachelor bridegroom,—

he must be a person capable in law of sustaining an injury; a person towards whom duties are to be acknowledged; the genuine crim. con. antagonist of the villainous seducer, Joseph. To realize him more, his sufferings under his unfortunate match must have the downright pungency of life; must (or should) make you not mirthful but uncomfortable, just as the same predicament would move you in a neighbour or old friend. The delicious scenes which give the play its name and zest must affect you in the same serious manner as if you heard the reputation of a dear female friend attacked in your real presence. Crabtree and Sir Benjamin, those poor snakes that live but in the sunshine of your mirth, must be ripened by this hot-bed process of realization into asps or amphisbænas; and Mrs Candour, oh, frightful! become a hooded serpent. Oh, who that remembers Parson and Dodd—the wasp and butterfly of the 'School for Scandal'—in those two characters; and charming, natural Miss Pope, the perfect gentlewoman as distinguished from the fine lady of comedy, in this latter part; would forego the true scenic delight; the escape from life; the oblivion of consequences; the holiday barring-out of the pedant reflection; those Saturnalia of two or three brief hours, well won from the world; to sit, instead, at one of our modern plays—to have his coward conscience (that forsooth must not be left for a moment) stimulated with perpetual appeals—dulled rather, and blunted, as a faculty without repose must be,—and his moral vanity pampered with images of national justice, national beneficence, lives saved without the spectator's risk, and fortunes given away that cost the author nothing?'

But it is so tempting looking over these sketches, and so really approaching the next best thing to seeing the actors themselves, that I shall ask pardon for giving a few more; that, at least, those who act and those who see acting may feel that, in those old-fashioned times, there was another ideal altogether, and may set it beside what they are now so contented with.

Bannister was about the last of the Garrick school, barely touching that famous era, and was instructed by Roscius himself. We have on our stage the conventional type of old man, played by every one in the same way, according to certain meagre canons,—a queer dress, gray hairs, quavering voice, and tottering gait. Let us see how acutely

Leigh Hunt refines on, and illustrates, this matter. 'The state of old age is a condition, of which no man perhaps can enter exactly into the personal feelings: it has no desire of motion; but a player is always wishing to be in a state of action, and acquires a habit of exercising his limbs momentarily, as may be seen sometimes in his gestures off the stage. The principal deficiency in the representation of old age generally arises from this propensity to motion. Thus an indifferent player, who naturally thinks that a stick will add to the decrepit appearance of age, forgets his support in the eagerness of winning applause by a show of energy, and thumps the floor or amuses his chin with it. An actor named Purser, who is very well when he plays the fool, and then only when the fool is a footman, sometimes misrepresents old age in this manner, and beats his mouth with his cane when he would affect an attitude of thought, like a young beau in a room who does it for want of thought. But Mr Bannister in his old age is not Mr Bannister in his manhood: he loses at once all his natural vivacity and robustness of manner, and sinks into that dependent feebleness which seems at once to fear and to look for protection from every surrounding object. Other old men on the stage take off their hats or pull out their handkerchiefs as composedly as young men; but Mr Bannister has the perpetual tremulousness and impotent eagerness of superannuation: if he takes out a paper, he quivers it about before he can open it, and if he makes a speech of any length, he enfeebles it by frequent breaks of forgetfulness and weariness, with that sort of pause, which seems as if he were recollecting what had already been said, or preparing for what remained to be said. One admirable mark of the feeble impatience of age must ever be remembered as one of the most natural originalities in Mr Bannister's personation of the 'Old Steward.' In thanking the heir of his deceased master for continuing some family favours to him, and in promising to overcome the violence of his grief for so heavy a loss, he trembles through four or five words with tolerable composure; but suddenly bursts out into a weeping of impatient recollection, and exclaims with rapidity—"But when I think of my poor master my tears will flow." An inferior actor would have added these words to his promise of patience in the same tone; but Mr Bannister understands that violent grief becomes only the more violent from temporary repression.'

What fine shades of distinction in his sketch of Elliston, especially in that description of a special gift, which it is not too much to say any intelligent actor of our time could make nothing of. 'All art acquires its greatest effect from contrast, and particularly the art of humorous ridicule, which in a grave dress pursues an end to which its means are apparently inadequate. It is full of contrast: its manner is easiest when its intention is most violent; it appears to be absolutely indifferent when it is absorbed in attention; it says one thing when it evidently means another; and its meaning, instead of being dissipated, is peculiarly embodied and enforced by this confusion. It might appear at first, like attempting to reach a goal by running away from it, or endeavouring to grasp a sword by putting your hands in your waistcoat pockets; but in an instant the goal is reached, the active sword is grasped.

'The end of an actor, in the management of this humour, is to talk in two languages; one, the language of the tongue; and the other, that of the manner and aspect united. Charles Kemble sometimes exhibits much nature in the lighter intermixture of these opposite effects: he assents, for instance, to a ridiculous proposition with a very easy gravity that contradicts its necessity by its indifference: but he cannot reach the perfect conviction of Elliston, who, with half-shut eyes, an opened mouth, a shake of the head, and a nasal depth of affirmation, perfectly cheats his interlocutor without deceiving the audience a jot.' In the representation of 'ludicrous distress'—a very simple notion to the modern histrionic—and easily enough portrayed—he was no less unrivalled.

'It is extremely difficult,' says Hunt, 'to manage this expression so as to render it agreeable to the spectators, because it is calculated to excite their contempt. The only method is to unite with it an air of good-nature, for good-nature is a qualification in the possession of which no degree of rank or of sense can be altogether unpleasing.' Nothing, indeed, is more conspicuous among the shortcomings of modern acting than the utter absence of these double currents of humours, existing side by side, and which are founded in human nature. There is not this logical consistency in every one's temper: the misers of life are not all misers *au bout des ongles*, villains are not villains through every successive instant. There is a fitfulness in our tempers which is not subject to iron laws. There is another of these delicate principles, also quite lost sight of, 'that peculiar self-command of action, which is half the secret of gentility . . . it gives him (Elliston) an unequalled grace in the polished gentleman. Blest with the proper medium between the extreme vivacity of that restless actor, and the extreme langour and reserve of Mr Charles Kemble, he appropriates almost exclusively to himself the hero of genteel comedy, that character which attracts the regard of the fair and fashionable; that, in its happiest point of view, unites the most natural attractives of social pleasure with the nicest repellants of familiarity.' A common situation on our modern stage is where fine ladies, or wits, are 'chaffing' some one of inferior station, their raillery being mingled with 'regulation' stage-laughter. Speaking of the delightful Dora Jordan, he says, ' With this frankness, too, she unites a power of raillery, seldom found in a performer of her honest cast. Mrs Jordan manages this raillery with inimitable delicacy; yet it does not carry with it an air of contempt, though such an air is one of the severest weapons of the ironical humorist; it is not delivered with an indifferent air, though such an appearance gives irony one of its most excellent reliefs; nor does it assume an air of gay acquiescence in the proceedings of its object, though the object may thus become doubly ridiculous in its misconception and unconscious furtherance of the ridicule. These three kinds of ridicule, considered with regard to the speaker, form a contrast with his manner only, since we can always discover his real meaning and mind, and are not surprised at either; but raillery becomes much more effective in the mouth of frankness and simplicity from the contrast it presents with the usual good-nature of the speaker, and from the peculiar obnoxiousness of that object which can rouse so unexpected and unusual a reprover. Mrs Jordan utters her more serious ridicule with the same simplicity and strength of feeling that always pervade her seriousness when it does not amount to the tragic, and she gives it a very peculiar energy by pronouncing the latter parts of her sentences in a louder, a deeper, and more hurried tone, as if her good-nature should not be betrayed into too great a softness and yet as if it wished to get rid of feelings too harsh for her disposition. Her lighter raillery still carries with it the same feeling, and her laughter is the happiest and most natural on the stage. If she is to laugh in the middle of a speech, it does not separate itself so abruptly from her words as with most of our performers; she does not force herself into those yawning and side-aching peals, which are laboured on every trifling occasion, when the actor seems to be affecting joy with a tooth-ache upon him, or to have worked himself into convulsions like a Pythian priestess; her laughter intermingles itself with her words, as fresh ideas afford her fresh merriment; she does not so much indulge as she seems unable to help it; it increases, it lessens with her fancy, and when you expect it no longer according to the usual habit of the stage, it sparkles forth at little intervals, as recollection revives it, like flame from half-smothered embers.'

But here is a picture of Sir Fretful Plagiary, worthy of Zoffany, as played by the elder Mathews, when the severe criticism is detailed by his malicious acquaintance. 'While he affects a pleasantry of countenance, he cannot help betraying his rage in his eyes, in that feature, which always displays our most predominant feelings: if he draws the air to and fro through his teeth, as if he was perfectly assured of his own pleasant feelings, he convinces everybody by his tremulous and restless limbs that he is in absolute torture; if the lower part of his face expands into a painful smile, the upper part contracts into a glaring frown which contradicts the ineffectual good humour beneath; everything in his face becomes rigid, confused, and uneasy; it is a mixture of oil and vinegar, in which the acid predominates; it is anger putting on a mask that is only the more hideous in proportion as it is more fantastic. The sudden drop of his smile into a deep and bitter indignation, when he can endure sarcasm no longer, completes this impassioned picture of Sir Fretful; but lest his indignation should swell into mere tragedy, Mr Mathews accompanies it with all the touches of familiar vexation: while he is venting his rage in vehement expressions, he accompanies his more emphatic words with a closing thrust of his buttons, which he fastens and unfastens up and down his coat; and when his obnoxious friend approaches his snuff-box to take a pinch, he claps down the lid and turns violently off with a most malicious mockery of grin. These are the performances and the characters which are the true fame of actors and dramatists. If our farcical performers and farcical writers could reach this refined satire, ridicule would vanish before them, like breath from a polished knife.' This is admirable.

The 'testy old father' of the stage takes its place as a proverb or cant phrase. But Dowton, one of the old trained actors, was above all conventionality. 'Who is so impressive, so striking, so thrilling, as this actor in scenes of angry perturbation, *or of anger subdued by the patience or pleasantry of its object?* His Captain Cape in the 'Old Maid' is a rough miniature of his Sir Anthony Absolute in the 'Rivals,' and both are imitable portraits of a mind naturally good, indulging itself in bursts of extravagant anger. Most actors are content with straining their eyeballs, protruding their lips, and pounding the air with one arm, to express their rage; in Dowton you see all the approaches, the changes, and the effects of that passion, which becomes impotent by its very power. Most actors are content to stare with stupid inaction at their interlocutor, while he is combating or deprecating their rage; Dowton still preserves the great feature of rage—impatience: he twists about his fingers, changes his attitude and gesture, mutters hastily with his lips, turns away at intervals from the speaker with a mouth of contempt, or seems unable to wait for his conclusion. The scene with his son, Captain Absolute, in the 'Rivals,' where he insists on the latter's marriage, is for this reason the masterpiece of extravagant anger. But then, when his son has won upon his feelings or suddenly complies with his demand, who at the same time can drop with such a fall of nature from the height of passion to the most soft emotions.'

In reference to this subject, a curious theory was held by Charles Lamb, and enforced with a strange persistency that seems to hint at its approaching the affection borne for a hobby. It is hard to dissent from any one of the fantastic speculations of this charming humorist, which are really always founded on some truth, though put extravagantly. In praise of his idol, 'Jack Palmer,' and of others, he would insist that the grace of his airy acting lay in a sort of undercurrent of by-play—addressed to the audience—the whole purpose of which was a continued protest against their accepting the business of the scene as anything approaching to reality. It was as who should say, 'You must not take me *au grand sérieux;* this is not earnest.' He enforced this by some ingenious arguments drawn from the nature of what he called 'artificial comedy.'

'But, tragedy apart, it may be inquired whether, in certain characters in comedy, especially those which are a little extravagant, or which involve some notion repugnant to the moral sense, it is not a proof of the highest skill in the comedian when, without absolutely appealing to an audience, he keeps up a tacit understanding with them; and makes them, unconsciously to themselves, a party in the scene. The utmost nicety is required in the mode of doing this; but we speak only of the great artists in the profession. The most mortifying infirmity in human nature, to feel in ourselves or to contemplate in another, is, perhaps, cowardice. To see a coward done to the life upon a stage would produce anything but mirth. Yet we most of us remember Jack Bannister's cowards. Could anything be more agreeable, more pleasant? We loved the rogues. How was this effected but by the exquisite art of the actor in a perpetual sub-insinuation to us, the spectators, even in the extremity of the shaking fit, that he was not half such a coward as he took him for? We see all the common symptoms of the malady upon him; the quivering lip, the cowering knees, the teeth chattering; and could have sworn " that the man was frightened." But we forget all the while—or keep it almost a secret to ourselves—that he never once lost his self-possession; that he let out by a thousand droll looks and gestures—meant at us, and not at all supposed to be visible to his fellows in the scene, that his confidence in his own resources had never once deserted him. Was this a genuine picture of a coward? or not rather a likeness, which the clever artist contrived to palm upon us instead of an original; while we secretly connived at the delusion, for the purpose of greater pleasure, than a more genuine counterfeiting of the imbecility, helplessness, and utter self-desertion, which we know to be concomitants of cowardice in real life, could have given us? Why are misers so hateful in the world, and so endurable on the stage, but because the skilful actor, by a sort of subreference, rather than direct appeal to us, disarms the character of a great deal of its odiousness, by seeming to engage our compassion for the insecure tenure by which he holds his money-bags and parchments. By this subtle vent, half of the hatefulness of the character—the self-closeness with which in real life it coils itself up from the sympathy of men—evaporates. The miser becomes sympathetic, i. e. is no genuine miser. Here, again, a diverting likeness is substituted for a very disagreeable reality. Spleen, irritability, the pitiable infirmities of old men, which produce only pain to behold in the realities, counterfeited upon a stage, divert not altogether for the comic appendages to them, but in part from an inner conviction that they are being acted before us; that a likeness only is going on, and not the thing itself. They please by being done under the life, or beside it; not to the life.'

The truth is, Lamb had in his mind the *effect* of the acting of his time, which he so reprobated, and which gave a coarse grossness to wicked parts. He also mistook that 'airiness' of Palmer for a sign of intelligence with the audience. The stupidity that can only see the gross villain in Joseph Surface, coarse and marked in his hypocrisy, as coarse in his servility and insinuation, belongs to our day also; but without keeping up any correspondence with

the audience, a true actor would remember that
Joseph Surface was a gentleman, carrying out his
schemes among gentlemen and ladies, and as such
would differ little from those about him in manner,
expression of face or line. If anything, he would
try to disguise all thoughts of the kind. But
how are the audience to pierce through his disguise? *There* lies the actor's art. Studying real life
and human nature, he will discover that there are
moments when the most trained are off their
guard; that when people are acting a part they
do not always put on solemn hypocritical faces,
and run into extravagances of servility and whining; that, on the contrary, they often assume a
light, cheerful manner. But to analyze all this
would amount practically to being a great actor.
The lightness and airiness which 'floated' Jack
Palmer over the gross parts of his character, was
never so understood by others who had seen him.
It was in truth, with Joseph Surface, the airiness and
unconcern of a man whose sense of honour or of
conscience was quite dulled by selfishness, and on
whom his hypocrisies sat lightly. Further, like so
many in real life, though inconsistent in his fine
hypocritical phrases, for the moment he believes

in them, or thinks only of the end in view; and this unconcern gives him that gay, natural, gentlemanly air, which so enchanted Elia.

Again, if there be a character in which the British actor is at home, it is that of the rustic, so often burlesqued with his red waistcoat, and dialect, and ostentatious virtue. There are hard and fast lines, almost inflexible, within which such a part lies; and every actor, according to his degree, plays it after the same fashion. Yet such a player as the great Emery, whose Tyke has long been one of the traditions of the stage, had *distinct* characters of this order—the serious, the comic, and the tragicomic. And while speaking of this wonderful power, Leigh Hunt makes a very acute remark, and which—it cannot be repeated too often—shows the histrionic vice of our time. He speaks of 'that expression which diverts with its manner, while it raises a serious impression with its sentiment, and which is therefore so difficult in its complication,' and of which Emery's *Farmer Ashfield*, in the spirited comedy of 'Speed the Plough,' is an instance. 'Inferior actors,' he says, 'indulge their want of discrimination in representing every countryman as a lounging vulgar boor, *for as they catch* externals only, they are obliged to exaggerate them in order to supply the deficiency of a more thorough imitation.' Nothing can be more just than this, for a meagre and unfurnished mind can well believe that there are these fixed types distributed in their own minds, into 'Leading Lady,' 'Chamber-maid,' 'Walking Gentleman,' 'Yorkshireman,' 'Irishman,' and the rest; whereas true genius will delight in acutely observing shades of difference, and subdivide nicely these various species. Such discrimination is far higher art, and gives one more pleasure.

Again, it may be asked, Where do we see the following refinement carried out? 'Comedy,' says Leigh Hunt, 'deals more in equivocation; the humour of which is enforced by the *opposite* expression of look and tone, or by the agreement of both differing from the speech itself.' This, too, is founded on observation of social life; for we are so vexed with contrary and inconsistent humours, so fitful in temper, that there is nearly always going on this discordance between various modes of expression. Being in critical situations where we are obliged to do what is distasteful, the bystanders are suffered at their own leisure to have every opportunity of closely investigating or searching calmly into the very faces of those before them, and probing their very hearts.'

We could not find a better illustration of the sacrifices caricature demands from its slaves, than the exaggerated close with which one of the most original grotesque players of the day mars his performance. Mr Rowe's admirable performance of Micawber illustrates how buoyancy and exuberance, tempered by judgment, will carry onward a good part. But after being perfectly true and dramatic all through his part, at the end, when Micawber becomes nautical, he comes out in an absurd burlesque yachting dress, buttons the size of plates, and all but buffoons with that new idea. The result is an utter loss of effect, and the part is at once vulgarized. The charm of the actor had been his perfect *genuineness* all through, his conveyed belief in the flourishes of Micawber. His deliverance of five words only, 'My foxy and diabolical employer,' showed this nice sense. The ordinary actor would have delivered this strange description as something comic, labelling it, as it were, as a joke. He would have shown that *he* felt it was an absurd speech. Not so this actor. That combination of 'foxy and diabolical' was the genuine Micawber view, *his* idea of odiousness, and so the actor conveyed it. The greater the surprise when we find him lapsing into such misplaced and ill-judged caricature. The true test would have been to speculate what sort of clothes Micawber would have procured when seized with this nautical eagerness. Probably clothes of the ordinary sort— a pea-jacket, and hat. There would have been a greater and more comical contrast between such, and the odd Micawber character, than between those pantomimic garments, and their buttons large as soup-plates. Trifles like these are dwelt on here, chiefly because they help us to get at real dramatic principles.

But it is surprising how completely astray writers are in their notion of the means necessary to convey an idea to their audience. We may take an example from a popular piece lately playing, and entitled 'Uncle Dick's Darling.' A fine gentleman, Mr Lorimer, is 'paying attention' to a married lady, and finds a low 'Cheap Jack' with her, who interferes with his plans. The 'swell' begins to address him as 'my bucolic friend;' and to show his vexation, superiority, and satire, speaks to him in a most offensive way, ridiculing his manner and occupation to his face. Now, the meaning of the writer was of course legitimate enough,—to explain to the audience that this 'swell' was much put out at the intrusion, and wished to show that he felt a supreme contempt— as the manner of his order is—for a sort of 'chawbacon,' so much his inferior. Now, the direct way was of course to make the 'swell' say so in plain terms to the common fellow, and thus the audience were, in the shortest way, put in possession of the fact. Yet only apply the test of real life, and there will be found a much more artistic and dramatic way of doing this. No gentleman in real life, and in a similar situation, would behave in that way. A gentleman, or a man of ordinary sense who was *not* a gentleman, would scarcely choose that fashion of conveying to a bystander that he felt a metropolitan contempt for a countryman; viz. by telling him to his face that he was a boor, an ass, 'a bucolic friend,' &c. There is a far more effective way than this; and the true *sneerer*, who acted according to the rules of society, would be apparently perfectly courteous and deferential to the object of his ridicule: his intention would be evident only to the *bystander*, or rather to the audience, who would feel they were not addressed directly. But instead, we must have the old stage vice so denounced by Charles Lamb: the shortest, coarsest way is the best; the actor must be considered, and not the piece. He gets in a little bit of personal effect, bringing himself in contact, by some telling sneers: whereas, by the opposite principle, the audience would not so much think of him, but of what he was saying, and of its effect on the object sneered at. We may be excused dwelling on trifles like this, and these remarks are not made in disparagement of the piece, which is a good one, but to show how the writer is obliged to follow the vicious customs now laid down by the actors. In short, it comes back to what has been so often dwelt on in these pages, that the stage has become a raised rostrum, on which the players bid with each other for the attention and interest of the audience: and the latter have been gravely taught that they are *to go to see players, and not plays*. Let any one visit the theatres bearing this statement in mind, and he will own its truth.

Again I say, how different the whole theory of French dramatic art. How different the view of even the educated stranger who takes interest in foreign literature. Two Frenchmen bring out that exquisite dramatic picture, 'FROU-FROU,' which is exquisitely acted, is seen by all France, and is now making the round of civilized Europe. It comes to this country merely in book shape, and is read with more delight than any novel, by every one of true taste and refinement. The impression left is as of something added to the common stock of recollections: it is as though we had been privileged to be admitted to know such a person, and had witnessed some such series of incidents. By-and-by we long to see it on the stage and get a new impression.* It is simply necessary to state these few facts, and the idea of the contrast will at once suggest itself. We have no piece of similar dignity that would bear treatment of the kind.

But players will say all these refinings are too delicate for the stage. We must now exaggerate to produce any effect. We must lay on our colours and strokes as our brethren the scene-painters do—thick, large, and strong: which at a

* Mr H. Sutherland Edwards prepared a good adaptation of this charming piece; but the French authors, by a scandalous legal quibble, reaped no advantages here.

distance look delicate and refined. There is some truth in this, but there is a misapprehension too. There must be an exaggeration to produce effect, as we can see by comparing an amateur actor's walk, and a professional's: but this must be governed by the same nice rules, due allowance being made. Thus there may be an exaggeration of facial expression, but it must be such as when it reaches the audience will appear moderate and natural. Can our players' scowls, bellowings, furious gestures, stridings, and stampings, be matched with anything known or seen? In fact, the whole rules, traditions, conventionalities of the English stage are radically false, unmeaning, and monstrous. We accept them from habit and helplessness. To begin at trifles, how ridiculous the practice of a mixed company of ladies and gentlemen at a party, trooping off *en masse* when some secrets are to be disclosed; and all trooping off arm in arm! How absurd the bringing forward the two chairs to the front when a conversation is about to begin, or a story to be told. Why, too, are hats kept on in drawing-rooms, and taken off in forests and streets, with a number of strange ceremonies and habits adhered to as religiously as if they were the religious rubrics of a church? When wine has to be drunk out of a pasteboard goblet, why is it put to the lips in a fashion that shows it contains nothing? There are a hundred traditions of this sort which will suggest themselves to every reader, and which, though scenery and dresses have made such vast strides, are really as antiquated as anything in the days of Garrick.

Again, there are little marks and tokens which prove that the actor only thinks of himself, not of his part. Not so long back we saw a clever actor, the son of a brilliant actor, playing groom in a piece, where the master is shocked to find that his bride has a wooden leg. The groom is supposed not to know this, and some humour is to be got out of his unintentional allusions to the secret. 'I suppose, sir,' he says, 'when she sees you, she will put her best leg foremost;' any point in which remark consisted in its being made with a stolid unconsciousness, and genuine gravity. But no; the groom winked at the audience, gave a grotesque flourish with his leg, tapped it, and grinned at his master—of course producing a roar. At the end of the scene he began to ' gag,' returning five or six times to ring the changes on the same subject. 'Sir, a messenger from Cripplegate,' 'Get out, sir!' 'Sir, there's a cove of Cork below.' 'Get out, sir; how dare you?' 'Sir, some one has left you a legacy,' &c. All this was utterly false, and a sacrifice of whatever real humour there was in the situation.

Again, amid other things lost to the stage in these days, is the important one of facial expression and utterance of the voice. Have we ever wondered how, in days when Drury Lane and Covent Garden were the chief theatres, the most delicate change of expression was seen aloft in the galleries, or across the vast pit, and that too by the light of dull oil lamps and candles? Now we look across Drury Lane, and far smaller theatres, and see but the two or three conventional expressions of alarm, joy, or sorrow, forced into faces so smooth and unmeaning, and in many instances so positively marked with unintelligence, that we wonder what could have introduced them to such a profession. We turn to the old portraits of actors, perhaps some of the most delightful portraits of all, and are amazed at the speaking intelligence, the bustling vivacity, the lines and channels of thought, and restless ideas, worn into their very cheeks; the roving brilliant eyes, the lips about to move. From these 'character' pictures we see how, by sheer training and power of intellect, they forced their features to signify what they represented. Nothing is more remarkable than this, and from the descriptions it is certain that this dramatic power and training triumphed over distance and dimness, and carried into the heart of the farthest pittite the end of an electric chain. So with the voice. In this matter there is now no training at all. There is no practice of elocution, no training of the voice to that fulness and roundness, which, without effort, helped it to fill the largest building. And this at least was the advantage of the two great patent theatres in the days of Garrick, when the monopoly was almost equivalent to a direct foundation at the expense of the State. There was a subordination, a reverence, a beginning with the lowest class, a rising in the ranks, a training pursued, as well from having the best models before one, as by the all but certainty of a fixed provision and dignity if the foremost ranks were reached. There was a steadiness, a massiveness, in both the acting and playing of those times. There was learnt the almost mechanical art of pitching the voice and making the features play; arts that are completely neglected now. There was found the invaluable service of a real true dramatic school, viz. a *répertoire* where there were the stock plays, each with its stock cast in readiness, and a different piece every night. What variety, what delight both for public and players, and what economy for the theatre! As shown before, our costly spectacles draw their motley audiences for a time, when a fresh and vaster outlay must be incurred for a new one. Under the old reign of intellect the play-goers attended their favourite plays, and of themselves nearly filled up the house,—the balance was brought by curiosity and chance. There were the stock scenes, which did for nearly every play indifferently, and perhaps from their generality were more theatrical and better helped the delusion. There was a genuine, healthy, steady support, and there was no need of stimulants. The actor, like a physician in a hospital, was trained by the variety of his cases. But what chance is there for educating an actor, say at the Prince of Wales' Theatre, where a single piece runs more than a year, and where he has but a single part to play? The result must be positive detriment, a dwarfing and stunting of the capacity.

Another strange deficiency in our players is
the impossibility of finding any young fellows who
when called upon to play the lover, or youthful
hero, about whom the attraction of romance is to
float, shall not present an appearance extremely
uninviting, and even coarse. Their necks rudely
shaved, their air clumsy, their voices horny, and
extra declamatory for the occasion, these are the
only elements with which to make up an English
Jeune Premier. There is no attempt at the tenderness of voice and manner, that chivalrous air which
a Frenchman, even elderly and plain, can throw into
such a part, when his 'je vous aime!' thrills
through the house. This is a most mysterious deficiency, but the truth is that we have hardly a
single presentable lover. It is not surprising, then,
that the providers of burlesque are driven into filling
every attractive male part with female performers.
To see beautiful young princes played by coarse
veterans would be a disenchantment indeed. But
it may be pushed too far. A really good burlesque lately playing had its three young princes
played by ladies: and the course of the plot
obliges them to disguise themselves as girls. So
here is confusion worse confounded,—girls off the

stage, then youths on the stage, and these youths again disguised as girls — bewildering reversion. But, as audience, we dislike such tricks, and the result is we dismiss the intervening stage of manhood, and look on them as girls, what they are really. This seriously affects the plot. The point of the situation turned on the intrusion of young men disguised as female pupils into a pastoral College of Ladies, and all the humour sprang from this unrecognized opposition between the two sexes. As usual, dramatic propriety and dramatic interest gave the *pas* to fine clothes, pretty faces, and 'a good leg part.' In France, at any sacrifice, men would have played the parts.

PART VI.

THE ACTORS OF THE DAY.

WE may now proceed to take store of our actors and *players*, and classify the leading artists of our time. Taking a true and legitimate school of acting as a standard, we must place in the first rank, Mr WEBSTER, Mr COMPTON, Mr PHELPS, and Mr LIONEL BROUGH. These are identified with round full-coloured characters that linger on the memory, richly painted and carefully studied, qualities which give the actor who follows the laws and traditions of a logical school an admirable advantage over his fellows,—distinctness and variety in every character. In inferior artists with the most grotesque diversity of 'make up' and dress, there is always a tedious sameness. They rely on external differences, trick, manner, voice, and dress, which are limited. While the storehouse of nature within is literally inexhaustible. Mr CHARLES MATHEWS and Mr WIGAN stand alone in representing the light airy school of comedy, founded, however, more on French than English traditions; Mr Buckstone also stands alone in a humour— broad yet restrained,—chastened by the playing of good characters of comedy, and by the influence of a theatre which has classical traditions of its own, with whom might be classed Mr Hare. Mr Toole, Mr Belmore, and Mr J. Clarke represent the semi-broad type of humour. Mr Sothern, the American Mr Clarke, with Mr Rowe, his countryman, stand for a line of specially grotesque characters. Mr Vining belongs to melodrama, Mr Vezin and Mr Barry Sullivan to tragedy, while Mr Fechter is the only representative of the romantic school unapproached in that line.

As we look back to a list of really good actors now living, they recur to us in the shape of some remarkable figure which they have personated. With such genius it is impossible to despair of the English stage. Mr Benjamin Webster comes before us associated with all that is powerful, conscientious, solid and yet elaborate, trained in that capital school of the old Adelphi, which has traditions of its own. Pleasant memories are associated with what was once called ' the Adelphi

Drama;' 'Victorine,' 'The Wreck Ashore,' 'Green
Rushes,' 'Flowers of the Forest,' 'Willow Copse,'
and many more. Such things were most entertaining in their way, as the most perfect effect, from
careful acting, was given to them. His characters
are all 'round' and full, well coloured as the old
portraits that hang upon the walls of the Garrick
club. The figure of Richard Pride, the sensitive,
witty, and pompous tippler, passes before us; the
honest, feeling rustics, like Fielding in 'The Willow Copse,' and his strange, all picturesque, half-
grotesque, and most touching picture of the decayed
music-copyist in the 'One touch of nature,' will
always be associated with the name of the manager of the Adelphi. There is but one character
which we must own he has made nothing of, and
from no fault of his; the Eastern in the 'Nightingale,' the last he has attempted.

Mr PHELPS and Sir Pertinax are convertible.
That amazing performance will never leave the
memories of those who have witnessed it. It is
simply perfect of its kind, perfect in its vitality, in
every motion, look, and tone. Charles Lamb would
have turned away from it, as too genuine, too
disagreeably real. It holds us enchained while we

look on: and while we live we carry about with us the impression of having met with some cold, dry, heartless Scotch 'politician,' whose ingenious schemes for advancement shocked yet interested us. With no other character has he so identified himself, and his other performances, though vigorous, are of a conventional sort.

With a portrait as living and spirited must we associate Mr LIONEL BROUGH, in 'Tony Lumpkin.' This spirited, artistic, and sustained performance has placed him in the foremost rank. It is virtually an anachronism, for it is a bit of the old acting, and conceived in the true spirit of the old models. That unctuous humour, always being distilled, always oozing out in abundance, that surplusage of fun, which when the work is done shows there is a reserve—is a gift scarcely known to our present comedians. Anything so rich in colour, so spirited, as Mr Brough's acting of this character, has not been seen for many a long day; and he, and he alone, has carried Goldsmith's play through its run of over a hundred nights, in spite of one of the most ludicrous misconceptions of character, in reference to Marlow, that could be conceived. That most delightful and airy of parts and gayest of rakes has been presented to us as a serious practical gentleman. Yet, thus weighted, this brilliant play has floated buoyantly, and gone on its course. But it has made the reputation of the performer of 'Tony Lumpkin.' One could hardly have expected that the quality described as 'breadth,' so hard to define, and which gives importance even to some trivial remark, could be among us still.

Mr COMPTON makes a fourth among these sterling players. He too has that invaluable gift of *weight* and soundness of style, which by instinct or diligent training on true principles, makes the most insignificant sentence *tell*. His London servant in ' The Unequal Match ' is a most amusing performance; and his Doctor Ollapod in ' The Poor Gentleman ' is one of the most enjoyable treats conceivable, and worthy of that most enjoyable comedy. The only occasion when this fine actor failed, was when he was thrust into a part translated from the French, rough-hewn and mauled from a part that in the original was one of a delicately drawn French adventurer, but which became a coarse tipsy ' Captain Mountraffe.'

There are two 'Mr J. Clarkes' who enjoy popularity. The one is an American, who for some four hundred nights, 'uninterruptedly' say the bills, has drawn crammed houses to the little theatre in the Strand; and during this period loud and most hysterical shrieks of laughter have been extorted, more uproarious and sustained than were ever heard in any London theatre. On a careful analysis, and after several visits due to piqued curiosity, the cause of these bursts could be traced to the actor's well-expressed fear of bursting a tight trouser, or to an assumption of oily volubility, and to a coarse exhibition of the stage of drunkenness known as 'beastly.' As he shakes a pump handle and bows to it—and an elaborate model is set up to enable him to do this, proving Mr Crummles' notions to be not so far-fetched—and as he staggers over a paling, or, missing the table, falls prostrate, the frantic shrieks of painful laughter rise higher and higher; and one feels something like pain and shame, as the British audience interrupts the scene, and calls forward its favourite, like a singer, to receive homage for this degrading exhibition. Very different is the other player who bears the same name, who has that wonderful art, so rare now, of merging himself in his character. He lately took a part called Mr Mould, that of a low, dirty, decayed, good-for-nothing old clerk, and anything so dirty *in mind*, so mean and pitiful and spiteful, it would be hard to conceive. Another good actor took up the part later at another theatre, whose abilities are as good but do not run in the same direction; and the result was the strangest failure. The part became a mere card figure. Laughter was indeed produced, but it was extorted by the conventional tricks, which never fail whatever be the part.

This brings us to Mr BELMORE, a very clever comedian of the solid and legitimate sort. His 'Grumley' in 'Domestic Economy' is a most entertaining and natural piece of acting—a dissatisfied grumbler finding fault with everything, and who, when invited to take the direction himself, throws everything into confusion. The real dramatic touch here is the blind self-complacency, the stupid insensibility, which, in spite of all blunders and mistakes, will not let him own that he is wrong. There is a benevolent attorney in 'the Long Strike' with a rough and savage demeanour purposely assumed, but with the warmest heart underneath. The struggle between these two principles was a very finished piece of acting. In short, this good player makes the most out of every part he attempts, though at times he is fitted with a very unsuitable part.

But for something eccentric and original, something of the spontaneous richness and luxuriousness of detail which real good actors import into their parts, an abundant unctuousness of touch, commend us to that American Mr Rowe, who has been presenting Micawber to the audience of the Olympic for some months back. About this performance there are many opinions, some holding it to be mere caricature of the Dundreary order; some, a misconception of Mr Dickens' character; but with all drawbacks it is a most amusing and original performance. There is such a racy enjoyment, such an exact correspondence and natural relation between the interior character and the outward acts and gestures by which it is manifested, that we feel it to be a mere accident his playing the part in this particular fashion, and that on another night he would illustrate the same emotions and humour by agencies wholly different. To convey this wealth kept in store as it were, seems to be the sign of a good actor: just as the idea, that he had but that one way of expressing him-

self, is of an inferior one. Micawber is a most
enjoyable performance ; the player seems to revel
in the unctuous platitudes and stick-flourishings
—the fitful changes—from hopeless despondency
born of 'pecuniary embarrassment from his cradle
upwards'—to pleasant and eager spirits, on the
mention of punch; his strange and original attitudes, and quaint gamut of tones, make up a
very quaint and racy picture. All these oddities of
speech and attitude give the notion, that they are
an honest expression of what is within. Had
Mr Dickens' Micawber never been written, this
stage character would have been a very original
performance, but it shows what a vast dramatic
force lies in all Mr Dickens' characters.

Mr Toole always enjoys an extravagant popularity in the provinces; a popularity said to be
valued at a steady income, to be measured in thou-
sands—the curious result being that a mere con-
tinuous metropolitan engagement might not be
nearly so valuable. This author's genius lies in the
old Liston vein of humour, broad native fun ; and
his Simmons in the ' Spitalfields Weavers ' must certainly be on a level with the performance of any of
the old acting humorists. Unhappily he thinks

his strength lies in compound parts, made so popular by the late Mr Robson, old men, half pathetic, half comic, a mixture of fun and querulousness. Of these he has a whole list, from the Toymaker in Mr Dickens' Christmas Story, down to 'Uncle Dick's Darling.' In 'Dearer than Life,' he gave a very artistic performance of a character of this description; but caricature is his failing.

Mr HARE, of the Prince of Wales' theatre, is an actor worthy of belonging to the old school; all his characters are so finished, and nicely touched. Every one is familiar with his old 'Beau Farintosh' in 'School,' which is as forcible as it is delicate, and marked with innumerable touches which show the most accurate observation. He has attempted nothing that has not been conscientiously worked out, and which has proved thoroughly successful. As Mr VINING chooses for his characters figures of low life, London cads, and reprobates, and Jew theatrical speculators, he has necessarily chosen a very limited range. There is no vitality in street slang or street manners. The professors servilely copy one another, and have no originality. The changes to be rung are therefore few. But in the Jew music hall proprietor of

'After Dark,' it must be conceded that Mr Vining has power, and a perfect identification with his character; in dress, voice, bearing, the transformation is complete. But then it does not go much beyond. There is little character in the part. It is all on the surface. A man who is master of mere surface peculiarities, worked out however elaborately, will find himself at home only in surface dramas. But we now come to Mr SOTHERN, perhaps the most successful actor of the last twenty years. His Lord Dundreary was one of the most amazing triumphs, and it must be said, in spite of 'pshas!' and contemptuous dismissal, as a bit of mere buffoonery, it was a well-deserved triumph. It was, unquestionably, original and elaborate, and also inexpressibly laughter-moving. By constant overlaying and repainting, it grew into caricature, virtually in obedience to the requirements of the audience,—very hard to resist. But still there was the basis of *character* underneath, the air of vraisemblance, with the idea that we had seen something strangely like all this earnestness in absurdity, this belief in one's own superior wisdom, this fatuous laying down the law. The whole represented a state of mind, the evidences of which were skilfully exaggerated; and had there been a strong plot to have brought out its follies and absurdities, the development would have been most natural and dramatic Although everybody in the kingdom must have seen the piece, its vitality seems literally boundless, and it has only to be announced, to bring the old crowds. One tribute to its popularity of a very questionable sort, is perhaps unique; namely, that a comic actor at another House should attempt to imitate what was an imitation: reproduce not Lord Dundreary, but Mr Sothern. This seemed a low stage indeed to which to go down. Mr Sothern has made a reputation in parts of another description,—the gentleman-lover; and in an adapted German piece, 'David Garrick,' he played with great vigour and versatility, and against the dead weight of a story, that in its historical sense was ludicrously false. An actor gifted with such nice observation for the details of eccentricity, should devote himself to finding out a part based on some of the follies which obtain in fashionable life; in which there are as many, and as marked *species*, as there are *genera* in the collection of broad characters. For instance, the weak and unconscious self-sufficiency of the *militaire*—his respect for knowledge

and learning, and delight in affecting to judge of
such matters, the excessive *personality* and pleasant
egotism that runs through his talk—the hail-storm
of 'I's,' his detailing of his own experiences, and
genuine belief of their interest for all the world,—
this done with sincerity is a character that might be
new, and would certainly bring out Mr Sothern's
powers. Mr VEZIN is a good conscientious actor,
with a certain power, and a great deal of that romantic *tone*, which belongs to the foreign school.
Of Mr BARRY SULLIVAN it is impossible not to
speak with respect, especially after his last gallant
struggle at the Holborn Theatre, where he fought
the battle of legitimacy with boldness and spirit,
and, it is said, with disastrous loss. Yet the cause
of the failure was in a measure owing to himself.
If he chose to revive the older dramatic pieces
there was no need of reviving the old-fashioned
school of declamation—the stiff pedantry of elocution which used to accompany it, with traditional
stalkings and stridings, and the whole collection
of old illustrations, long since exploded; which,
taken together, interposed between the audience
and the play. This is the mistake—thinking it
necessary to restore such an antiquated style of

acting. Thus with 'The Gamester,' that really heart-rending play: the long, stiff soliloquies were delivered in the dry, solemn tones which have been handed down from the days of Mr Kemble: while the dying agonies, the tremblings and howlings, and contortions on the ground, which only too faithfully exhibited the physical agonies resulting from the workings of the poison, were really a spectacle to excite uncontrollable laughter, rather than sympathy. This was the old regulation shape of presenting a violent death, a sort of caricature of which still provokes amusement at theatres 'across the bridge.' A truer sympathy with the tone of the revived pieces would lead an actor of tact to ask himself, how would the gentleman of the present day, brought into such sore straits by gambling, behave; how would a chivalrous officer in one of the Queen's Regiments behave? This should give the whole key to the piece. But no; vanity, applause, the actor himself, his lusty lungs, his points, his rounds of applause—these are the grand points to be looked to. To see the same actor in the romantic 'Lady of Lyons,' and his strange, monstrous style of elocutionary love-making, was a no less antiquated spectacle. Quite a false principle here obtained: the treating the play as something to 'show off' the 'star' actor. Hence the favourite passages, where traditional points are made at all risks, and at all sacrifice of propriety, with suspension of the dramatic interest while the leading player harangues the audience and ignores his fellows, challenging the duly-earned 'round,' by the traditional striding across the stage. How stiff and stale are the conventionalities of business which are made to cling to this charming drama,—the absurd dress of the 'Prince of Como,' and that no less absurd hiding of his features behind the enormous general officer-like plume, when Claude returns from the wars! With many an actor, except with Mr Fechter, this drama itself would lose its whole flavour and charm were this bit of business withdrawn. As Mr Sullivan describes his 'Palace' and its 'Gee-ardins' not to Pauline, but to the galleries, it is impossible not to recall the famous sketch of another actor, by the bitter Churchill:

> 'Mossop, attached to military plan,
> Still kept his eye fixed on his right hand man,
> Whilst the mouth measures words with seeming skill;
> The right hand labours, and the left lies still;

For he resolved on Scripture grounds to go,
What the right doth, the left hand shall not know.
* * * * *
In monosyllables his thunders roll,
HE, SHE, IT, AND, WE, YE, THEY, fright the soul.'

What can be said of Mr BUCKSTONE, save that he is always welcome, always delightful, save when he condescends to poor parts. His very face makes one in the long gallery of humorous faces, like those of Suett, Liston, Wright, with the curious twinkle in the eye and lines of humour in the cheek. He has the true *vis comica*, the genuine buoyancy; and though he lapses into extravagance, it is the extravagance of an artist.

Miss HERBERT is perhaps the only lady who claims to be what is called a classical actress, and she plays with great elegance and animation. It would be well, however, if she could get rid of a certain artificial tone, as well of manner as of voice; though this may seem an unreasonable demand, when an actress has long since formed her style and manner. To some parts she has the art of imparting colour and tone,—in other words, of conceiving it. She is apart from the rest, and bears with her the traditions of an excellent school. For a pleasant interesting actress, with at times certain tenderness of passion, and a sort of general level of steady playing, there is no one to compare with Mrs VEZIN. That charm which makes up for so much that is wanting, *sympathy*, an evidence of heart, she commands in a great degree, and in the established heroines of the stage, Pauline, Juliet, Mrs Beverley, ' the Wife,' Julia, she is at this moment without a rival. She is just old enough to have weight, just young enough to impart interest; her Pauline is an exceedingly graceful and interesting performance. Her Mrs Beverley is something very natural and womanly, in its passion and despair.

Miss MARIE WILTON has a finished style, and a certain brilliancy founded on training, and is perhaps the only actress on the stage who has caught the French tone. Miss OLIVER in her latest part, as Mrs Onion in Mr Halliday's piece, may be congratulated on a firmness of touch that is really classical. But where are we to look for *genius?*— that something which draws every one when no one thinks of theatre or company or scenery, and only of that one charm! The stage presents but one dead level of female talent. Even Mrs Charles Kean, in her decay, grown stout and old, was worth a legion of these genteel *soubrettes*, so popular with the young men.

There are surprisingly few actresses,—none that approach the type that is called *ingenue* in France; names that are associated with triumphs like 'Frou-frou' and the 'Famille Benoiton.' Our skilled and trained actresses have too heavy a touch for such airy delineations, and when training and experience have placed them in the front ranks, have to face a new difficulty, that of age and physical defects. But in truth this ludicrous disregard of propriety is common to both sexes and to all ranks of the profession.

'Superfluous lags the veteran on the stage,'

is a line unfamiliar to its ears, and it is not so much the French public, as the nice sense of self-respect in its actors, that makes them choose a part exactly suited to their age.

There is a class of actresses on the stage who have a noisy *clientèle*, and whose reputation is chiefly based on physical attractions, and agreeable, unassuming histrionic powers. To this belongs Miss Furtado, Miss Lydia Foote, and many more, who play in a lady-like way, but without decided power, or genius. The existing theory of realism

on the stage leads them to believe, that it is only
necessary to reproduce the tame, tranquil bearing
of a lady, to be dramatic. The result is, the stage
is crowded with a number of young ladies, who
offer agreeable and even pretty faces, and who
play, in a nice unobjectionable, unobstrusive way,
the various Susans and Marys, the suffering daughters and injured wives of the modern drama.
Supposing the standard to be no higher than the
point at which they have fixed it, *they* may be satisfactory. But even their greatest admirer must
admit there is no genius, no power, no training:
the play moves on in the conventional way, and
the heroine is lady-like and ' nice.' The drama
requires far more than this,—it demands situation,
and the exhibition of character produced by the
situation. And what is the result?—parts of this
description now must take a shape corresponding
to the powers of those that act them, something
unobtrusive and tame. Neither the actresses nor
the parts they play hold the stuff sufficient to produce an O'Neil or a Jordan. A Jordan indeed!
To hear old playgoers rave of that silvery joyous
laugh, heard ringing out behind the scenes, her
inexhaustible spirits that made every one joyous

and enthusiastic; and then turn to this race of average *couturières* without even the function of such—styled affectionately 'Kate this' and 'Polly that!' The strange thing is, that they and their audiences are more than content, and both believe that the highest standard has been reached. The average type in most plays is that of an insipid mediocre young girl, sempstress, or young gentlewoman in distress, whose soft voice and 'quiet' manner draw the fullest approbation. But it need only be repeated, that a vast deal more than an inoffensive mediocrity is necessary to make the stage *entertaining*. There is actually a conviction in the profession, that such a one gives the most perfect type of the gentleman of social life, and such a one of the lady, because they are 'quiet,' and get their stage clothes at a fashionable maker's. They walk about the stage, and talk with the pleasant indifferent carelessness of a well-bred man. As was laid down before, we do not go out to the theatre to see this servile copying of an original, which would itself be more agreeable. The advantage of the stage is, that it presents, within the compass of an hour or two, rare situations, rare views of character which we may only read of, or hear described by others, and which may never fall within our own experience. To see therefore 'ladies and gentlemen' merely performing the conventional every-day round of their life, is nothing; but to see how the special habits and characters of such a class act and react on each other; now what is evil, and now what is good in its works—this is a very different thing from a genteel or 'nice' carriage and walk, or well-cut suit of clothes. This false notion has in truth resulted only in producing a crowd of these tame decent young girls, without talent or training, or any real gifts.

Miss NEILSON, after many circuits of the provincial stage, has now come prominently before London audiences, having taken a sort of fixed classical position, through the indifference or languor of the public. She is eminently correct, and what may be called a steady actress, but is highly artificial and without much genuine passion, as any one will discern for himself who listens to the 'charnel-house' tone of her voice.

Mr Vincent made a reputation in one play, the 'Ticket-of-leave-man,' but has not advanced beyond that one character. Mr Coghlan promises well. A new actress has just been added to the ranks,

with such singular natural attractions, and a face,
voice, and manner so powerful for drawing sympathy, as to make it very difficult to pass an im-
partial judgment on her acting: moreover Mrs
ROUSBY, such is her name, has had the disadvantage of receiving the most extravagant eulogy,
and we must wait to see how she will establish a
position. Mrs SCOTT SIDDONS, who had the
same remarkable advantages, as well as the particular one of relationship with a famous name,
has proved to be little more than an elocutionist,
with an indescribable coldness in all her acted
characters which verges on the artificial. This
sort of sympathy with the character played—a sort
of *tone*, like that of a picture—is what is sadly wanting to most English players, and is found invariably in foreign artists. And to illustrate it again
from painting, it is the dashing sketch which some
careless dashing idle genius will throw off, set
beside the highly-finished, correct, well-drawn, but
tame and mediocre picture. Mlle BEATRICE, im-
perfect as she is in many points of her acting,
has this charm of sympathy to a wonderful degree, and over her Juliet, unskilful and perhaps
unshaksperean as the performance is, there is

a singularly human air and tone, to which even her foreign accent contributes. The scene in the garden, with Juliet's passionate expressions of love, seemed to the writer of these notes to convey, for the first time, the complete idea of a young Italian girl, with whom that otherwise forward confession of love seemed almost natural. Miss BATEMAN, it has been discovered, is an actress of but one character; Leah, the Jewess, and herself are, as it were, convertible. That is, indeed, a wonderful performance—wonderful for the acting, and helped by a genuinely dramatic play, even if tried by the test, that it remains on the memory as a strange and distinct picture of human passion. There is Mr H. IRVING, who played at the Gaiety Theatre, in a singularly satisfactory fashion, and who, in a rather meagre part, that of a stage Mr Dombey, has exhibited much delicate touching and knowledge of human nature. Miss Amy Sedwick, in certain pieces, as in '*The Unequal Match*,' shows finish, and a lady-like conception of the part. But there is nothing striking. It was different with Mrs STIRLING, whom to see, so spirited and coquettish, in the little French trifle called '*A Subterfuge*,' was simply delightful. Her store of 'tricks,' as we might call them, and *agaceries*, was unbounded, and gave a richness to the part. Miss Carlotta Leclerq, who has caught much that was French and dramatic from association with Mr Fechter, touches a chord of sympathy where passion is concerned, and has a certain tenderness in her voice. There is a romantic *tone* over all her characters, which, whatever defects there may be in details, is like colouring to a picture. Perhaps this may be due to some French blood, which her name would seem to indicate. Let those who would see something finished, who would see acting and expression, nicely significant of character,—let such go to the Gaiety and see Mr Alfred Wigan in that exquisite little chrysolite of a drama, 'The First Night,' booty, of course, from the French, where it is known as 'Le Père de la Débutante.' There are many who may never have met an old Frenchman speaking broken English, and helping himself out in a foreign tongue with a whole museum of shrugs and smiles, and vividly expressive motions. Yet to such, Mr Wigan's old actor would be an old and familiar friend. The protean vitality of that single figure; the many shapes of expressing the one idea; his quaint and grotesque figure and dress, not assumed to extort a guffaw from the galleries, but really in harmony with, and the legitimate expression of, the mind within, his agonies of doubt, his little flatteries, his affection, his cleverness,—all these things absorb us, and make up a most delightful and interesting character, which, it is to be suspected, could never have found its way to the English stage, unless by way of theft from the profitable French. Actors would do well to study this wonderful impersonation of Mr Wigan's, which is founded on the best French traditions, and which is also fortunate in having such an admirable little piece to work on.

Many actors aim at a merely correct and tame standard, a sort of dead level of mediocrity, that neither rises nor sinks; and quite flatter themselves that they have attained a natural and easy bearing; and to this class belongs Mr Clayton, who has besides a want of sympathy, not to say stiffness, in both voice and movement. Witness his blacksmith in 'Uncle Dick's Darling,' who is more a clerk than a blacksmith. Mr H. Neville is the titular lover, but though an agreeable actor, his tones have a peculiar affectation which is unpleasant. Mr Honey is a comedian of the old broad, boisterous, exaggerated school, with an obstreperous prominence, and an engrossing, for the chief comic character, the whole attention and applause of the audience. This, however, is but the fault of his school: pieces were written expressly to bring out this rather selfish conspicuousness. It must be said that his Wormwood in the 'Lottery Ticket,' is an exceedingly amusing and spirited performance, supported with unflagging vivacity and activity.

There are a number of players who, though not in the first rank, are good serviceable performers, who, if they had opportunities for training, would turn out excellently. Another, Mr Irving, is one of this class, for his excellent identification of himself with the part of Uriah Heep, in spite of caricature in the over 'foxiness' of the head, and the eel-like twistings of his body. The former toned down, and the snake-like twistings indicated, would have produced a far more powerful effect. A first-rate actor would, in fact, reverse the process: he would make his conception as 'crawling' as possible, and his bearing would unconsciously illustrate this feeling. But on the stage, at present, its

The Actors of the Day.

mimetic gestures are the end, not the *means* to express the end. Still, in Mr Irving the reproduction of Heep is wonderful. Miss ADDISON, who plays the coldly malignant Rosa Dartle, shows talent, and that gift of 'cleverness,' a word of which theatrical critics are so fond. Yet here again we have that rigid iron application of a principle which is so false in practice. The aim was to exhibit a savage, unrelenting hatred; and the existing teaching of the stage laid down that this was only to be done by an exhibition of black hatred, never relaxing, colouring every emotion, word, and look. But this is not nature: and the audience should be admitted to see the feeling of love for Steerforth which produced that hatred to the boatman's 'Little Em'ly.'

PART VII.

THE MUSIC HALL QUESTION.

IT might seem at first sight, that such entertainments as are offered to a crowd, in the act of eating, drinking, smoking, and talking, could not be of an intellectual sort, and would, at least, be below the dignity of serious examination. Yet there can be no doubt that what is called the Music Hall question is intimately connected with the present decay of the stage, and, humiliating as is the confession, bids fair to rise into equal importance with the drama itself. For the music hall and its entertainment now represent a principle of false and spurious dramatic effect, and therefore cannot be foreign to what we have been investigating. In this place we propose examining the rights of the curious and rather interesting dispute which has arisen between the parties concerned, but which, as will be seen, really involves a question between true and false dramatic art.

Viewed by all the principles which we have been weighing, this point becomes a very simple one. The conclusion to be arrived at is that 'protection' of dramatic art is unfair, as unmeaning as it is unfair, and that the music halls, or any houses with proper license, should have their plays and actors. How can it be explained to a foreigner visiting a place like the Alhambra, and lost in admiration at its wonderful scenery, stage effects, and ballet, that the place dare not go one step further and have dramatic dialogue? But the fact cannot be disputed, that for this sharp music hall competition, and this threatened invasion of the dramatic province, the stage has only to thank itself. Once it took up a lower and debasing style of performance, it invited competition.

At the present time, when the whole spirit of monopoly is passing away, and when the idea of any special privilege being guaranteed by the State to any class or kind, is always protested against, it could not be thought of for a moment, that dramatic protection should be revived or maintained; and therefore under the present condition of things, the confusion and laxity which exists, with every sort of *performance*, as it were, running riot, is utterly unworthy of any legislative countenance. It may be fairly urged by the conductors of such places of amusement, that the theatres are competing with *them*, and have invaded their special department of dancing, tumbling, comic singing, and general buffoonery. If there is to be protection at all, they say, let a marked line of division be preserved, and the theatres be kept in the strictest way to legitimate business.

This, of course, would be the mere technical way of viewing the matter. But the time has come for the removal of all such antiquated restrictions, and, as the public wishes for any kind of *show*, under any combination, all should be allowed to compete for its support without any unfair advantage being allowed to either party. The question will then be solved in a way that managers will little dream of; and though the advocates and admirers of real dramatic art might wish that there should be an arbitrary line drawn, and that theatres should be obliged to keep to their province, and music halls to *theirs*,—still, such a distinct separation may, strange to say, be only looked for where there is unrestrained competition. Managers will find that they cannot compete with the resources of places like the Alhambra, gigantic *restaurants*, whose profits from food and drinks alone would be enormous; and yet cannot offer the same inducement, as the wit or words even of a comedy could not be followed, amid the distractions, suppers, &c. On the other hand, the enfranchised music halls would be debarred from the same class of entertainment for the same reason. The real play-going public would still demand plays, and it is certain that for that minority good actors and good plays must be found. Then let the burlesque theatres become restaurants, and, working up their position, flourish honestly.

It is curious to think how this division between mere unintellectual *shows* and the true drama has always been maintained, and, that whenever the stage has degraded itself, it has always been confounded with the meaner class of performances it was aping, and been chastised accordingly. I cannot but think that a retrospect of this nature will be useful at the present crisis, and act as a wholesome warning to both players and managers. That unerring evidence of all social relations—the Acts of

Parliament—will prove this view for us. We can start from the days of Elizabeth, when a Vagrant Act was passed (39 Eliz. c. 3), which was meant to deal with all 'rogues, vagabonds, and sturdy beggars, fortune-tellers, fencers, bear-leaders, and common players of Enterludes,' who were to be taken up, 'stripped from the waist upwards,' and sent back to their own parish. There was an exception, however, in favour of such players as belonged to a Baron of the Realm, and who could produce his license. This exception, however, is as degrading as the rule, for it classes all as servants. Old text-writers, like Bacon or Hawkins, have much the same view, classing stage-players with something 'disorderly;' and it is actually laid down that a play-house may be a nuisance 'like any *other disorderly house.*' Now without leaning very much on the strict primitive meaning of the interlude, which was clearly a sort of irregular dramatic performance, a mixture of singing and farce, it will be seen that it was something of a 'music hall' pattern, and the legislature seemed to think, as indeed most modern justices have done, that anything in the shape of 'strolling' accompanied with mere buffoonery, must be classed with what is disreputable, and is against law and police.

In the days of James I. the law was made more severe (1 Jac. c. 7), and even the protection of a nobleman's license was taken away. Two years later an Act was passed, fining heavily, which was virtually imprisonment, any stage-player using holy names profanely. It is indeed hard to give an idea of the tone used towards these players of interludes. From the time of Edward IV. downwards, we find many sumptuary Acts, relating to costly dressing, at the close of which the nobleman's players and servants are always contemptuously excepted. Various Vagrant Acts succeeded that of James, until we reach the reign of Queen Anne, when (13 Anne, c. 26), the cost of transporting vagrants to their parishes was made lighter, and again it was carefully defined that the law should apply to 'fencers, jugglers, bear-leaders, minstrels, and common players of interludes: who, if found wandering, begging,' and mark, 'or misordering themselves as aforesaid, were to be apprehended, whipped, and passed on.' All this might not seem to apply to the players in London; but not very long after, in the year 1733, their extravagance, quarrels, rivalries, and vanities, their opening of new competing houses, their fighting with managers, and appeals to the public, and above all, the scandalous personality and license of their performances, brought them into contempt. The barriers too between the stage and the audience were broken down, and all the speeches and newspapers of the time were full of complaints of the 'disorder' of the stage. And in that year the bold step could be ventured on of actually arresting a player, one Harper, under the Vagrant Act of Anne! He was actually brought before the justices and committed to jail as a rogue and vagabond. He was indeed released when brought up on *habeas corpus* before a superior court of law, but this was done on a mere point of law, he being able to show that he had a settlement in town. But it is curious, that it was actually contended by the prisoner's counsel that he did not come within the description of the Act, 'players of interludes,' he being a comedian: thus fortifying the view I have taken, that it is with entertainments of the music hall order that the legislature dealt so severely. Indeed we have only to look at the stage itself, on the night Garrick first appeared, to see evidence of this confusion: for there was a concert of vocal and instrumental music, with 'an entertainment of dancing' by some

French artists, a ballad opera, and Richard III.! So with the theatres, at the time of the actor's arrest as a vagabond. House after house was being opened, solely from quarrels, secessions, and competitions, not because they were wanted as schools for acting.* Precisely as at the present day.

It was now high time to put some check to these disorders, and a private member of the House, Sir John Barnard, in 1735, brought in a bill to regulate the number of theatres, but owing to an attempt on the part of the government to introduce certain clauses, establishing a censorship of plays, the authority of law instead of custom, the mover preferred to let it drop. The question of censorship was of course a distinct branch, and without going into antiquarian lore, it may be stated that there was always *assumed* by the Master of the Revels, and then by the Chamberlain, a control over the pieces to be acted, and then over the stage itself. This would of course arise out of the control over the theatre itself, derived either under patent from the king, or license. Two

---

* The reader will find a curious picture of this state of things in Sir John Hawkins' Life of Johnson, where he says every new theatre was surrounded with a halo of Bagnios.

years after the withdrawal, Walpole, who was then first minister, introduced a Bill of a very severe sort, and actors should bear in mind, that only four years before the appearance of the greatest star of their order, they were once more brought under the terrors of the Vagrant Act, under which they remained until very recently, so late as fifty years ago. That famous Act, known as the licensing Act, and entirely directed against the players, was yet, rather offensively, entitled a Bill to explain the Vagrant Act. It was felt that the words 'players of interludes' offered a loophole for escape, so the words 'rogue and vagabond' were enlarged and made to include any one who should act tragedy, comedy, opera, play, farce, or other entertainment of the stage, being at the same time without legal settlement, patent, or license. Even supposing he *had* a settlement, he was liable to a fine of £50.*
It became law, and thus it will be seen that the actors owed this severity to their own desertion of the true dignity of the drama, by putting themselves on a level with showmen and mountebanks.†

---

* They had even a forecast of the future music halls, for when any interlude was given where liquor was sold, it was to be dealt with as a theatre.

† Fielding's Pieces, with their personalities on the ministers and

Fortunately after this crisis rose Garrick, whose splendid talents, and admirable *dignity* of administration, raised the stage and its actors to the highest social condition. The competing houses decayed away rapidly, for in the face of the talent collected at Drury Lane and Covent Garden, they could have no *raison d'être*. This 'palmy' state of things continued until Garrick's retirement, when disorder and confusion again broke out.

It was not until the present reign that a comprehensive view was taken by Act of Parliament of the stage, and the whole system relating to players and playhouses was solemnly regulated by the 6th and 7th Victoria, cap. 68. The licensing of theatres was divided between the Chamberlain and the magistrates, and the 'Stage-Play' which they licensed such houses to perform, was enlarged to include 'tragedy, comedy, farce, opera, burletta, interlude, melodrama, pantomime, or other entertainment of the stage.' Though indeed explaining a 'stage-play' by an entertainment of the stage, recalls the well-known definition of an archdeacon.

others, were the immediate cause of the Act, but Sir John Barnard's first Bill was levelled at the actors, and at the disorders of the playhouses. Personality and mimicry does not belong to true dramatic art, but to the showman, or ' interluder.'

On this Act have turned all the recent disputes between encroaching music hall directors, and managers of theatres. Music halls are literally nothing more than gigantic restaurants, or, in England, more public-houses than restaurants. Our magistrates have always found it necessary to regulate places where crowds resort to take drink, on account of the great disorders which may naturally grow out of a crowd and stimulants in combination. When an entertainment of any description is offered which shall *detain* the drinkers, and induce them to drink more, the probabilities of disorder are increased, and a stricter control, with fresh license for music or dancing, is necessary. Now though large halls where men and women may go and drink must be tolerated, and can never be dealt with further than in the direction of control and restraint, and since it is conceded that they are fruitful in many sources of evil, direct and indirect, it would seem that the tolerating of *fresh inducements* to invite and detain people in such places, is against the pronounced policy of the State, its laws and police. It seems strange that with one hand public-houses should be watched with a jealous severity, and licenses be served out with strict caution, while with the other it presents them with this seductive bonus, in the shape of the attractions of music and dancing. In France such things take a more rational shape. There is the *Café Chantant* in the open air, where the real object is national enjoyment of good music, with a little *refreshment* in the shape of coffee, or *limonade gazeuse*, or the tiny glass of cognac. It is indeed but another shape of going to the play, and the refreshment is secondary.

In England a consistent police administration would refuse singing and dancing licenses to gigantic public-houses altogether, or it should at least interpret the license in its most strict terms, and allow nothing but 'shows,' such as juggling, rope-dancing, dancing pure and simple, and music. This ought to be the course, if the administration of the law was consistent with itself. But as it is not, and as there is utter confusion of the two provinces—theatres exhibiting music hall business, and music halls encroaching on theatrical business,—it would be best to abolish the farce of apparent restriction, which is administered only in justice, and let there be free trade in entertainments of all kinds.

The meaning of a music hall license was surely

founded on the old legal distinction between 'a common player of interludes'—classed with bear-leaders and jugglers—and a comedian. The former would find his proper place in the street, at a fair, or in any raised and conspicuous place. It was in short the difference between intellect and matter, between what was addressed to the mind and to the senses. The legislature felt there was no danger of disorder from a crowd gathered for intellectual entertainment, no more than from a crowd gathered at a concert or at a lecture. But music hall managers have gradually gone on advancing in their encroachments, and it would be impossible to visit the one, which for its splendour and popularity holds the first place, and distinguish it from a theatre. There are private boxes, pit and stalls, though not thus officially styled, galleries, a noble stage, and orchestra. The scenery is unrivalled, in or out of England; the ballet equals that of any opera house, exhibits a story, and is accompanied with gorgeous scenic changes, perfect transformation scenes, and groupings, not to be matched by any regular theatres. It was not surprising that theatrical managers should attempt to make a stand against these gradual encroachments. When a formal pantomime was attempted, with the regular *personnel* of harlequin and his companions, they interposed. The word pantomime was actually used in the Act, so that attempt was put down. Later when the 'ballet of action' was represented, and an amazon story exhibited, without dialogue, with scenery, groupings, and changes, as at the Italian opera, the interference of the courts was sought; but strangely enough it was held, that it was not within the province of the judges to decide whether such amounted to 'other entertainment of the stage,' and that the question was one for a jury. After such an intimation it was considered imprudent to take further steps, and ever since, this house has gone on producing a series of these magnificent *spectacles*, worthy, as has been said, of any opera house in Europe.

Yet it is impossible to doubt that such comes within the meaning of a stage entertainment. It is certainly within the meaning of the word interlude, used in the Act. Even long ago, when it was laid down by Lord Kenyon that he could not interfere with 'tumbling,' no more than he could with fencing, it was for the reason that no written copy of the performance could be sent in to the Lord

Chamberlain—one of the requirements of the Act. Now here is a test; for there is a written story or programme for every ballet: and, taking a more æsthetic view, a ballet elaborately prepared, such as Saconthala, an Indian tale, got up in Paris, and written by a poet, such as Theophile Gautier was, told a story, and left the impression of a story on all who witnessed it.

It could of course be urged by the music hall advocates, that any amount of elaborate scenery, *by itself*, could not amount to a stage entertainment, any more than a panorama or diorama would; and that the dancing of a woman, or of any number of women, *by itself*, would be fairly in their province. We may grant these positions: but it is the combination that imparts the *dramatic* element. The most elaborate transformation scene, if we went merely to see it alone, at one of the patent theatres, would be pronounced to be no more than a diorama. And if the public flocked to a concert room to see a Taglioni, or a number of Taglionis, go through steps, they would only go to see an exhibition of dancing. But the two elements in combination produce another effect. The scenery begins to tell a story; it is a mountain dell, or the palace of fire, where a *succession of events is to take place:* and the dancing, instead of a mere series of muscular leaps and graceful attitudes, utterly without meaning, brings out the significance of the mountain dell, and of the palace of fire.

In short, summarizing the result of this inquiry, we arrive at these conclusions. The State should act logically, and either enforce the distinction between these two departments of entertainment; or remove all restrictions, and let the public, as it would surely do, bring about a separation between these confused elements. In the first case it should remove the word interlude from the Act, which, in its strict sense, belongs to the Music Hall, and should mean the unassisted entertainment of posturing, buffooning, mimicry, with or without music: it should draw a line between what is intellectual and dramatic, that is, the operation of mind working on mind or material objects, thus bringing out a story, and that mere physical enjoyment, the entertaining of ears and eyes, produced by material means. Or else, let protection of all sorts be abolished, and a general license of performance, subject only to conventional police restraints, be granted to all. The present arrangement is unfair to all parties; unfair to the manager, who sees stage performances allowed at certain Houses, which are allowed to combine the profits of restaurants and public-houses,—a privilege unreasonably denied to him:—unfair to the music halls, who may have theatre and stage, scenery, and all that belongs to a theatre,—and are unreasonably checked when they attempt to go a little further, and have dialogue. Legislation of a broad, sensible sort is wanted, and, it is hoped, will soon be applied.

The managers of the other Houses have made a desperate resistance, and say that such a concession will be their ruin. They protest that a simple theatre cannot compete with a theatre and public-house combined. Yet managers have brought this threatened mischief on themselves. For many of them have been all but turning their theatres into music halls, wanting only the pipes and pewter pots in the pit, by exhibiting shows that appeal chiefly to the eye, and in which, if the dialogue be missed, the loss is small. Why should they be protected *in the interests of the drama*, when they have virtually departed from the drama itself? But if we look at the result of removing this restriction we shall see that it will actually *benefit* the drama. For this change will certainly take place. A number of the weaker theatres will be forthwith invaded by capitalists, and converted into public-houses with stages, on which the entertainment will be of a broadly-marked kind, and the jokes exhibited strong enough to overpower the din of pewter, and the chink of glasses. Others will be built specially for the purpose. Many of the actors too will not be able to resist the temptation of higher salaries. Then there will remain the theatres that are now devoted to the corrupted drama—the spectacular and burlesque. The latter will flourish in a renewed prime, and become really worth seeing. For it is quite a different thing to witness one on a broad music hall canvass; and it will be quite intelligible, even satisfactory and humorous, when looked at now and again, between morsels of the 'devilled kidney' and refreshing draughts of ale. These weeded off, there will remain the sober legitimate Houses, who, relieved of competition under false colours, will draw together the scattered host of real appreciators. For the others, new audiences—music hall audiences—will multiply: but things will be on an honest footing

and called by their right name. Further, these
'*spectacle*' pieces can then be produced on a scale
of stupendous splendour, as the additional profits
from food and drink will be so large.

No one, of course, can advocate the extension
of places of amusement of the music hall pattern;
as at present conducted, their theatrical entertainment is but a cloak for bringing vast audiences of
young men, who come for quite different ends. *That*
is a question for the magistrates who issues licenses
for music or dancing. But the existing illogical
restrictions are quite another matter. The 'two
branches of the profession,' as they are now virtually
considered, should be treated on equitable grounds.
If these are unmeaningly allowed to run to the
very verge of stage-representation, and, after using
scenery, dresses, pantomime, dancing, with a ballet
that leaves the Opera House behind, are then
checked abruptly; the same rigour should be dealt
out to the theatres, and they should be restrained
from encroaching on the tumbling and dioramic
business of the music halls. The result of free
trade in the drama would, I conceive, be beneficial
even to music halls, and raise the tone of such
places. At the Alcazar at Brussels, a sort of

gigantic theatrical public-house, on the model of the Alhambra, we may see Offenbach's operas given for the entertainment of an audience enjoying their cigars, and wine, and other drinks. And though that sort of social fungus 'the cad' does not spring up abroad with the unwholesome fertility it does in London, and our music hall, and the earthy sort of pleasure it offers has much to do with its cultivation, in the presence of good acting, and under the influence of good opera, his intelligence would become refined. Offenbach, and his gay music, agreeable dramas mounted with the magnificent resources of such places, would be a restraint. But with tumblers and 'scurræ,' real and genuine 'buffoons,' beside whom the honest clown of the pantomime is a gentleman and an artist,—in such a presence we cannot blame an audience for feeling no respect.

The case of *Wigan* v. *Strange* (1 Com. Pleas Rep. p. 175, 1865) exhibits that timorousness and over-refining which is such a blemish in English law. There one of the managers attempted to put down, at the Alhambra, a spectacle in which amazons advanced and retreated and engaged in mimic conflict, and in which the conventional 'ballet of action' was exhibited. In the course of the argument an acute distinction was taken, and which seems to me almost conclusive, namely, that the phrase 'entertainment of the stage' is a different thing from 'entertainment *on* the stage:' for the latter would comprise many species of entertainment which the Act would allow, but the former must mean something purely *dramatic*. Thus rope-dancing, fencing, juggling, concert singing or playing, *tableaux vivans*, acrobatic exercises, dancing, like that of 'the great American clog dancer,' the Highland fling, Irish jig, or English country dance, all these might be entertainments given *on* a stage, or in a theatre, but they could not be called 'entertainments of the stage.'

Such seemed to be the view of the judges as to the law of the matter, but they declined to decide on a matter of fact, whether the incidents of the Alhambra performance amounted to a regular ballet. With all respect to this view, it seems hard to understand their hesitation. The facts were before them on oath; were virtually admitted by both sides, between whom the real question raised was, did a *ballet d'action* come under the Act? There the question has remained; and with such judicial authority in their favour, it seems surprising that the managers have not taken a further step. There are some technical difficulties in the way, as I believe the matter would have to be decided by 'the justices,' who have already pronounced in favour of the music halls, overruling the magistrates' decision, which was the same as that of the Court of Common Pleas. Any one who had seen 'Flamma, or the Child of Fire,' at the Alhambra recently would have no hesitation in pronouncing it an 'entertainment of the stage.'

We must now conclude this rather desponding review, whose aim has been to contrast the high standard of dramatic excellence of old days, both in writing and acting, with the very modest requirements of modern audiences. One thing alone ought to disturb the placid public conscience, and make it doubt if it be getting value enough for its money, and long hours of attention: viz., the fact, how easy it is to become an actor. No one asks for training or for study. Excite a laugh by some new familiar trick, and the ear of the public is secured. It may be fairly asked, then, are there no remedies to be suggested, or how is reform to be brought about? The audiences are content with what they get: why should any one interpose? But here is the truth: people may grow accustomed to, and even relish, what is always being presented to them, but they may all the time be losing what is infinitely more enjoyable. The tone of the public mind is now to follow like sheep. If managers will not learn, English audiences will, later. One would have thought that even the commercial principle of competition would tempt managers to follow the lead of the Prince of Wales' Theatre, and open pretty little theatres, daintily decorated, with actors that act, if without genius, at least with tact and even elegance, or pieces of the same stamp as 'School.' Even now a new theatre was lately opened, and announced as being devoted to the furtherance of pure comedy; but very soon two burlesque players of the most extravagant sort were associated with a genteel comedian in the management; and as these gentlemen must have their 'gags' and women's clothes, and the rest of the 'business,' we may be certain of having lost a favourable chance of reform. Can it be that no English writer is capable of depending on his own resources for presenting a successful little comedy to the public.

The view of anything going on upon the stage is always attractive, even from associations. Still, however, there are signs of reform and reaction. The astounding success of that little picture of manners, 'School,' is a hopeful symptom; for even the languidly genteel, who have had their interest so much excited as to go and see it seven or eight times, unconsciously bear testimony to the force of dramatic principle, and show that the spectacle of their own habits and characters pleases and entertains them. While this comedy of manners has had an extraordinary 'run' at the Prince of Wales', at the Olympic an extract from Copperfield and a burlesque, of a most agreeable and legitimate sort, are enjoying a no less extraordinary popularity. But the most healthful token of all is that glorious comedy of Goldsmith having now passed its hundredth night; propped, however, on the crutch of a poor burlesque. This is not much, but it is something. We are now also having a regular French dramatic season, and our players, if they are wise, will find opportunity for picking up some valuable lessons, useful for this reason also, that they are founded on correct principles of human nature. It really looks as though such were the solution of this universal borrowing from foreign countries. It is as though they confessed to the French. 'You alone know how to treat character, and the dramatic changes consequent upon character; we must therefore take from you:' just as certain manufacturers import the wheels, &c. of watches from Geneva, and put them together as an English watch. It might be safely affirmed that were new theatres opened with such a programme as elegant comedy, and tolerably trained actors, they must always succeed. And though bidding our actors copy the French in some matters, I may mention as a fact, a certain compliment that has of late been paid them, and which may encourage them. Some influential representatives of the *Société des Auteurs Dramatiques* came over to us in reference to some copyright matter, and went round the theatres. They reported one point in which they owned that the English stage had begun to leave them behind. They said that the stage gentlemen, in pieces like 'School,' were better dressed, and in general appearance and 'get up' were far more like gentlemen than theirs.

POSTSCRIPT.

WHATEVER reception the reader may be inclined to give to the conclusions drawn from this little essay, there is, at least, one, founded on those pieces of criticism quoted from writers like Hunt, Lamb, and Hazlitt, which is certain to be accepted; namely, that stage critics of that day were tolerably skilled in human character, and could support their judgment of mimetic passions and eccentricities by principles drawn from the study of human nature. This gives their work, and the stage which they illustrated, a vitality and substantial dignity, which makes the criticism itself not only valuable, but highly interesting and instructive. It is impossible to look at the criticism of our own time without feeling that it proceeds on quite a different principle, the fault of which rests not so much with the critics as with the meagre material they are called on to deal with.

There are, indeed, men of taste and culture, like Mr Oxenford, who could deal with the drama, and test it by the true and correct standard of human character; but the average criticism is very inferior. This, it must be owned, is not their fault. There is no substantial material for them to deal with. It is impossible to exhibit nice discrimination, to express in words a picture of human passion or emotion, where none such has been before us, or is indeed intended.

Since the French company has visited us there has been a valuable opportunity for lessons of critical and histrionic wisdom, and nothing is more deserving of note than some admirable remarks of Mr Tom Taylor, which illustrate better than any words of mine some of the principles urged in the preceding pages. Such criticism could scarcely be applied to the case of our own players. There is no 'stuff' to work on. The following remarks will be found so just, that I have no scruple in inserting them here. He is speaking of Regnier.

'After the kindly senility of Noel, the old servant, in *La Joie Fait Peur*, and the perplexity of Balandard in *Une Chaine*, it was well we should see how perfectly at home this master of his craft is in the humours of an entirely different type and time. As the parvenu of 1700, in flowing periwig and crimson velvet coat, laced on all its seams, a second-hand *Grand Seigneur*, always ready for an adventure when his friend and exemplar, de St Héreur, shows him the way—nothing could better illustrate than did this performance the difference between a master of the craft and a pupil. Not a word or intonation of Regnier's was lost by the audience; not a point missed fire, thanks to the admirable clearness of his elocution and incisiveness of his delivery, though so entire is the absence of strain or palpable artifice, that his utterance seems the easiest and most natural thing in the world.

'It is now 27 years since Regnier first played "Dubouloy" at the Théâtre Français with Brindeau, then a very young actor, for the Comte D'Anjou, and Firman, then in his prime, as St Héreur. Regnier seems still as full of spirit, his humour as buoyant, his movements as lithe, as he did then. It is difficult to believe that next April will close his 40 years of uninterrupted service on the first stage of Europe. He retires from the active practice of his profession with unimpaired powers, and he leaves no superior even among the excellent *troupe* to which he bids farewell. But mark the difference between French theatrical administration and our own. Regnier ceases to act, but does not cease to teach acting. He still continues as a Professor at the Conservatoire, to train pupils for the profession he has so long adorned. The rich fruits of his experience, his intelligence, his good taste, his culture, have a chance of being transmitted, where they find a congenial soil, through the actors in whom he sows their seeds. And he retires, for his good work, on a pension almost as large as the salary he is now receiving as an actor. So much for his future. Then for his past. Look what his career has been. A member for 40 years of the same company, always composed of the best actors and actresses of the time, in pleasant and cordial relations with the most cultivated society of Paris, acting on an average from 10 to 20 nights a month, *with frequent intervals of leisure, and abundant time for study, never obliged to undergo the deadening and depressing influence of those wearying runs, which, when they do not wear out the actor's strength, inevitably lower his personation to a mechanical act.* Esteemed and beloved by the public, working under the constant sense of close, exacting, and intelligent criticism, in the pleasantest relations with familiar and congenial comrades, feeling himself part of an establishment in which his art is honoured, and which plays an important part in the culture of his generation, can we wonder that the actor so treated, so influenced, so surrounded, gives to his work an impress of refinement and self-respect which we can only expect to find by a miracle in that of our own players, buffetted from theatre to theatre, making part of companies that change with the season, if not with the piece, under no control of severe criticism from press or public, scuffling through careless and undisciplined rehearsals, followed by wearisome runs, with neither leisure nor opportunity, in most cases, for self-culture or society, having neither recognized connection with literature, nor part in the work of national culture, treated too often in the theatre without respect, and out of it neither claiming nor receiving much consideration? How, under such conditions, is the English actor to maintain his faith in himself, or keep in view high ideas of his art? Of course there are exceptions to this general rule; but the general rule, as we have described it, is, we fear, beyond contradiction.

'And that it is so goes a great way to explain the marked and painful inferiority in refinement and intelligence in English acting and actors to French of the corresponding degree. Believing in the importance of the theatre as an instrument of national culture, we make no apology for this digression, suggested by the presence here of such artists as those who have just closed these performances at the Princess's.' All this is excellent, as well for those who have witnessed the performances, as for those who have not: pleasant to read, as embodying principles and reflections.

SINCE writing the above I have had the advantage of seeing some comedies of mark, and which have significance as illustrating the Principles which I have tried to lay down clearly in the foregoing pages. These pieces are Molière's 'Malade Imaginaire,' 'Englished' by Mr

Charles Read, and Mr Robertson's new comedy, 'M.P.' It may seem scarcely fair to the modern writer to consider two such pieces together; though, on the other hand, it is all but certain that the new piece will run for a period about ten or twelve times as long as the old one. And yet in this instance, as well as in that of Goldsmith's 'She stoops to Conquer,' there is a precious opportunity for our modern play-writers to learn the true broad Principles of Comedy, and the secret of exciting the interest and sympathy of an audience.

Mr Robertson's 'M.P.' is very pretty and agreeably written, and 'laid out' with the refinement which is his characteristic. But it has the same defects which most of his other pieces exhibit—a want of story, a want of that conflict of passion, or human weakness, with other passions or weaknesses, with the consequent suspense, and the practical *effect* of one character in the other. In short, it seems to be little more than a series of pretty tableaux, in which the ordinary ladies and gentlemen of our day might frequently find themselves *posé* with those average, less marked types of character, which we often encounter. This is all agreeable, but it is not the drama—not *comedy*. That oft-quoted and misunderstood principle, 'holding the mirror up to nature,' has many other sins besides this on its shoulders, and has led many a writer astray.

Even now when we would wish to describe the plot of 'M.P.' it seems to elude the grasp—it fades away. It is more an exhibition—a pretty background — an old country house, a ruined squire, his daughter, her admirer, seeking to be elected M.P.; scenes in the garden, scenes in the house, and the final election. So with the epigrammatic dialogue with which it is garnished, and of which I took down a few fair examples; those, too, which seemed to meet the greatest applause. Suppose Shakespeare were abolished by an Act of Parliament, 'the bill might pass the House of Commons, it never would the Lords.' A coarse, low character in a piece is 'a money-bag with a dialect.' The heroine says 'she would make a bad wife,' because 'she has had no practice.' 'It is a pity that courtship always ends in marriage; it would be much better that marriage ended in courtship.' The heroine says 'she never can argue after travelling by railway.' A fair quakeress is described as 'looking like biscuit-china.' One of the gentlemen is 'so big, but *he'll tone down* after he is married.' 'Flesh is grass, and mowed away by time.' (This a very old joke.) The coarse 'money-getting character is addressed as 'a ready-made man;' 'no, self-made, sir,' he answers. The same person affects a gentleman in this way; 'He leaves a dirty taste in the mouth.' 'Of copper?' 'Not of clean copper,' is the answer; 'but of dirty manufactured half-pence.' 'Actors may marry according to law. In fact, I know several actors who are married, &c.' A Quaker girl adopts the conventional worldly dress, and is described as 'Pennsylvania of the past transformed into Paris of the period.' A lady says she would wish to see her lover in Parliament. Why? 'Because she would like to hear him called to order.' (This produced a roar of laughter that lasted some time.) Some one remarks, 'What a pleasant sound the river has.' 'Yes,' is the answer; 'sounds like water.' A gentleman in love called attention to the forget-me-nots. 'See these flowers up-side down,' says the lady. The answer, 'That is because their heads are turned,' which produced another roar. The old squire, taking some soda-water, remarks that 'life is very like soda-water; youth is all effervescence, corked down and wired; manhood is, &c.; old age the empty bottle.' Again, 'She won't forgive me,' says the lover. 'Yes, she will,' remarks his friend, 'because you are in the wrong. Women always forgive men when they are in the wrong. Now, if you had been in the right,' &c. Then apropos of some one 'he kissed me, I set my face against him.'* The lover addresses his flame as 'Miss Dunscombe.' 'Don't call names,' she answers; 'it sounds so dreadfully abusive.' ''Pon my word, women ought to have no votes because *they are so sharp.*' 'I got your four votes,' says the lady. 'How?' 'By kisses.' 'No voter,' says the coarse man, 'would give me a plumper *if I offered to kiss them.*'

There is a violent crowd outside. 'Not our side, but the other—in fact, *very much* the other side.' 'These are the things,' says the heroine contemptuously, 'they send to Parliament to keep us out.'

At the end, the old squire says to the coarse

---

* This, by the way, is the old riddle, 'Why do ladies dislike moustaches? Because they set their faces against them.'

man, 'Skoome, give them your blessing. It's cheap and—nasty.'

Now it would take too long to go over these 'epigrams,' and show that they will not stand the test which genuine wit would. First, it is the author who is speaking, not the character; as for instance, that last 'hit' which produced a roar, and has been quoted with praise by the papers. No staid, sober squire, or *gentleman*, would make such a remark in his own house. It is 'out of character,' and the strangest thing in these 'biting epigrammatic hits' is that the victim never resents them, but the conversation goes on. Thus is proved the fact that it is only the author who speaks. So with that making a bad wife 'because I have no practice:' there is no 'epigram' here, as it is simply a statement of a truth, which, if enunciated *gravely*, would be equally effective. Then, what is the meaning of a man being 'so big, but he'll tone down after he's married'? Making every allowance for some witty *arrière pensée*, what does it *mean?* What is the figurative or even the literal sense? But it would take long to analyze all these quips and cranks.

The bold experiment of reviving Molière's

'Malade Imaginaire' again presents an opportunity of studying what should be the true principles of dramatic effect. The subject might seem a pretty one — a hypochondriac invalid, preyed on by doctors, and whose eyes are at last to be opened to their imposture, to his own imaginary diseases, and to his domestic slavery. We know what farcical treatment this theme would receive at the hands of our modern playwrights; how cleverly it would be worked up; how comically the invalid would run about with a sheet around him; what a comic manservant there would be; how Doctor Bolus would order one medicine, and by a mistake the patient would take another; or, more probably still, how Mary and Thomas, the two servants, fond of 'master's' wine, would take, say an embrocation, by mistake, or think they had taken one, and run about, their hands on their stomachs, in all the agonies of supposed poisoning. This is no exaggeration, and the play would be worked out according to a fixed prescription taken from the dramatic 'pharmacopœia.' This really shows what is the vice of the day in the drama, dealing with mere surface peculiarities, instead of going lower, to the grand principles common to every nation and to every age. It is really worth a few moments' reflection to see how so great a writer as Molière handles a subject that to poorer minds would seem merely farcical and trivial. To him the mere hypochondriac's complaints and the foolish guffaws they induce, were as nothing. There was another side—the miserable self-worship, and sacrifice of all other things to that idol, which such a delusion fosters. Again, while the delusion seems to give an apparent despotism and tyranny, it creates in reality a miserable slavery, first to one's self, one's humours and fears; secondly, to others—to the second wife, for instance—who rule through those humours. See, again, with what artfulness and with what truth the master works. Such a character depicted boldly could not take with it the sympathy of the other characters, or of the audience. It would be simply repulsive. It was a fine idea to show that this was but the decadence of a fine and really *un*selfish nature—that the heart was sound, the affections strong, all the time, and that when the invalid's eyes were opened his real character asserted itself. And again, how naturally that moral cure was brought about. In modern plays how violent, how improbable is the reflection we make in analogous pieces? The sick man pretends to have died in his chair, and the behaviour of those interested in that event reveals to him those who like him, and also reveals to us his own natural affections. The whole minor details of the working out of this *motif*, the delicate *nuances*, the glimpses of human nature, all strictly subservient to the main incident, and growing out of it, the true humour, the wit, the little *situations* constantly arising, the originality of the 'jokes,' unite to make up a most delightful study. There is also present, as there should be in true comedy, a certain weight and seriousness in parts. What a fine and artful touch that is when the 'Malade,' wishing to test his family by the pretence of his death, agrees with alacrity in the case of his false wife, but hesitates with almost pathos in the case of his little daughter. In the former instance there was perfect security, from the confidence that she was devoted to him; in the latter a faltering hesitation, from the fear that though he loved his child, she might be thus proved not to love him. Again, when the servant enters disguised as a doctor, how artfully is her natural objection that she would be recognized by her master, met. He *does* so recognize her, and calls for the maid, and by a sudden pantomimic change outside, she appears *as* the maid, indignant at being taken away from her cooking. This quite bewilders the master. But the whole play is a 'masterpiece.' Not the least of its merits was the reintroduction of a first-rate actress, who brings the traditions of the old school—Mrs Seymour, who in 'Toinette' was literally charming. Anything more spirited, more firm and solid, than the rendering of this part could not be conceived, and it would be well if some of the free misses who consider 'Toinette' to be in their line, and who would 'get it up' in a day, had been there to see, and feel ashamed of their own poor, feeble, and scratchy rendering of a *soubrette*, beside this brilliant oil-painting of Mrs Seymour's. It was easy to trace the training and traditions of an older school in the play of feature and expression—the 'note' of a good actor or actress. Instead of the usual weak pertness, there was earnestness and force, and a controlled sauciness; and no one with a good ear, or who has heard good acting, but must have welcomed those unfamiliar elocutionary cadences of a trained voice, which, a sure instinct told us, gave the best and most spirited expression to Molière's speeches, and to Molière's humour.

Mr Tom Taylor's ''Twixt Axe and Crown,' an historical play, has had a prodigious run, and has the real elements of success—interesting story and grand character. The same writer's comedy, 'New Men and Old Acres,' after some hesitation, was accepted by the public, and followed during its career with real enthusiasm. Later again a new writer, Mr Alberry, has brought forward a very pleasant and interesting little comedy, 'The Two Roses,' in imitation of Mr Robertson's pieces; and having one really good character in it, was fortunate enough to find an admirable actor, Mr IRVING, whom it has all but placed in the first rank. At this moment there is nothing so delicately finished, so elaborated, so controlled or so spirited, that can approach this performance on the English stage. And this success only helps to fortify the conclusion which has been urged all through these pages, namely, that good plays are necessary to produce good acting, and that with scenic effects and properties, but without characters, a Garrick or a Clairon could do nothing. But there are hopeful signs abroad; already there are symptoms of a better taste; and with wonder managers have recognized the fact, that at this moment the only *paying* houses open are those where reigns the LEGITIMATE drama, that is, a faithful picture of human character and human emotions.

APPENDIX.

EVEN as I write, the evils noticed in these pages grow worse, and the observer can scarcely keep pace with them. There are some points revealed occasionally in newspapers and other directions which speak significantly for the thoroughly mercantile and shop-like character of stage transactions at the present time. A provincial theatre was lately duly advertised, and one of its recommendations was announced to be a level avenue leading from the road on to the stage, so that an omnibus or other vehicles could be driven on to it with the greatest facility. Again, let any one look at the play-bills, and say whether it is an advertisement for wares and trades, or a puff of the merits and callings of various persons directly or indirectly connected with the House. Every bill seems to be the property of an enterprising perfumer, who has a whole page to himself, and to his perfumes. Thus we read that 'the registered JEWEL LANTERNS in the dress circle lobby, and the illuminated BOUQUET MIRRORS in the dress circle, are by —— and Co.' 'The —— valses between the first and second act, published by —— and Co.' Then we are told that the refreshments are, not 'supplied by,' but simply 'by' Messrs —— and ——. Surely gas and gas-fitting is an ordinary enough handicraft, yet there is given the name of the gas-fitter to the House. So with the 'florist,' where flowers hang in baskets. So with the dressmaker; and 'the masks by ——,' the prompter, treasurer, stage-manager, scene-painters, house-decorators, 'the ornaments in *carton pierre* by Messrs ——,' '——, box keepers,

Appendix.

&c.' 'The furniture and mirrors in Act II. by Messrs —— and ——.' All this is based on a mercantile view, and springs from the present dedication of the stage to the gratification of the eye. Where intellectual effects were produced, it was natural that we should desire to know the name of the producer. Now, where the grand effect of the night is a conflagration, or some mechanical structure, it is very fair that the handicraftsman, who has had the labour and trouble, and *is* the actor, should not have his name suppressed. Further, there is here an attempt to use the theatre for making money in other ways besides its legitimate one; for these 'lustres by Messrs ——' are supplied gratuitously by the firm, in return for the advertisement. More detestable still was the spectacle exhibited last Christmas at many theatres, where whole scenes were covered over with huge advertisements, and it shows the supineness and helplessness of an audience when, having paid its money, it could allow itself to be affronted by such an exhibition. The system of self-puffery, too, in the newspapers, where it is not enough to announce the play for the night, but there must be added 'roars of laughter at the new song;' 'the Mill Scene, pronounced by the united press the grandest triumph of realism ever attempted on this or any other stage;' has now become so universal and necessary, as to reduce all to the same level and give no advantage to any one of the number. But here, again, this flows from the character of the entertainment. Anything in the nature of a *show* must follow the ordinary rules of mercantile dealing; and where theatres are established like shops and houses of business they must be 'pushed' like houses of business.*

But, in truth, it is impossible to look in any direction without

---

* In proof of what was stated in the body of this essay, that the large number of theatres are the result of mere speculation, and subject to the incidents of speculation, it may be mentioned that at this moment no less than *twelve* have been obliged to close, or are about to close, their doors, through failure of business, or managers. This is nearly one half the number of existing theatres. These are the Surrey, Charing Cross, New Royalty, Holborn, Lyceum, Haymarket, Astley's, Globe, Belgravia, Royal Alfred, Princess's, Drury Lane.

finding evidence of this perverse taste. Witness the following. The 'Era' says :—' A "Wee dog" dinner was given at Richmond on Tuesday, to celebrate the extraordinary success of this famous song in the Burlesque of 'La Belle Sauvage.' Among the company were Mr Barton Hill, who wrote the original words of the song; Mr W. H. Montgomery, who arranged the music; Mr Hingston and Mr Fiske, who composed additional verses; Mr A. W. Young, who has sung the song over one hundred and eighty times; Mr J. G. Shore, who has understudied the song; and Mr Lionel Brough and Mr Grainger, who appeared in the burlesque.' But the reader will recall many other curious freaks.

THE END.

JOHN CHILDS AND SON, PRINTERS.

www.ingramcontent.com/pod-product-compliance
Lightning Source LLC
Chambersburg PA
CBHW020233240426
43672CB00006B/514